White-haired Melody

Michigan Monograph Series in Japanese Studies
Number 61

Center for Japanese Studies
The University of Michigan

White-haired Melody

Furui Yoshikichi

Translated by Meredith McKinney

Center for Japanese Studies
The University of Michigan
Ann Arbor   2008

itle: *Hakuhatsu no uta*
Copyright © Yoshikichi Furui, 1966
Originally published in Japan by Shinchosha Co. Ltd., Tokyo
English translation © Meredith McKinney 2007

Published by the Center for Japanese Studies,
The University of Michigan
1007 E. Huron St.
Ann Arbor, MI 48104-1690

This book has been selected by the Japanese Literature Publishing Project (JLPP), which is run by the Japanese Literature Publishing and Promotion Center (J-Lit Center) on behalf of the Agency for Cultural Affairs of Japan.

Library of Congress Cataloging in Publication Data

Furui, Yoshikichi, 1937–
    [Hakuhatsu no uta. English]
    White-haired melody / Furui Yoshikichi ; translated by Meredith McKinney.
        p. cm. — (Michigan monograph series in Japanese studies ; no. 61)
    ISBN 978-1-929280-46-9 (cloth : alk. paper)
    I. McKinney, Meredith, 1950– II. Title. III. Series.

    PL850.R74F87   2008
    895.6'35—dc22

                                                                        2008021900

This book was set in Palatino Macron.

This publication meets the ANSI/NISO Standards for Permanence of Paper
for Publications and Documents in Libraries and Archives (Z39.48—1992).

Printed in the United States of America

White-haired Melody

1

THE AROMA OF SUSHI

I wonder when the practice first began in Tokyo of serving sushi to guests at a funeral wake. I've never gotten around to finding out, although for more than twenty years the same question has occurred to me every time I'm at a wake. I say "in Tokyo" because I can't imagine that the practice would have started in any of the other old areas of Japan. I also feel that it wouldn't have sprung up in the old downtown area of the city; my own sense is that this practice may have originated in the uptown Yamanote district and then spread into the newer areas, making itself at home by slow degrees among those who had drifted in from the provinces over the years. In any case, the custom has a forlorn feel to me—the sort of expedient measure that breathes the same dejected air as the transient world of makeshift lodgings.

I remember the first time I experienced a wake in my own home—it was in 1949 or '50, when I was in fifth or sixth grade. The house we lived in was in Shiroganedai-cho, in Shiba, a two-story house with somewhat sloping beams that stood at the end of a little lane off a main street, which our family shared with an assortment of other households, each family to a single room. Our landlady, an old woman who lived on her own, took to her bed one day and died in the evening three days later, after half an hour of agonized groaning. I seem to remember it was early spring, but it may in fact have been late autumn, since I have a memory of the sweet taste of the big pickled *daikon* radish—no doubt a piece of leftover food from the wake—that my mother, still caught up with the bustle of post-funeral activity, thrust into my school lunch next morning. Whatever the season may have been, I recall that the air of the house at night wasn't the deep cold of winter, but did have a chill edge to it. I have a child's memory of sitting in the room next door, separated from the gathering by sliding doors, and of the way the aroma of sushi overlain with the scent of incense smoke crept in through the heavy chill, provoking in me a melancholy hunger. It was late into the wake by that time, and the room in front of where the body lay had grown very noisy. I don't think the sushi had been ordered in beforehand on that occasion.

It must have been about two years later that sushi deliveries first became available. I would have been in middle school then, although in my memory I don't feel at all like a middle-school student. But if it was the late autumn of 1951 or early spring of 1952, this would fit with the fact that, with the death of the irascible old landlady, things started to go awry with the house's inhabitants. Disputes arose, people grew listless, and soon we too found ourselves at an impasse and were forced to move on.

So anyhow, as I sat in the room next door, plunged into the melancholy of hunger, I puzzled over how people could eat this raw flesh in front of a corpse. The raised voices of the tipsy men and women in the next room sounded to me suddenly desolate. Dread and sorrow became one for me— and even now, as a single sensation, they are evoked by the pungent aroma of sushi wafted within the scent of incense.

I think it was when I was at the wake for my mother that I began to puzzle over when the practice first began in Tokyo of serving sushi to wake guests. That puzzlement belongs to myself in my thirties, some twenty years ago. The detached, faux-erudite probing of the past for facts and evidence must have been a response to my inner bewilderment. Facts and evidence were utterly beside the point, of course. It's perfectly obvious that I had arrived at this question in flight from the need to confront a family member's old age, illness, and death. Yet when it came to the moment of my mother's funeral, utterly unprepared though I was, I conducted myself with an accomplished, almost sordid degree of calm. With each new occasion, my bewilderment was only a momentary occurrence, and the skeptical ponderings about the sushi were but a passing thought. The idea would simply flit through my mind, as I gazed at the tray of sushi lying there barely touched, its aroma slowly diminishing in the glare of the fluorescent light, that this practice still continued, though even now it hadn't quite risen to the level of an established custom.

In this sort of situation, the best approach is to spend some time diligently questioning more elderly people about their personal experience. Even if you can never pinpoint the exact moment a practice began, at least you should be able gradually to work your way back up the years, with the memories of others serving as your guide. This method enables you to gain more knowledge than you can hope to get by simply consulting a book on the subject. Formally interviewing the person with prepared questions is likewise a rather dull approach, but that said, it's not easy to find an appropriate moment to introduce such a subject with someone you hope to question. Thus, one way and another, the years passed without the task being accomplished. I missed my chance to ask my father. This was because I held back, sensing that no satisfactory answer could be had from him. In fact, it was at my father's funeral that I noted with surprise how time had slipped by without my ever pinning down any answers to this question of the origin of sushi at wakes, though for the last ten years I'd felt I was fairly knowledgeable on the matter. Then, slowly over the course of time, I found myself increasingly counted among the more senior people at gatherings, and it was brought home to me that if I wanted to ask others about this, I'd better move fast. At this point, however, a strange scruple arose; namely, that it was surely those still in the prime of life who should be asked to discuss wakes, not the old. Yet, since the experience of people this age had been interrupted by the wartime food shortages, when such luxuries as sushi were virtually unheard-of, it seemed to me that their memory would unfortunately antedate my own earliest memory by only a narrow margin.

My sister and brother had both died recently, still in what could be called their prime. I did have regrets over not having put the question to them, but our household had never had much to do with Buddhist ceremonies and the like, so they would certainly have had no prewar memories of such matters.

But then one day I was startled to find myself asked by a young person, "Why do people serve sushi, of all things, at wakes, anyhow? When did this tradition start?"

The sound of a suburban train receding into the deepening night had caught my ear, transporting my thoughts to the garden of a house by the tracks, where an old plum tree held a sparse scattering of white blossom, when footsteps came in through the gate and went around to the kitchen entrance, a soft woman's voice was heard, and the next moment, from beneath the smell of incense that permeated the house, the aroma of sushi came wafting sharply in to me.

"I remember sushi being served in 1950, or perhaps it was 1952. Before that it was wartime, and I have barely any memory of eating sushi at all. . . . In any case, it must be a fairly new practice."

This reminded me of a memory of being taken by my father to a sushi shop near Meguro Station, in a little lane that would have led to the entrance of the Naval University. It was just coming on evening. We were about to turn the corner when large drops of rain began to spatter down; in no time at all it had turned into a summer downpour. The sushi cook, whose name may have been Tetsu, had been hit by a car some months earlier, and his right hand was not yet fully functional. "I'm exercising it a bit each day," he said, as he slowly closed and opened his big hand for us. It turned out that the place was full up with customers who were there to escape the downpour, and at the owner's suggestion we raced out through the white sheet of rain to a tempura restaurant diagonally opposite. So I missed out on the sushi. That would have been about 1943. Back on the main road before the rain began, I remember, I'd stared at a train decked out with flowers and lights for a celebration of some sort.

Recently the faint shadow of another memory has begun to stir in me, of

5

being taken to a wake in some other house by my mother. I kneel there, small and quiet, in a corner of the crowded room, and I even begin to glimpse the woman, apparently the lady of the house, who emerges from among the guests and comes over to me, holding a little plate, and tearfully welcomes me and offers me some sushi. But there wouldn't have been a funeral in our immediate family, and it's highly unlikely that my mother would have gone off to someone else's wake taking her youngest child with her. It must be a false memory.

In any case, I felt sorry that I couldn't satisfy the young man's interest with any personal recollection worth relating. It also occurred to me that one of the benefits of being approached like this as an older man was the freedom to display a little pedantic erudition. Searching vaguely through the various novels I'd read, I found a scene in which a young woman has died in a lodging house near Hongo, and the other students in the lodging house and their friends, even those with no connection to the young woman, have been brought in to serve as mourners—a big jug of saké goes the rounds, and they pass the freezing night singing silly songs and having a boisterous time together while the wind howls outside. The story is set in 1937 or '38, around the time I was born. On such an occasion you might think it would be quite appropriate for the people in charge to take the easy option and order in sushi, but in the scene the guests are all served individual meals on little tray tables. The meals contain grilled fish-paste cakes and the like, but apparently no sushi. I then recalled another scene, one that would have been set around the turn of the nineteenth century. The house is in the old style of the tradesmen's homes of the Tsukiji area, but the people are transplants from the provinces. The wife has died that morning, and now in the afternoon the women are busy cooking and preparing things for the wake, worrying about the next day's funeral clothing as they work. In the kitchen are bowls of tempura on rice and plates of sushi that have been brought in to tide the women over during their preparations. All it will take is a little more relaxation of attitude, and we will see at least the sushi make its way into the room where the wake itself is held.

I couldn't retrieve any other scene of relevance. With no further associations springing to mind, my inclination to talk failed me. Besides, the young man apparently had no interest in novels, so more of this talk would only annoy him. Even the beginning of the 1950s must have seemed a long time ago to someone so young—well over a decade before he was born. When you've been asked about the origin of something, I thought with a sigh, any tale of a time long before the person was born, even if it doesn't answer the question, at least serves as a source of knowledge for him. Then I was puzzled to realize that I knew this young man's age, and then, as if waking suddenly from a drunken stupor, I cam to my senses and understood with fresh astonishment that this was his house, he was the host, and I was a guest here. It wasn't, after all, the night of a wake.

In my bewilderment, I found myself remarking rather abruptly, "So a young person can be interested in this sort of thing too, eh?"

"It wasn't actually my question originally," replied Yamagoe as we listened to footsteps ascending from the living room. "I just happened to remember my mother telling me at my father's wake that he had been puzzled about it at the wake for my older brother."

I realized I knew the year his father had died, and had also heard that Yamagoe's elder brother had died in childhood, when he was just six.

It was also odd that I had the feeling I was on the second floor of this house. In fact, we were at the rear of a single-story building, in a little room that had apparently been added on to the old main house years before. From the front door, I had been shown past a long row of old sliding paper doors along a creaking corridor with a verandah beyond, then turned left at the end into an odd wooden-floored bit of room, and finally entered this room with an abrupt step up. Then, when the saké had begun to take effect, Yamagoe had said, 'May I encourage you to move over there toward the window?" Beguiled by his rather old-fashioned turn of phrase, I did as he suggested and moved over to settle myself back diagonally by the base of the window—and sure enough, as I leaned my elbow on the fashionably wide windowsill, I immediately slipped into a posture of easy familiarity, and a relaxed contentment came over me. In the old days, a breeze from the bamboo grove at the back would have come through the open window, the young man explained apologetically, but about ten years earlier the area had become crammed with houses, and at one point there had been a noisy stereo nearby, so they'd taken to keeping the shutters closed, and this had now become a habit. I'd already begun to assume that an elevated view lay beyond the shutters, so now it seemed my sense of hearing interpreted sounds as if from a second-floor room.

Yamagoe would be just turning thirty this fall.

·　·　·　·　·

My relaxed pose led the woman to put the sushi plate down right next to me on the tatami mat. She then sat for a while in the corner of the room and chatted before she left, and the scent of her skin that lingered, mingling with the aroma that rose from the sushi, swelled faintly within the night air that was slowly darkening inside the room. The nape of her neck had grown still whiter than before.

I was the one who abruptly asked about age—in two weeks it would be exactly two years ago. It was in the hospital common room, well after the time for the lights to go out. The young man was in a wheelchair, his leg in a plaster cast and propped on the small table affixed to one side of the chair. As for me, I had a white headband-like bandage around my head, and I was pushing a walker that looked like a tall version of a circular playpen. I was strapped into a bizarre harness that went from the back of my head around to the chin and down the chest, to stabilize the vertebrae that had been joined in a recent operation.

I'd been seeing the young man in the corridor since I'd started my countdown of the days left till surgery. What an unusual, clean-cut probity there is to his features for a youth of today, I thought as I gazed at him. I, on the other hand, was finding it all I could do to walk straight, back lengthened from the hips and stepping along with an almost specterlike stiff correctness. I kept my mind from dwelling on the post-surgery future—my anxiety was focused simply on whether I could just maintain free movement of my limbs, and I suppose this mental tension must have had a severely restrictive influence on my gait.

Later, while I was being kept flat on my back in the harness after the surgery, the world beyond the single door of my room merged with the world of my imagination. When at last I was able to grasp the walker and set off down the hall, I was surprised to see the young man still about. I must have assumed he would long since have been released, but as I gradually looked around me I discovered a number of other patients also still there, looking just as they had before my surgery. Then it finally came home to me that in fact I had been confined for a bare couple of weeks.

I had much painful difficulty getting to sleep each night. During the day I managed to propel myself around the hospital with my walker, so I could sustain a state of relief from the predicament of my useless limbs, but all this changed once the lights went out at night and I lay down. By now, I was allowed my usual face-up sleeping posture, but once I had settled into it I couldn't easily turn over, owing to the harness that held my body rigid from neck to chest. Suddenly deserted by the drowsiness that had at last settled over me, I was beset by a breathlessness that seemed to echo my post-surgery reaction. Anxious now to prevent my sleeplessness from hardening into something more tenacious, I grasped the rail around the bed with one hand and slowly drew my incapacitated body into an upright position, but as I did so my sense of gravity deserted me in the darkness, and a sudden urgency overwhelmed me. Finally I managed to set off down the corridor as if to the bathroom, disturbed at how my face felt creased with the effort of breathing with my jaw, despite the fact that the jaw was held rigid from below by a metal fixture. I skirted the nurse's area, and arrived at the empty late-night common room.

That night, Yamagoe had placed his wheelchair in the shadow of a long bench in the darkened common room, and was gazing at the dead television screen. Perhaps the pale light shining in through the window produced this illusion, but his long, soft, youthfully luxuriant hair looked for a moment like white hair to me. At this moment, his boyish face turned toward me and our eyes met. I pushed my walker over to his wheelchair. It was still a little difficult to sit on the bench, so I stood looking down as I addressed him.

"What year were you born?"

I have no idea now how I could have spoken like that, but at the time I didn't have the leisure to feel astonished.

"1963," he replied instantly.

Not only was the reply immediate, but then this apparently taciturn young man proceeded, quite unprompted, to talk about himself. It was an extraordinary self-introduction.

"That was the year when the double train crash they call 'the Tsurumi accident' and the gas explosion in the Miike coal mine both happened on the same day. More than 160 people died in the Tsurumi accident, you know, and over 450 in the mine. I'm told that was the very day my mother came home from hospital with her newborn son.

"In my family, it often happens that a birth or death coincides with some big accident, you see. My sister was born the year before me, at the time of the Mikawashima accident—that was another double collision, with about the same number of deaths. I was only three when my brother died at the age of six, and all I remember is my mother's wailing, but during the previous month that year there were no less than three passenger plane accidents, and a total of more than 320 people apparently died. And then there was another crash that autumn. My father died the year I went to college, so I remember that well—there was a big fire in an Akasaka hotel that February. The people on the upper floors were visible through the windows, engulfed in flames, I remember. Another boy taking entrance exams just like me was actually one of the victims.

"That was on the eighth, and then on the ninth there was that accident where the Japan Airlines plane went down in the bay right next to Haneda Airport—you know, the "Exit! Exit!" incident, where the crazed pilot plunged the passenger plane into the sea. My father was already sick then, in bed at home, and he watched every single report of it, without a word. He never expressed how he felt about it later, either.

"When the forty-ninth day memorial service for him was over—it must have been the end of July—one night my mother and I spent a long time watching the television reports of that disastrous flash flood that resulted from the big Nagasaki rains, again without a word spoken. Neither of us wanted to watch, but we sat there endlessly without turning it off. Both of us were too courteous to make the first move. My sister wasn't there at the time. She died at the beginning of summer three years later. She was only twenty-three. That summer it really was my mother and me, just the two of us. 'Let's keep our fingers crossed nothing happens,' we'd say to each other, and of course in that way we were already anticipating the worst. And sure enough, in the middle of August there was that Japan Airlines accident. It was past seven in the evening. As she watched the latest reports coming in, my mother was shivering in the hot summer air, I remember. 'All perished, every one,' she was muttering to herself. My father died of cancer, but my elder brother and sister died in car accidents. All I'm served is this civilized case of broken bones in a skiing accident, so I get off lightly. The Gulf War seems to be over now, too ..."

There in the darkness, it was as if each of us was alone; he spoke softly, so as not to call down on us a scolding from the nurses. Perhaps it was this situation that allowed him to speak so freely, or perhaps before my arrival he had been sitting there staring at the blank television screen, mentally reciting this tale to himself. It was not just that his tone was old beyond his twenty-seven years—I listened to him with a sense that I was hearing echoes from the language of his parents, who would have been about my own age, coming through the somewhat outdated turns of phrase such as "passenger plane" that littered his speech.

"So, you've had something wrong with you?" Yamagoe inquired at last. "I caught sight of you being wheeled back from the operating room."

Thoroughly preempted by his tale, I now had to tell the story of my own illness. He seemed interested in my description of the way a constriction in my cervical vertebrae had suddenly produced a nervous paralysis of the limbs, and he asked the cause. I laughed and told him briefly. "The accumulating years lie more and more heavily on the body, in much the same way that snow piles on a branch till it breaks, you see. I had no inkling of the illness till it actually began in earnest, but looking back now I think the first faint beginnings of the symptoms were there ten years ago."

He peered up into my face with eyes grown suddenly deeper. "How old are you?" he asked in a thin, somehow hazy voice. Then we discovered that his father had been two years older than me. I couldn't deduce the year he would have died, however.

At that stage, my ability to calculate the passage of years and months was slowly returning to me. No, it began with the calculation of days, in fact. Before the surgery, my only calculations were of the number of days remaining until the operation. Two days before it was due, the one day that separated me from it felt to me absurdly long, a time that would never pass. Once the surgery was over, I was sentenced to lie on my back for three weeks, and the only calculation I could manage was of the days that had elapsed since then. For the first ten days I managed to maintain a fair degree of equanimity, but from the moment the doctor promised that if my pace of recovery continued I could be up the following week, the remaining days suddenly grew enormous.

My present calculation difficulties were no doubt a result of this experience. Even after I began to walk, although the number of days since my operation was clear to me, I would suddenly grow confused if I had to recall further back than two days. Sometimes expressions such as "three months ago" or "for three years" suddenly invaded my mind as pure concepts, free of all contextual content, and as I gazed at them from the spot where I lay on the bed, a breathlessness seized me, a sensation like being sucked down inside a bottomless hole in which time had stopped.

Under the circumstances, the years that the young man had swiftly arrayed before me like a little riff of song were far beyond the bounds of my grasp at the time; it even felt arbitrary to hear myself speak of "ten years ago," and this sense of arbitrariness was accompanied by a faint whiff of fear. Yet some days later, as I lay dozing, beset by the weariness of recovery, I found myself counting up the years in the young man's story, and found that I simply couldn't recall the various dates. Even the simplest attempts at addition and subtraction confused me. Each tragedy that he had related was clear in my memory, I knew these events, I remembered them, but by reason of this they also appeared before me clouded with memories from my own life at each of those times. Each memory stood alone, however, unconnected to the others. When I tried to add a context to them, they seemed to positively resist me, and faded instead to a featureless dullness. If I attempted to pin them down by relating them to events in my life that coincided in time, they began to peel away to reveal a deeper layer of almost demented delusion. And yet I counted. To count where counting offered no salvation constituted a kind of compulsive ascetic penance.

From time to time, a young woman came to visit Yamagoe in the hospital. Going along the corridor, I would cast a glance into the large room and see him lying faceup on the bed, eyelids closed, while the girl bent over his face, lifting his head and combing his long hair, her back twisted somewhat to reveal a suppressed quickening of her breath. Then one Sunday afternoon I saw them sitting in a far corner of the rowdy visitor-filled common room to escape the blaring television, deep in quiet conversation, foreheads almost touching, and for a moment I thought they must be related. True, Yamagoe had lost his sister and brother, and there was no facial resemblance between them. Yet there hung about these two a particular atmosphere, completely separate from their surroundings, that was like the atmosphere around people I had seen in this room many times, when relatives are talking in a hushed voice to a patient who is seriously ill. Each would speak earnestly for a time, while the other listened, giving brief nods. They appeared somewhat bewildered but above all tender with each other, and not at all like a young couple having an emotional discussion. Her tiredness was visible in her hair. After a while there was a pause in their conversation, and in the next instant a trembling sound like a sob rose from the girl's throat and she burst into laughter. I was fearful lest this was some kind of fit, but as the laughter continued it grew clear and relaxed. With each deep breath, the voice faintly swelled. Yamagoe too softened into a wry smile.

11

"Are you two living together?" I asked him that evening, when we met again in the now quiet common room.

"Not living together, no," Yamagoe replied with odd directness, then looked a little nonplussed. "But she's in the house. Lately she's been coming to the house on a daily basis. She stays over from Friday night on. I'm a bit worried about my mother, you see. She sometimes says some peculiar things, things about the days when my father was still well. No, it's because she's got a tendency to high blood pressure, and she's lonely. Because I'm not at home, we've decided to check her into a nearby hospital, starting tomorrow. A place we've been familiar with for years. She can go in anytime, they say. I've asked my friend to help with this. But it's odd, you know, to be in this place, and be asking someone I didn't even know a year ago to look after my mother."

"How difficult for you," I said. "But you must be happy that she's such a cheerful person."

"You're talking about her laughing today, aren't you?" said Yamagoe, quick to catch my reference. "I had blurted out to her that if something happened to my mother, and if things went badly with my next round of surgery, there'd be no one left, so she should consider living in the house...."

I'd had no idea he was waiting for a second round of surgery. He told me it was scheduled for the following Thursday.

"There's Monday, Tuesday, Wednesday, three more days to go—it'll be two days tomorrow morning, but I haven't slept tonight yet, so three more days. The surgery itself is nothing big."

I was silent.

"Where do you live?" Yamagoe inquired after a while, somewhat absently. "You'll be going home any day now, won't you?"

I told him the approximate area where I lived, but he pressed me for a more precise description of the location. He seemed for a short time lost in thought, and then gradually, in a low voice that seemed to rise of its own accord out of the darkness of the room, he began to laugh.

'Good heavens, so we're in the same part of town! From this perspective, we're virtually neighbors. As a kid I often used to walk to the area where your house is. I remember the sun going down while I was walking among the vegetable plots ...'

His bright laughter rang on and on. My ears grew intent as they detected, from a corner of the darkness, what seemed a woman's voice that rose and wove through his.

· · · · ·

Occasionally I would catch, from within the shadows of the voice that talked quietly on, a swelling sound of muffled women's laughter, as if from the lively gathering downstairs, and I realized that I had grown a little drunk-

12

er. I learned from Yamagoe that three young wives from the neighborhood to whom the couple owed favors of one sort or another had been invited over for a girls-only lunch with "the wife," and were gathered in the living room.

Yamagoe stayed in the hospital two months longer than I did. The card he sent informing me that he was out mentioned that his mother had been released too. Let's get together for a drink nearby sometime, I suggested in reply, and there the matter was left between us, while one year and then another passed.

It was on a Saturday evening a couple of weeks before that I had bumped into Yamagoe in front of the station. I had crossed the tracks and was heading towards the exit when I came suddenly face to face with him as he stepped absentmindedly in off the street, and we stood there awkwardly by the track crossing, talking against the clamor of the warning bells, while one after another three trains went by. He told me that his mother had gone back into the local hospital again soon after New Year's, and that he would be heading there for the second time today, after he stopped at the local store.

His voice was difficult to hear above the din, but what he more or less said was, "It looks as if she'll be in hospital for a long time, and I've decided if I stay this busy I should quit my job and get myself some work in a little local company instead. I've looked around and noticed that there are still a few small businesses around here. I feel like it would suit me better personally as well."

At that point the warning bells stopped, and the crossing gate opened.

"Why don't we meet round here tomorrow and have a drink?" he added with a smile. "There's a place that's open on Sunday evenings."

For some reason, I found myself attracted by the somewhat depressing thought of spending a Sunday evening drinking in a local bar. But tomorrow would be difficult. The following Sunday, Yamagoe was busy, and as we set off walking together we agreed to meet on the Sunday after that.

While I was on my way to meet him at the station, Yamagoe slipped in beside me. He was wearing sandals and cradling a large bag from the local store. We walked along together and had gotten to the lowered gate of the railway crossing when he said, "My mother has died." He said he had spent all his time at the hospital since the evening of the day we'd met a fortnight earlier, and that she had died the following Sunday just after noon.

"She went quite suddenly, when the day was at its brightest."

"So today would be the day for the second week's memorial service, wouldn't it?"

"Everything's done."

First a rapid express train painted up like a colorful toy box, and then a limited express train passed right in front of our noses.

"This seems the moment to tell you that that injury of mine was actually

13

from a traffic accident," Yamagoe continued. "I was behaving like a delin-
quent kid, out on a spin on the motorbike, riding round just to cheer myself
up one night. It was about the time the land invasion was beginning in the
Gulf War."

When we crossed the tracks he turned left, away from the station, and
set off walking parallel to the railway line. I fell silently into step beside him,
deciding that I would either walk with him till he was satisfied, or have a
quick drink before I left, since I guessed he might be longing for a friendly
face from the hospital days. I was aware that the slight aftereffects of our
injuries were apparent in both of us as we walked. Eventually we turned
right and entered a long narrow back street. We passed a church, the front
facade of which was painted white, but which looked from the side like a
normal apartment building. Next was a medical clinic—probably the hospital where his mother had stayed—that looked like it might once have been
a tuberculosis clinic and that faced onto the faded blue paint of the wall of a
Western-style building behind it. Finally we came to a point where the road
began to twist about in a way reminiscent of the footpath between fields it
would once have been. Yamagoe spoke again.

"Could you come back to my place? It sounds funny, but I've been looking forward to having you there ever since the time of my mother's last
service, at the end of the first seven days since her death. The women are
gathered there to cook for the event, but we've arranged not to get in each
others' way, so there'd be no problem."

We were already standing in front of his house. My eyes were immediately drawn to the deep, narrow, single-story building with its simple gable
roof and warm brown horizontal siding boards. Sandwiched cozily between
newer houses, it looked to be a remnant of the type of house built just after
the war, timeworn but still intact. There was a modest wooden gate, and
between it and the entrance hall, as well as in the thin strip of garden that
stretched like a little lane along what would be the shaded southern side,
plants grew in such profusion that there was scarcely space to tread. Potted
plants were crowded in as well. Early spring though it was, the place was
dark with dense greenery, though on closer inspection the plants appeared
quite well tended.

"How old was your mother?"

"She was almost sixty-one. Still young."

"You've married."

"No, but she's been living here in the house with me for the last six
months."

"Living together, eh? I see … Would there be a flower shop nearby?"

"Don't worry about flowers for the altar. And anyway, it's Sunday, so
the shops are closed."

When the entrance door was opened, there was a sudden rush of rich

14

feminine laughter from within, together with a pervasive scent of incense. The laughter suddenly subsided, and the girl I had seen in the hospital emerged to welcome me. She recognized my face, and lowering her limpid eyes as she knelt on the mat, she said, in the standard greeting, "It has been a long time." Her head was lowered before me as if she were for a moment shyly disconcerted in the presence of a guest, and I recalled being surprised before as well at the pale transparency of the skin at the nape of her neck, suggesting that she too might be recovering from some illness....

. . . . .

"Apparently the low-frequency noise from roadways can carry quite far, and interfere with people's sleep."

"You're not talking about the overhead expressways?"

"At night the Tokyo-Nagoya and the Central expressways are both close enough to carry this far. If you strain your ears and listen to the noise of the Kanbachi Expressway, you can make out a different noise, a kind of hissing like rain. It sounds shrill, to my ears."

"Well, I don't drive, so maybe that's why I don't notice these things. What was it like in the hospital at night?"

"The night I had my accident," Yamagoe began. His voice thinned to a singing intensity. "The noise from Kanbachi seemed unusually loud. My mother felt something evil about it, and she was harping on and on about her memories of the air raids in the war. Finally I got mad and declared I was going out to contribute to the noise, got on my bike, and tore off. That was how it all began. Even while they were taking me away in the ambulance, I was just so scared that something might happen to my mother."

I was realizing that this young man was the sort of person who would keep his mouth shut for hours when he was in the mood, but who could also talk and talk, quite oblivious to the silence of the listener, when he was so inclined. He sat there cross-legged in front of the forgotten sushi tray, back held straight though his face was lowered, maintaining a trim upright posture despite the gloomy depression that threatened to engulf him.

"When my sister died, my mother took to bed. I remember I was watching TV with her, my ears alert to the fact that one ambulance after another was going by out there, when the telephone rang behind us. My sister's accident had already happened two hours earlier. She'd left home the year before. But it felt scary to have someone in the family who'd left home return to the house as a corpse, from a place very close by. My mother blurted out that she must have been drawn back to the area to die. Actually, the car was heading away from the house."

I'd heard in the hospital that she died the year of the big jet crash, so now I was able to calculate that it would have been 1985. Yamagoe's brother had been killed in his car accident the year that there was a succession of plane crashes, so that would make it 1966. He'd been an infant, so the tragedy must have happened close to the house. How far did the Ring Route 8 extend at the time? I wondered, as I listened to the story unfold. Thoughts of this series of deaths in the family must stir Yamagoe to rage from time to time, given his youth. But there was no sense of any anger building in him as he talked. He would launch abruptly into speech, talk at length in a thin, keening voice, and then just as abruptly break off again. The pauses never seemed to anticipate any response from the listener. As for me, it may be the result of increasing age, but I have developed a habit of listening in complete silence as someone talks. It isn't that I'm coldhearted or indifferent, so my lack of responsiveness strikes me as strange.

The women's muted laughter swelled softly again. We should all be heading home before long, I thought, beginning with the guest in this room, or we'll overstay our welcome—but when I looked at my watch with the expectation that it would be quite late, it was only just before ten.

"She's become really close to the local women during the six months she's been here," remarked Yamagoe, listening to the echo of laughter. "All the young married women around here have recently moved to the area after marriage, so apparently they sometimes assume that she was raised locally. I can sort of understand it, knowing how she is."

"Did your father build this house?"

"No, the story is that my grandfather bought it, then after he and my grandmother died my father lived here alone till he married my mother. That was in 1960, and it seems she was already pregnant with my brother, the one who died. My mother was three years older than my father."

"Ah, is that so?" I said, finally understanding the situation, and amazed at how stupid I'd been about the relative ages of the people involved. I changed the subject. "The extension to the house seems old too."

"Apparently it was here when my grandfather bought the place. The story goes that there was a family of eight in the place before him. This room was the place where we kids studied while we were living here, and it was where my father spent his last illness, sometimes in bed and sometimes up. The noise from the living room doesn't carry into this room much, you see."

I had relaxed into the window seat he'd offered me, and was now settled leaning in against the sill. Slumped here like this, chin on propped arm, I had the sensation that I was in a deeply familiar place, and the disconcerting thought occurred to me that if this young man were suddenly to add, "He always used to sit there just like that," I wouldn't know quite what to do with myself. For the moment, however, there seemed to be no avoiding the sensation of rather gloomy ease that was enveloping me as I sat. Yamagoe continued to talk.

"We would hear him calling from this room, day and night, for my mother. His voice wasn't loud, but it had a sort of stern ring to it that penetrated the whole house. He'd call and call, but my mother would just sit on where she was. You'd think she was angry, but no, it seems she was afraid. Her head hung, and she was awkward and flustered with her hands. My father never used to be one of those tyrannical head-of-the-family types, you know, and my mother wouldn't have been a particularly submissive wife either. Sometimes, when I couldn't bear to witness it, I'd urge her to go to him and stop the noise, and then she'd rise grudgingly to her feet, with the air of a tearfully reluctant young girl. Whenever she came in here, she'd firmly close that door. All we could catch from beyond was the sound of my father's voice, talking in a tone of patient remonstration.

"Sometimes his tone would grow severe, and then my mother would respond in a weak little voice. She sounded as if she was soothing and lamenting at the same time. I don't know about the others, but I at least had no idea why he treated her like that. She always ran the household with wonderful efficiency. But when she emerged from that room, she certainly had the look of a woman who'd received a scolding. She'd sit dejectedly in a corner for a while afterwards. I just hated seeing her like that, and sometimes I said dreadful things to her, things like 'Just be patient, he won't last much longer.' I was only eighteen at the time. My father was forty-seven."

I thought with a sigh how young his father had been. His mother too—three years older, so only fifty at the time. With a cancer diagnosis at this age, he would have felt the future shut against him, and clung to his wife, pouring out his fear and resentment to her; I could imagine how this might well be interpreted as irritable haranguing, if heard at a distance and through several walls. His distressed wife's attempts to pacify him might also sound not only soothing but also apologetic. Even at fifty, she would surely have been aware of herself as a woman, as this man deprived of all future clutched at her and railed against his fate. I also had no trouble understanding why her still-adolescent son should interpret as gloomy the image of this woman sitting alone and filled with despair after she left the room.

I really must be going, I thought. It was only thanks to the gratuitous connection of having been patients together at the hospital that Yamagoe now felt he could say as much as he had; if I pressed him further, I warned myself, we would be in danger of destabilizing the slightly unnatural degree of openness between us that had carried over from our hospital conversations. In my imagination, I began to trace the way home from here. The road diagonally connecting my own street with the ring road that had caused Yamagoe's family such grief, veered off well before the railway crossing. It was a relatively quiet one for this part of town. It snaked gently to and fro, following the curves of the canal that had once run here through vegetable plots … and along it walked the figure of a man returning from an evening's drinking, his hair starkly white even in the darkness—become, unawares,

17

almost completely white, the season still too early for the cherry trees lining the road to be in bloom, the man almost like a solitary blossoming among the unblossoming trees, I thought in wonder as I watched him go … and the women's laughter swelled up again as if from below.

Yamagoe said, "If a man's been jealous for ten or twenty years over something that never happened, do you think the woman might come to feel that it no longer mattered whether it had actually happened or not, and after he died she might even cherish the fact that he'd thought this of her?"

I paused over "cherish," a word you don't hear much these days. Well, I muttered mentally, if you mean something like "feel grateful for," I suppose I could imagine it, yes. I looked at his face. Yamagoe was still sitting poised, back straight and head bent. He turned his eyes in the direction of the women's laughter, as if waiting for it to swell again.

2
SPRING EMBANKMENT

"It's prettier over here!"

The girl's voice came from behind me, and the young girl who had just skimmed past me turned briefly in her seat to look back. It was a fine Sunday morning. The two, who looked to be of about high school age, stopped their bicycles at the edge of the sidewalk and gazed at the row of cherry trees, already past their full flowering, lining the street that twisted its way north from the nearby main road. When the traffic signal changed to green, they lightly pedaled away together, heading in under the blossoms.

You only have to go on a little further and you can see all the cherry blossoms you like in the park down the road, I thought, as I paused to look at the row of trees. Then I realized that they had in fact grown into quite impressive trees without my noticing it. Living in the neighborhood must have dulled my eyes to such changes. I watched the girls winding their way down the road until they disappeared, imagining how a girl of sixteen or seventeen, speeding along high on the seat of her bicycle through the light of the scattering petals would be aware of the gloss of her black hair and of the way her face would glow whitely. I suddenly decided to change the route I would walk today, and waited for the traffic light to turn green again.

It was twenty-six years ago that I had first come along this road. That day, I walked down it from the station with my wife. She was pregnant with our oldest daughter then, and we had come to look at the model apartment that had been set up at the construction site of the building where we lived now. I seem to remember her holding a parasol. The street looked the same as it does today. The cherry trees lining it were perhaps a little taller than the height of an average person. Even the cherry tree seedling we had planted in our little garden, brought back from elementary school by our eldest daughter as a memento of her graduation, had grown quite big and was now covered in blossom.

About four years after we'd come here I heard from a neighbor, who had moved to the area when she first married long ago, that this road followed the course of an old buried canal. I then looked at its curves with new interest. She described how the water did not flow, but lay like a long, stagnant swamp, and how people on either embankment eventually took to tossing rubbish into it, till finally it was filled in. Even so, if you went down to the water's edge in those days you could look up and see nothing but sky between the embankments. I recalled all this every time I went along the road. Seventeen or eighteen years ago, however, a subway station had been built less than twenty minutes' walk to the south of our house, in the opposite direction, making it more convenient to come and go from the city center, and as a result I began to use this road less and less. When I occasionally walked through this area in recent years, I was struck by the number of houses that had been torn down and rebuilt. It had become one of the many new developments that sprang up along the route of the railway line, and it was in these terms that I saw it. Then one day it struck me that even before I had moved here in my thirties, the street would slowly have been filling with the homes of owners in the prime of life, for recently I seemed to be seeing everywhere along it the signboards that marked a wake or funeral in progress inside the house.

Some time ago, a sign had been put up on the roadside explaining the street's history as a canal, and I had several times paused and taken a photo, but each time I would somehow forgot to read it, and the photograph would disappear. It was only a month earlier that I had noticed a new and more detailed sign there, and finally read it.

It seemed that the canal had drawn its water from the Tamagawa Aqueduct and had first been constructed in the mid-seventeenth century, so it was impressively old. It was originally known as Togoshi Canal, and later as Shinagawa Canal. Apparently various water supply outlets were set up in Setagaya to avoid sending water through the area, but this canal was originally used to carry water in to the city as far as the present Togoshi area in Shinagawa Ward. This meant that it had extended as far as the area where I was born. In 1932 the Irrigation Water Association that supported the canal had disbanded, said the sign, and then between 1950 and 1952 the canal had become reclaimed land. The explanation was accompanied by a cross-section diagram of the embankment, showing how the water had run along a bed cut into embankments that were raised quite high above ground level. The line of embankments running through the fields had apparently been a distinctive feature of the local landscape.

As I stood picturing the scene of those hefty embankments snaking their way through the unremarkable fields, I felt a sudden rough wind blow through me. Had I perhaps seen this sight myself? Near where I now lived there was an equestrian park, which had been completed in 1940, when I was three. At the time, it was a place where children from the kindergartens and elementary schools in our area would be taken for picnics, and both my elder brother and elder sister had come there, I remembered. Perhaps

20

my parents had taken me there too? Everyone was now dead, and I had never asked them. Perhaps they had silently thought, when I came to live here, that it was owing to some odd attachment to a place whose name had been familiar to me from early childhood. You're wrong there, I thought as I walked away from the notice, making a show of scratching my head to demonstrate my innocence to these invisible accusers. It was the beginning of March, and I was on my way to meet Yamagoe at the station.

The road I took to his house followed the original canal route upstream.

"Apparently that street was an old canal embankment," I remarked, modeling my tone on one he sometimes used himself. "If you followed the canal right on down, you'd arrive at the area where I was born. I moved to this area the year you turned five, you know—in other words, two years after your brother died. It's funny, but once I was living here, I felt that the place connected me to my own dead in some way. If you go along the lane from your house to the street out front—which probably also started out as a canal, by the way—and then turn right, there's a Buddhist temple on the left, isn't there? That's where my mother's funeral was held. Relatives arrived from her hometown, and they would have gotten off at the station nearby. Several have died since then. If you go on from the temple and cross north at the lights before you get to the Kanbachi Expressway, you'll be on a street a few blocks west of the one in front of your house. It runs more or less parallel to it, and if you go along there you'll see a hospital on your left. That's where my father died. Our family had no connection to the area originally. It all happened quite by coincidence. His funeral was held elsewhere, mind you."

I found it odd that I was speaking more rapidly than Yamagoe tended to, although I was the same age as his parents. I gazed into the distance along the winding road....

Draw the waters from above, they grow faint below. Must have been a gruesome fight, I'd say. Turning your back on a sinful world is the least of it ...

I approached the corner, my thoughts veering again. The path that branched off to the north there ran between the back edges of the university and the middle school grounds. I turned in towards a row of brilliantly blooming cherry trees, petals scattering in quiet flurries, whiteness at last pervading my being....

The surname of the woman who lived in that house with Yamagoe was Torizuka. I didn't know her first name, since he never spoke it, always referring to her as "Torizuka." This may be a fashion for young couples living together these days, but there was something in Yamagoe's tone as he spoke the name that was different from easy familiarity. There seemed to me a note of reserve or even of warning there. While we were in hospital together he'd told me how, when Yamagoe came in with his serious injury, at a time when

21

his mother was slowly growing sicker, Torizuka spent most of her time devotedly going to and from the house rather than visiting him, staying over sometimes to look after his mother. Apparently she even consulted with Yamagoe and moved his mother to a nearby hospital herself. Later, after both he and his mother had been released, the relationship had returned to normal, and they had met outside the home as before, but the girl had also continued to visit his mother at the house two Sunday afternoons a month, to listen to her by-now rather incoherent talk and look after her in various ways. She would then stay on to have the evening meal with them, returning late at night to her distant apartment. He told me she occasionally stayed the night and went straight to work from there the next morning.

This went on for a year, and then, about six months ago—suddenly, over the course of a week or so, it seemed to Yamagoe—his mother had completely lost her mobility. Then her speech became peculiar. At this point, Torizuka began to spend most of her time at the house. Yamagoe pleaded his mother's illness as a reason to take all the time he could from work, and Torizuka too set aside what time she could to be there, but they could only maintain the situation for ten days before they had to put her back into the same hospital. Two weeks later, Torizuka moved out of her apartment and came to live at the house. His mother then began to wait anxiously for her morning and evening visits, he told me.

I didn't know what her circumstances had been, but as I listened it did seem that it was possible to hear this story as a happy tale of the way a young man and woman of today might come to live together. However, Yamagoe also told me this: that just before she went into the hospital, his mother had taken to referring to Torizuka by her first name, though of course with the polite addition of "-san." This pleased Yamagoe whenever he heard it. But then he discovered that even when they were alone together, he himself could no longer use her first name. This didn't mean that he now began to use her family name, but rather that for the moment he stopped addressing her by any name at all. This caused no difficulty. She, meanwhile, always referred to him outside the home in the manner typical of young couples, while to his mother she used "him" or some such vague term; but when his mother began to use her first name, she in turn started calling him by his first name, Hitoshi, both when speaking to his mother about him and when addressing him directly. Yamagoe said that at times her voice as she spoke his name had the proprietary ring of a relative who had come running to her mother's rescue and taken control of the household.

While he was telling me all this, Yamagoe never spoke her first name, even in indirect reference. I knew his first name from having seen it on the name plate of his door at the hospital two years earlier. He had also talked about it one night in the common room, when he told me that his father had called him "Hitoshi" for reasons of his own, and had been quite unaware of any possible associations until someone had astonished him by remarking that I must be named after the famous comedian Ueki Hitoshi. Yamagoe described the scene vividly, almost as though it were before his eyes. I remember that the story struck me as quite funny, recalling as I listened that he had been born in 1963, when Ueki's popularity was at its height. His father did indeed seem to be a serious and earnest sort of man, who would never have thought of such a frivolous connection.

Yamagoe continued to avoid the name of the girl he had shared his home with until his mother died. And it had been only twenty-seven days later that I had come, unaware of all this, to visit the house the month before. The way in which Yamagoe had undergone this sudden change and begun to use her family name, and the reasons for this, I guessed would be connected to how she had behaved and what part she had played in the events following the death. This was speculation, of course. All I knew was that during the last six months of her life, his mother had spent much a great deal of time alone with Torizuka, and the young woman was still strangely reluctant to talk about what his mother had confided during that time. Yamagoe said that he felt he would be coercing her if he tried to pry the information from her, and he was waiting until she had digested it all and made her peace with recent events, to see what might develop.

What I then heard from Yamagoe is perhaps something that, being merely there as a listener, I should not have allowed myself to store away in my memory. Even Yamagoe stated that he was unsure of the facts.

Three times in those last six months, he said, his mother had mistaken him for her dead husband—once at home before she was hospitalized, and twice at the hospital. Each time she was more debilitated, but the things she said on each occasion were almost identical.

"There was nothing, really, nothing!" she had said, gazing up into her son's face, her eyes imploring. From the moment this first happened, Yamagoe felt instinctively that he was being mistaken for her husband. But at this stage it was too late for any attempt to point out to her all her mistaken ideas and delusions. Now, whatever extraordinary things she might say, you simply waited until the idea left her again, he told me. You didn't nod or make some vague response, but it was wrong to outright deny anything, either. You simply listened, your mind blank. After a while she would seem to become appeased and forget her delusion. Yamagoe said he always responded to this particular delusion of hers in the same way. It never crossed his mind to wonder about it.

After she spoke to him this way, her face would pale and she would gaze at him imploringly. Her eyes flickered and trembled, and she started to nod her head softly. The nodding went on and on, extremely earnestly.

"Yes, it's true," he heard her murmur, "everything you accuse me of is true. I remember now at last." Her voice was thin but bright.

She would say, "I had your children. I always did as you told me. I only left home that time because I went a bit crazy. Nothing happened then, nothing. Still, what you said was right." Then a faint glow of happiness would suffuse her face, and the delusion would finally pass.

The third time it happened, however, she wept irrepressibly for a while. Then, eyes fixed on him, she asserted firmly, "All three of my children died."

"That's not true!" Yamagoe found himself replying. Hearing this, his mother's face shone for a moment.

"Really? So they're alive, then? Yes, they're alive, aren't they! They come to see me every day. I'm so confused these days ..." Then she asked for water, drew in a mouthful from the feeding cup, and fell asleep in apparent contentment. This was about ten days before she died.

"Whatever may have happened before we were born ..." he began; he was speaking of the three of them, quite naturally, though his brother and sister were both long dead. "Whatever may have happened before we were born, we weren't in a position, being her children, to make it any concern of ours. Of course, as her son, I was rather disconcerted to discover how she loved him to the very end, but I was also moved." Touched at the directness and lack of flippancy with which Yamagoe spoke of all this, I listened without interrupting, sensing that the story was approaching difficult terrain. Whenever his talk faltered and threatened to fade to nothing, the sound of women's suppressed laughter would come swelling once more into the room where we sat. He would listen for a time and then begin to speak again. I had the impression that his story managed to maintain its even tone and continuity thanks to the protective presence of the women.

"Actually," he said with a wry smile, "as a son, I couldn't imagine how such a thing could be possible. Her life was pretty restricted, really—she never set foot in an airplane, only traveled on the bullet train a couple of times, and knew little about expressways. I've heard her babble on about there being 'shops along both sides of the expressway.' In fact, she had no interest at all in those things."

He sometimes teased her by asking whether she'd done anything at all interesting when she was young. "I never went to late-night coffee shops," she said, "or to any rockabilly concerts." Then, with the passionate intensity of one who had heard talk of such things but never experienced them, she would frown exaggeratedly and explain to him how popular things like that had been. "Didn't you ever go a bit wild?" he teased. When she replied that once, in her twenties, she'd dared to get her hair cut just like Audrey Hepburn's, he rolled about laughing.

But when he mocked her innocence of the world, she would come back at him. "Say what you like, but I've been through all kinds of hardship since I was young, so I'm capable of doing anything." And even if he didn't take this statement at face value, her son acknowledged its essential truth. She may have been dreadfully old-fashioned, but she was highly adaptable in many ways. After losing her husband at fifty, she began to work in a local store; then someone introduced her to a small company in the area, and she started out there as an assistant on a short-term contract. There it was discovered that with a little training she could do clerical work. She became a valued employee and stayed on for about seven years. She had continued commuting to and from work practically without any days off, dressed in the simple clothing typical of a local housewife, through the death of her daughter and her son's graduation and the start of his career, until at the end of 1989 she at last grew tired and quit.

She related how her father had died just after the war, when she was fourteen or fifteen, and she had gone to work in a factory in the Gotanda area. "It was one of those small-scale factories, the kind they used to have in the old days," she told him, "so everybody needed to do all kinds of different of work. That's why I can do just about everything, even now." This seemed a source of lifelong pride for her. "I only ever went to elementary school," she used to say. When she was about twenty, a nearby factory that was considered medium-sized by the standards of the day apparently became quite successful. It began to hire a lot of people from the neighborhood, and she moved to a job there. She could never explain the work to him, except to say that it had to do with electricity. Later the firm actually expanded into a large international company. One day, when Yamagoe was still in high school, she surprised him by mentioning that she'd been accustomed to using a tape recorder since she was young. She explained that sometime before 1955, the company had loaned what in those days was a large, cumbersome machine to each of the girls in turn to take home, together with some tapes, perhaps as a way of advertising its wares, and she had spent half a day or more on Sundays playing the hit songs of the day over and over. She was twenty-three when transistor radios first became widely available.

Two years later she moved to yet another small local workplace. It was by then about ten years since she had begun to work, and she had grown tired of large companies with many workers. The owner of this new place was old, so there were no real future prospects, but it was a pleasant environment, and the days passed easily. She liked feeling needed there, and working hard at all sorts of different tasks suited her style. While she was employed there, she vaguely expected someone to approach her sooner or later with an offer of marriage, though she couldn't imagine it being anyone beyond the local world she knew.

"It occurs to me now," Yamagoe said, "that in fact we had plenty of time together for her to tell me such things, with both my father and my sister gone. I'd often just be nodding and half-listening while I went on doing something else. I mostly forgot what I'd heard."

After Yamagoe's father died, she spoke more and more highly of him. After a few years, she even got to the point where she could blithely assert that he had been some kind of buddha. Her son sometimes felt a little uncomfortable at the indulgent way she spoke, but it was a minor irritation, so he would generally let her talk on, without interrupting. But his sister, who was only a year older, reacted very differently. Perhaps it was because she was a girl, but right from the time of their father's death, whenever their mother would start in on her nostalgic ramblings, her daughter would turn on her. After a while the girl seemed to tire of outright quarreling and began to say less, but this only made her message more pointed. Eventually she stopped talking altogether, and only her eyes would glitter poisonously. Right around the third anniversary of their father's death, as though she'd been waiting for this moment, she suddenly found herself an apartment and moved out. She was still a student at the time, but now she became financially independent.

For his part, Yamagoe had recognized that his father, who had been a steady worker all his life, nevertheless maintained a strangely stern, resistant attitude to the world. He had seen this attitude turned on his mother, who would in response lose all her usual courage and make flustered attempts to placate him. Yet he also knew, from those times when he had needed to consult his father on some matter, that although his father was never particular about the children's behavior and could even seem indifferent, in fact he was deeply caring. After his father's death, Yamagoe had begun gradually to sense something pitiful in this loving attentiveness, and to imagine that it could well be related to the death of his father's first-born infant son in an accident. But when Yamagoe was seeing his sister off at the station late at night after she had packed her final bags and was leaving the house, she suddenly said to him, "Did it occur to you that our father never took any joy in the fact that we were born, the way other fathers do? Mother realized it too."

He was astonished at her hardness, and only answered vaguely, "Well, I'm not sensitive enough to notice such things."

"Someone who secretly loathed the world the way he did wouldn't love even his own child, would he? Unless the child had died ..." his sister went on, and then she turned her face away in the direction of the railway tracks.

From that time on, mother and son lived alone together—yet while his sister was alive, perhaps out of some continuing deference to the absent girl, his mother now seldom brought up topics of conversation that concerned her husband. It was only about a year after his sister's death that his mother had taken to waiting up late for her son's return, and then falteringly embarking on her incoherent stories from the past. He would sit there in his pajamas in front of the television, surfing through the channels for interesting

26

news items, while she sat diagonally behind him. He listened to the various tales of her first meeting with his father and so on with half an ear tuned to the rapid-fire voices from the television, and generally with a head heavy with both sleepiness and the aftereffects of alcohol. It was his own lack of enthusiasm that made it impossible to remember whether he had heard a story last week or last month, and whether it was in fact the same story or another.

After graduating from the electronics college in a nearby suburb, his father had worked for about a year in a large company. Then, when he was around twenty-four, he could stomach life as a salaried worker no longer, so he supported himself with part-time work for a while. Both his parents had died while he was still at college, and he was an only child, so he was alone in the family home. He had met Yamagoe's mother at the beginning of December. Yamagoe's mother told the tale in a very euphemistic way, but the essence was that she had become pregnant the following year, before the winter was over. It seems that they began to live together here almost immediately after that. Before she moved in, he persuaded her to stop working, and since his part-time work was not enough to sustain them, he grudgingly searched out a job in an electrical machinery company that was already a bit behind the times, and there he spent the rest of his working life.

The first time he asked her out, near the end of the year, they were sitting on a cold park bench when he suddenly launched into a long speech. He began by repeating several times that she seemed a serious person, and then proceeded to talk fervently of how decadent the world had grown. Once infected by it, he declared, you would end up destroyed body and soul, and he drew evidence from examples from things he had witnessed at the company where he first worked. He denounced the world fiercely, proclaiming that everyone's head was filled simply with thoughts of money and sex, and that they could neither see nor hear the terrifying danger bearing down on them. "What terrifying danger?" she asked again and again, but there was no answer. Why is he criticizing me, she would wonder. And is it even me he's criticizing? She had no idea—she simply felt humiliated by his rebukes, and by the fact that she was three years older than he. But when he asked her out on subsequent occasions, though she felt a little oppressed, she went anyway. And then he would start in again on his rebukes. She was no coward, and felt that her years of employment since an early age had given her a good understanding of the world, but when she was with him her responses faltered, and she found herself listening with head bowed. She had never before been addressed so passionately, on such serious matters.

One night as they sat on the bench, he had risen to his feet and shouted, "I want nothing to do with the world! I refuse to go to any dinners, or weddings, or funerals!" Naturally she was astonished. As she sat there watching this man aswirl in the momentum of his own words, she thought how handsome his face was. "So I'll just have to quit work," he muttered earnestly, and hung his head. This was the first time she found herself laughing at him.

Once they realized that she was pregnant, he was forced into a position where he needed to go out into the world and throw himself into a working life once more. At first he seemed wounded by the experience, and tended to react violently, but with effort he eventually grew able to stay calm in the face of any provocation. That spring, Japan was full of unrest and demonstrations over the Japan-U.S. Security Treaty, but he would get up early and leave for work and come straight home in the evening, never mentioning what was happening in the outside world. They had no television set in the house, and they lived quietly, as if with breath held, she said.

Listening rather absentmindedly as she talked, from time to time her son tuned in. At first he dismissed any thought of being able to imagine this young man who had been his father—so different were they in temperament—but as the stories continued, he was unnerved to find that he was beginning to form a picture of the man after all. Each time he heard these tales, he was puzzled at how the whole thing seemed not quite to make sense, but he never checked the details with her. It struck him that the longer she rambled on in this fashion, the more the stories began to assume a mythic status for her, but he couldn't be bothered putting a stop to it. Five years or so passed while she kept on repeating the tales, in disordered fragments, and then one evening, when he was in a bad mood, he finally burst out angrily, "None of what you're saying makes any sense!"

"Women always leave out the most important parts, don't they?" Yamagoe then remarked, with a reminiscent chuckle. "But on the other hand they'll say things they should have kept quiet about."

He went on to tell me how his mother confessed to him one day that she had once worked in a bar. Looking at her, her son couldn't bring himself to imagine it. "What!?" he asked, disconcerted. It turned out to be an innocent enough story.

She had a friend, a girl who had grown up in the same area and in the same sort of circumstances as herself. This girl knew a boy, or perhaps it was her boyfriend, who had left school and had nothing much to do, and since he was a quick-witted and sensible sort of person, the owner of a small bar offered him the position of running it. He was actually the only one who worked there. The girl would go and help out in the evenings after work, and since drinks were cheap there, it gradually became popular with poverty-stricken students. His mother would sometimes go there with her friend for an evening, and when she had become quite familiar with the place, she would occasionally go around behind the counter and lend a hand. Things went on in this way until nearly the end of the year. Then her friend came to her, saying the bar was on the verge of having to close down and begging her to help. Although his mother was busy at the factory, she began to leave work as soon as possible and go in the evenings to lend a hand, at least for the moment. That was all there was to the story. At the end of that year she met her future husband, and after he had asked her out a few times, he made her promise to quit the bar as soon as possible. She added that while she was working there she would spend most of her time in the kitchen area in the back, seldom serving customers, so it was strange that he should have noticed her.

Some men do like to meddle in other people's affairs, don't they, her son thought as he listened. "Where was this bar?" he asked, and she told him it was right near one of the stations along this line, a few stops closer to the city.

This news somehow flattened him. "Why would you want to go all that way, just to work in such a dumb place?" he asked.

Her answer was almost childish. "But you see, I'd never gone to work on a train before, though I'd been working for ten years by that time." He burst out laughing at this, but then reflected that his flippant responses must actually leave her feeling quite helpless and alone. She seemed to take his laughter as a further rebuke, however, and began to speak regretfully of the past.

"There really wasn't anything low-class or seedy about the place, you know. Of course it was a bar, sure. I did work in a restaurant once before, when I was temporarily out of a job, a noodle restaurant that had just opened in the neighborhood, where I simply helped out for a month or so at the end of the year when things were busy. It was a lot like that. But I guess there was something frivolous about it, it's true. Your father got very angry about it. I couldn't understand, and I cried and apologized at the time, but then the next day I'd forget about it. Then when he got angry again and threatened to leave, I'd go through the same process all over again. I guess he saw me as a lost cause. Finally he declared that though I was a good person I was too careless at guarding myself from the world, so he'd never abandon me again, and would stay right there to protect me. I still regret it all. If only I hadn't gone to help in that bar, he would have been spared all that suffering on my behalf. But on the other hand, if I hadn't worked there, I'd never have met him. And you children would never have been born ..."

Her son choked with laughter again at this, though he noted her inclusion of the dead in the way she spoke of "you children." But then he nodded in response, hoping to keep her from repeating the story again. It was odd that she should be lamenting her mistake like this to someone who was the living result of that mistake. But he was also relieved to be able to reassure himself that there was nothing malicious in his laughter. Before long he managed to control his mirth, but found that he was at a loss for an appropriate response. Then he was startled to hear himself saying, "You worked far too hard in that place, you know, Mom."

His mother's eyes widened in surprise. Then her look softened suddenly, and she slowly nodded and replied, "Yes, I felt as if I was absolutely useless there at the time, but I guess you're right." She looked immensely relieved at the discovery of such a simple answer after all this time.

"Let's have a cup of tea," he said, to send her off to the kitchen for a while. The image flickered through his mind of that young man, little more than a student still, wracked with love and jealousy over a woman who was his senior and far more knowledgeable about the world than he, yet coming to view her as vulnerable and dependent on him. It struck him that the urgent thing he himself must grasp from this was that when this man wanted to sleep with her, given the kind of person he was, it would surely only be to this house that he would lead her, her head bowed in acquiescence. And as he realized this, he felt the quietness of this house, where the orphaned young man had lived alone and where now only he and his mother survived, draw in upon him. His eyes went to the stains on the wooden panel at the base of the old paper sliding door, and he thought how his mother seemed to be growing more infantile as she advanced in age. This was a couple of weeks before the evening he had had his bike accident, Yamagoe added, at a three-way intersection at the end of a winding back street on the far side of the Kanbachi Expressway.

In the house where his father had first slept with his mother, he now slept with the girl he lived with. His father had died ten years ago, the three children had dwindled to one, his mother had died, and now Yamagoe harbored suspicions that it was to his lover, and not to him, that his mother had divulged the details of his parents' original secret, details which the girl now kept to herself. Perhaps they were truths that could not be told in so many words to the opposite sex, or that, if spoken, could be understood only in terms of the words rather than of the substance. Or perhaps it was her feelings that stopped her speaking. But given this, to make love to the girl inevitably became a form of questioning for him. There was perhaps no other way to question. Her silence waited, neither encouraging nor rejecting, seeming to say, "If you really want to know, make love to me like this. If you do, you will surely learn the answer. Even if I don't speak, a voice will breathe from the doors, the ceilings and pillars, the whole house itself, to tell the tale, a tale of your father rather than your mother."

… I felt as if I were looking straight up, into the crown of a great hackberry tree, the fierce rays of the noonday sun beating down on me, although in fact the tree had been sawn off about a third of the way up its thick trunk. It was only a carcass, yet seen from this foreshortened angle it suddenly took on the dimensions of a vast tree.

The tree felt to me as if it must be one or even two hundred years old. The place seemed to be where an old milestone once stood, yet there was no sign of any road having once passed this way. It was a small suburban park, set among a maze of narrow, winding streets. I had come along behind the middle school, turned towards the back of the elementary school, and had just decided I'd come too far and should turn around when I glimpsed, down a little street that branched off at a nondescript corner, an old-fashioned L-shaped crossroad, the kind that were a feature of the highways of an earlier century. It had all the atmosphere an old-style crossroad should—a group of trees stood there, their cloud of spring leaves so luxuriant that it seemed almost like the dense heaviness of rainy season foliage. It must have been the zelkova tree in front of it that lent this hackberry the illusion of having its own flush of new leaves. Coming closer, I could now see that it was in fact just a meeting of three streets, one block of which formed a small park.

Yet looking still more closely I saw that at the corner of the park the roads did indeed retain the suggestion of an old-fashioned crossroads. It was odd to think that a place with the feel of an original crossroads should still survive like this, though it was only a bend in the road. Then, looking about more carefully, I discovered an old stone milepost close by. I crouched down to read it; the names of distant towns in the four directions were inscribed on its four sides. Yet there was no sense of the place ever having been a meeting of four main roads. It must have been a strategic point along the old highway, from which byways branched off.

Footsteps approached me from behind. While I had stood just now looking up at the hackberry tree, my mind once more mulling over those two making stealthy love in the empty house, I had noticed out of the corner of my eye a figure at the first-floor window of a house that stood above a set of nearby stone steps. The figure seemed to be gazing in my direction. But when I turned around, there was no sign of any house above stone steps, nor did the topography allow for any such place to exist. Instead, an old man with a head of wiry white hair had suddenly appeared in the middle of the park. He seemed to glare a moment when my gaze fell on him, then he came towards me, a vague smile hovering on his face. He wasn't an old man, after all.

"What a surprise! Do you live around here?" he inquired in a youthful voice. At just that instant, I recognized the face. He stood in front of me, nodding, and broke into a bewildered laugh. I realized he'd forgotten my name. And although I recognized my old classmate's face before me, I was likewise unable to retrieve a name to go with it.

"Er, Sugaike …" he said, another classmate's name stumbling from his lips.

"Ah, Sugaike …" The memory evoked by this unexpected name blocked my mind still more thoroughly from recalling his.

Hesitant to introduce ourselves by name, we stood together gazing at the hackberry.

3

A Human Figure

The image in my memory, of the old man with his head of wiry white hair standing there almost accusingly in the midday light amid the scattering blossoms, was in fact a brief optical illusion. On coming face-to-face—two men of the same age—I realized that my own hair was probably whiter than his.

When I turned to look back once we had parted just before the corner, there was no longer any sign of a human figure receding down the street, and the hackberry again seemed haloed in that pale hazy crown of spring leaves. Fujisato had mentioned that his house was nearby, but had not pointed to show me the direction.

It was one night about six weeks later that I went over to the bookshelf and took down the yearbook listing the alumni from my graduating class in college. I hadn't felt any particularly strong emotion the Sunday afternoon I had met Fujisato, but later a certain heaviness and preoccupation stayed with me. First of all, there was that sideways glimpse I had caught, as I gazed up at the thick trunk of the hackberry, of the nonexistent house on its stone wall, perched at the top of the stone steps. Why did I think, in the instant before I turned on hearing the approaching footsteps, that the man who had been glaring from the first floor window had immediately come downstairs, run down the stone steps from the house, entered the park, and begun to walk boldly towards me? Fujisato had said he'd been approaching the edge of the park on his walk when he noticed a man gazing up at the hackberry; he struggled for some time with a sense that he'd seen this man somewhere before, and it was only when I turned my face slightly that he found himself walking over to me. So I had indeed been under scrutiny.

"I felt as if it was quite a while since I'd seen someone just standing there like that," Fujisato remarked when we had walked together to the corner and were about to part. I instantly understood this to mean someone standing rooted to the spot, and at the phrase "quite a while," a sad sympathy rose in me. It's quite true, I thought, you don't often see people doing that these days. Still, it didn't make sense to me that the phrase referred to me.

That couldn't be how I had looked.

I sat there wondering about it as the afternoon began to darken towards evening. Suddenly the telephone in the living room rang. It was my eldest daughter's voice on the other end, cheerfully telling me about how she'd landed poorly from the sky diving parachute and broken her leg, and a friend from work was about to drive her home. She'd apparently been treated at a nearby hospital. "The parachute did open, didn't it?" I asked belatedly. She had told us the night before of this foolhardy plan to go skydiving today, saying it had to something do with work. It was arranged that she would go into the hospital the next day, and two days later she would have surgery on the leg. It all went smoothly.

She was in the hospital for a month, and the afternoon of the day she was released my second daughter, who had been walking in the mountains for two days, rang from the nearby train station to say that she'd sprained her ankle coming down a mountain and was about to catch a taxi home, so instead I went to pick her up and took her straight on to the nearest hospital for treatment. This was on a Saturday. When we got home, the elder sister with her leg in a cast and leaning on crutches and the younger sister limping along with her foot tightly bandaged looked at one another and burst out laughing. Nothing further happened on this occasion.

I was tired after working all day, and my eyes snagged at the S row. Recently, whenever I looked through the fine print in a dictionary or a list of names late at night, long before my eyes had reached the object of their search they would begin blankly to follow some quite irrelevant letters. Each name along this line now called up an adolescent face. The *Profession* column listed not only the company or office where the person worked, but also the post and managerial rank presently held. My only experience of work had been eight years of teaching, so almost all these professional details represented a world unknown to me. I had no concept of what the various departments and sections in a company did, and when it came to the smaller subsections or committees, forget about it. It was even worse when the names included foreign words.

My father and my brothers had been company men. Indeed more than half my friends, now that I began to think about it, worked in offices. However, I had almost never asked for details of their professions. On the rare occasions that I did, the other person would usually look dismayed. He would seem at a loss how to begin to explain to someone outside the field. An expression almost of bashfulness, occasionally even of private gloom, would appear on his face. Sometimes the friend would at length rather carelessly provide a swift explanation in a specialist's language, but of course it meant nothing to me. I would simply nod. I did feel a certain satisfaction at hearing the answer, yet I couldn't claim to have understood it. Ten years or more ago, I confessed to a friend who was a long-term company employee the astonishment I'd felt on realizing that I had absolutely no idea of other people's professions and indeed no longer even tried to imagine them, though I too had worked hard all my life to make a living—but he had replied by saying that he was just the same, and had no clue about anything beyond his own narrow world of work.

Given this, how must people feel, filling in the careful details of their profession and position on the questionnaires that arrive regularly from the alumni association? Even I could vaguely sense from these publications that there was a considerable shift in the status of these men from sometime just before the age of fifty. When I congratulated them admiringly on how far they'd gone in the world, I was sometimes met with a difficult smile in response. In recent years, there had been a gradual increase in messages informing me of someone's new job. Some were stiff and formal, but there were quite a few others written in an oddly youthful style. I used to have a ridiculous thought that perhaps someone seeing his own name with its profession and position listed there might sense that some other version of himself, like an actor in a play, had separated off from this present self at some point and put a final end to things. Then one day, running my eye down the *Profession* column, I noticed a sudden gap in the lengthy and detailed column of position names, and, turning my surprised eyes to the name on the left, discovered that it was Fujisato. In my own place in the column some names a bit further down, the simple word "writer" looked almost like a blank space that was communing with Fujisato's blank.

But surely Fujisato climbed quite high up the ladder in one of the big companies, I thought in surprise. Still, I couldn't claim to be really startled. We had never known each other well enough to do more than exchange an occasional greeting. We were in the same high school, but not in the same class, and though we also went to college together we graduated from different departments, so we probably hadn't really met face-to-face since our high school days. It would have been more than a decade or two since I'd heard news of him via others. Perhaps Sugaike had mentioned him in relation to something. Yes, that must be it, I thought, flipping through the pages as if to find and ask Sugaike himself.

And now another confusion astonished me. Sugaike wasn't listed among our classmates. Of course! He had gone to a different college. We had not met through our work, or through the introduction of a mutual friend. He was someone I had met by chance after leaving college. I hadn't had any idea that he and Fujisato knew each other. In fact, since it would have been almost forty years since I had even counted Fujisato among my acquaintances, it was odd even to be finding anything odd in all this. Suddenly, belatedly, the conversation with Fujisato in the park under the big hackberry tree that Sunday began to take on a dreamlike quality.

"I haven't seen Sugaike for a long time either."

"Come to think of it, it's been five years or more since I saw him too."

It was only when Fujisato murmured his remark as we stood together looking up at the hackberry, and I found myself responding without thought or hesitation, that the name of this man I had been struggling to recall suddenly slid neatly into my mind.

"You and I were in the same math class, weren't we?" said Fujisato, changing the subject. His own sudden relief was evident in his voice. "I sat right behind you, looking at your back the whole time."

"That's odd, though. We were seated in alphabetical order, weren't we?"

"Theoretically we were. But we must have sat out of order in the first class, and that's the way it stayed."

"Well, I would have felt pretty uncomfortable with you staring at my back. You were excellent at math, weren't you?"

"That's not really true. I just knew how to handle numbers, that's all. I was always interested in how you'd work out the problem on the blackboard. You took such strange ways to get there."

"Yes, I can see you must have been watching me. I did things pretty oddly, didn't I? You must have been thinking, 'If you choose such a stupid way to go about it, you'll make a mistake any moment now.'"

"No, actually I was really intrigued by the way you thought. It struck me as pretty strange. You thought like a mathematician."

"Oh, come on now. You were the one who could solve a problem in a minute without so much as looking, while I'd spent an hour over it the previous evening and still couldn't come up with a solution."

"But my seat was behind yours. How could you tell?"

"Don't you remember? We would often get to class before anyone else arrived."

"Oh yes, so we did … And where are you living now, by the way?"

Fujisato had changed the subject suddenly again, and when I pointed down the road and told him that my house was near the equestrian park, he set off walking in that direction. I half-expected him to pursue his reminiscences as we walked, but he didn't speak again.

Left in silence, I now vividly recalled the cold of the morning classroom where I'd been alone with Fujisato. It was on the third floor, and Fujisato had temporarily taken someone else's seat, right in the front row by the window. I was sitting diagonally opposite, in the back row and closest to the corridor, also in someone else's seat, battling before the morning math class began to get some sense out of the problem I'd finally flung away in defeat the previous night. Fujisato had his math text and notebook spread open, and was apparently working through the homework he hadn't yet done, but whenever I glanced at him he was looking out the window. From time to time, his pencil would move swiftly over the notebook. He seemed to be solving a number of problems in this way. When the class began and we were in our alphabetically ordered seats, and were asked to come out to the blackboard in pairs and solve a problem, before I was halfway through Fujisato would have tossed down his chalk and briskly returned to his seat. His solution was always clear and concise. I never had energy to spare to wonder why Fujisato, who had so little trouble with math, would bother to come earlier than me, or why he installed himself in the window seat like that, but when my gaze was led by his to the window beyond, my eyes took in the scenery he was looking at. It wasn't really interesting enough to deserve the name "scenery." Directly in front of the classroom, another wing of the building went off at right angles to our room, so all we could see was a wall and some windows. Ivy clambered up the wall, but the scene was drab. The old concrete wall was discolored here and there to a dirty red, and in other spots to almost white. Looking at the end of the building next door where the steel frame had been exposed by a bomb during the war, you could guess that these patches too had resulted from exposure to heat in the attack. It was nine years after the war ended. There was also a rooftop parapet with rusty wire fencing, and a narrow ledge below that where pigeons gathered, and I thought these might be what he was looking at. There were days I envied him—a clever boy who evidently had time on his hands and must be rather bored.

"I remember if I had a slight fever for more than a couple of days, I used to worry that my lungs were infected, like so many others' were," I remarked, saying the first thing that popped into my head, in order to keep the conversation going. However, Fujisato only relaxed the line of his mouth slightly and made no reply. Looking up at the hackberry, his face had been somehow youthful, but now his brow was slightly furrowed and his head down as he bustled along, half a pace ahead of me. He made me think of an irritable old man anxious to see an unwelcome guest to the door, and I was puzzled yet again to think that what I'd seen earlier now seemed like a complete illusion. Then Fujisato came to a halt, long before we reached the corner.

Turning to gaze at me, he asked, "Had you been transferred from another school?"

"Yes, I had, actually."

"That's right, I remember now. Ours was the first year when there was no one in the class who died from tuberculosis."

I couldn't work out what the connection was. But he went on, with the same shy smile and air of confusion that he'd had when we first met. "I'm surprised you even remembered who I was. I'd just got to the edge of the park on my walk and looked towards the hackberry because I noticed someone standing there. I had this feeling it was quite a while since I'd seen anyone standing still like that. 'Now, who is he?' I said to myself. I racked my brains for a long time. A long, long time ..."

. . . . .

We parted without any further words. I could think of no way to respond to this sudden leap into intimacy, this revelation of a sense of deep connection between us. Fujisato simply nodded understandingly, encouraging me to leave, and I seem to remember giving an answering nod as I walked off, taking my cue from his comfortable silence.

All the way home, after losing sight of him at the corner, I found myself repeating Fujisato's words: "Now, who is he?" They seemed both strange and at the same time completely natural; I felt I could almost grasp what was in his mind as he said them. Then the feeling would blur and grow distant again. "It was me he was looking at as he said it," I said aloud to myself, and suddenly I felt hungry. Walking along the old canal road, I was aware of the early afternoon sun beating down. Even my knees grew weak with hunger, and the last bend before I reached the three-way intersection felt strangely long.

I hadn't been standing still all that long in front of the hackberry. When Fujisato's eyes had been drawn to my figure, he must have projected something onto it. Concentrated gazing will make a figure appear differently to different people, I decided at last, and with this rather lame conclusion I finally gained some peace of mind after hours of puzzlement. Then the phone rang, and I found myself swept up in my daughter's unexpected accident. It was a strange experience, probably because the bad news was relayed by my daughter herself, and came with the assurance that she was all right. I was worried that fear might overcome her when she looked back on the accident, but three days later, emerging from the operating room on a stretcher just as the evening began to darken, she turned to my wife and I as we rose from the waiting room and came over, apologizing with a carefree laugh. I went to visit her the next morning. The anesthetic had worn off, the painkillers weren't working, and her face was drawn, but within half an hour her expression had relaxed and she was even beginning to feel bored. Marveling at this youthful resilience, I jokingly remarked, "If that parachute hadn't opened, today would have been your funeral, you know." Each time I visited, the feeling remained light-hearted, though at the same time I was slowly tasting and digesting the aftereffects of this ill-omened event.

Now, a month and a half later, it was my turn to find my eyes drawn by Fujisato, when I came across the blank next to his name in the *Profession* column of the alumni yearbook. Though gazing at it was not likely to help my ignorant imagination to supply the background details of this blank space, I went through the motions of thought. And I recalled again, with a bitter taste of something like regret, the moment that day when Fujisato had fallen silent. He wouldn't have approached me in the first place if he

37

hadn't wanted to, I told myself. He had been responding happily enough until that moment. I guessed that my mention of that time in the classroom before the lesson had stirred up some old unpleasant memory. I could only imagine that the reason this boy, who was so good at math that he was bored by the lessons, would come so early to the classroom must have to do with his home circumstances. Everyone nurses old wounds from their adolescent days. They can lie dormant for many years, but if something re-awakens them, they will still throb, and the pain can be fiercer for a while than that from more recent wounds. And as you approach old age, the scar tissue covering some of these wounds may well grow thinner. In any case, it was inconsiderate of me to suddenly say something that evoked unpleasant memories for him, when, as he put it, he had been drawn to me from a distance after all those years, and when he was in a happy, nostalgic frame of mind. The insensitivity of that long-ago self, slaving obliviously over his math assignment, had evidently been preserved unaltered in me all this time. Perhaps insensitivity also grows with the years, like old scars.

I checked the yearbook again. It had been published this March. Updated books were supposed to be issued every two years, but when the last one arrived, I had thrown out the previous edition to make room on the book-shelf. Every time I received the latest edition, I would run my eye quickly down over the names of my classmates. There were a few old friends who were still just close enough for me to wonder from time to time how they were doing, and as I dipped into the book I would be surprised at how easily my curiosity was satisfied by mere job titles I had no real clue about. Then, coming to my own name, I always glanced hastily away from the *Profession* column with the feeling that it had murmured to me the dreaded word "unemployed." I had no recollection of seeing any nearby blank that echoed this when I had looked two years earlier, indeed I had the feeling my eye had happened to fall then on Fujisato's name against some highly responsible-looking professional position, though I couldn't recall what it was. It said a lot about my level of interest in the outside world, that I threw away the previous yearbook whenever a new one came. On the page facing the publisher's imprint there was a full-page advertisement for a famous fu-neral hall company in the downtown area. They apparently delivered both fresh and artificial flower arrangements, in addition to handling funerals.

I thought of telephoning Sugaike and asking him about Fujisato, but it was after midnight, so I decided against it. And then I realized I wouldn't be able to find his phone number anyway, since I didn't know where he lived. Sugaike was the sort of acquaintance whose address and number I hadn't noted down, despite the fact that he was an old friend of thirty years' stand-ing. We normally had no communication with each other, and didn't even exchange year-end cards, but about once every three years he would sud-denly telephone and invite me out for a drink. He would speak in a tone that suggested we had met very recently—perhaps only last month—but for me his voice held nostalgic echoes of the distant past, and I would immediately be eager to make a firm time to meet.

I'd set off in the evening, and we'd talk into the night, mostly about the past. The past in fact consisted of only a single year, when we'd been young men in our mid-twenties with time on our hands in a regional city and had gotten together regularly in downtown bars. The connection had petered out after ten years or so, but then we had happened to meet one day in the Shinjuku area, and from our thirties on into our fifties the relationship had continued in its present form. Whenever we met, we would exchange business cards. My name and address remained the same, but Sugaike's name was always followed by foreign words describing his position, and as I took his card I would ask, "Still the same?" Sometimes he would give a wry smile and say that nothing had changed, but ever since, in his early forties, he had left the foreign company that was so big even I'd heard of it, he would often shyly reveal certain changes of professional course. However, he never went into any detail. I had the feeling that it was because I was the sort of person who didn't need to be told more, that he asked me out like this. He seemed to remember me whenever there was a shift in his life. He would spend the night talking comfortably about the past and go home satisfied. At the end of the evening he would thank me and sometimes add that meeting me helped orient him about his own present situation. I too was happy to be needed this way every few years, like some solidly supporting prop.

Then, five years back, he started out by frowning apologetically and saying that unfortunately there was some problematic business he had to attend to late that night, and he spent the next few hours more than usually attentive to the clock. As we stood on the roadside while he hailed a cab, his parting words were, "Oh yes, I always forget. My address isn't on that card I gave you. Now I come to think of it, you've been living in the same place for quite a long time, haven't you? Odd, that ..."

By then the cab was waiting, and as he was still searching in his pockets, I stopped him and told him to leave it till next time, and just call me again when he felt inclined. He went on to say something strange.

"Yes, I guess if you didn't hear from me for a long time you'd think, 'I wonder if he's dead.' Well that's okay. You know the saying, 'Even if you're not right, you won't be far wrong'— that's how things are going these days."

It was the year we'd both turned fifty. I'd assumed until now that any business he would have at this time of night must be with a woman, but as I watched the cab pull away, I thought to myself that judging from a certain rawness I'd felt in him this evening, he might in fact be on his way to the hospital. There are occasions when, despite the urgency of the situation, you can find yourself suspended for a while in an oddly detached moment in time. I detected in his wake a definite sense of one who is off to a hospital.

Then one morning some time later, just as I was emerging from a dream, I saw Sugaike suddenly turn and say: "That's okay. You probably think, 'He may well be dead.' But you don't then pull out that business card and call me at work to check, do you? Whether I was alive or dead, after all, the answer wouldn't be pleasant. And so the relationship from your point of view is growing more and more like a relationship with the dead, so long as I don't suddenly show up on the phone …"

"Yes, that's true," I heard myself reply. "There are vast numbers of the living consorting with the dead like this, aren't there? We'd say we were alive, but actually we're both equivalent to the dead for each other. You could almost say we were completed and ended as living people. Not knowing about each other means we're dead to each other, doesn't it? There's probably more transparency to this than if we knew about each other, you know …" At first I had assumed Sugaike's remark about the unpleasantness of the answer was referring to me, but now I wondered if he wasn't talking about himself. Then I realized it must be eight years or more since Sugaike had contacted me. I spent a long time trying to calculate, despite the sluggishness of my brain, till I woke thinking, Wait a minute—it hasn't even been three years! It was very soon afterward that illness overtook me.

The year I was in the hospital, I started thinking in March that this would normally be about when another call from Sugaike would be due. I was only in the hospital for about fifty days, but during that time the house was often left empty while the family was visiting. Sugaike's calls always came soon before eleven p.m., and when I came to the phone he would begin by apologizing for the lateness of the hour. His voice suggested that he had viewed eleven o'clock as the cut-off time, and that he had been hesitating to call, right up to the last minute. I was in the habit of picking up the phone as soon as it rang, if I was at my desk, but it was the living room phone number that was registered with the hospital, and so if the phone rang late at night in the study it would take a while for anyone to reach it, despite how small the house was. Knowing Sugaike, he would be inclined to hang up after about five rings, and if this happened more than twice, he may well take it as a sign to give up. And in any case, the impulse to see me would pass. We would become dead to each other again.

Three months after I was released, I wrote a small piece for the essay column of a certain financial newspaper describing my experience of illness. It was the sort of paper that Sugaike would probably look at. Fujisato may have caught sight of it as well, in which case it would be only me who was continuing the relationship with the dead. Of course it may be that they both read it and came away with the natural impression that the future looked bleak for me.

All this had happened almost two years earlier.

"Still," I said to myself again, "I hadn't the slightest idea that Sugaike and Fujisato knew each other." A reproachful sigh escaped me, and then I proceeded to lie awake for some time, astonished, mulling over this meaningless reproachfulness, my eyes alert as a startled bird's.

· · · · ·

One night about a month later, during the rainy season, I saw Fujisato's face reflected in a window. This reflection was only a momentary impression I had when I first turned to look; in fact, he was standing beyond the window, beckoning to me impatiently.

After my illness, I had taken to smoking a pipe. I provided various explanations when people inquired about it, but in fact I myself had no real idea what shift in my preferences or physiology lay behind the decision. One drawback about becoming a pipe smoker is that, though it's all very well if you commute to the city, someone who works from home like myself can find almost no shop in the local suburbs that stocks pipe tobacco. Luckily, there is one shop that provides an excellent range of pipe tobacco in my neighborhood, although it's about fifteen minutes' walk from my house. Once I had established that I could only buy it there, I developed the habit of buying three packets at a time, and when I opened the seal of the third, I would set off for the shop to buy the next set. I had only been doing this for the last few years, but somehow it had developed into such a strong habit that felt as if I had been doing it for decades.

This doesn't mean that I gave up the cigarettes I'd been smoking since the age of eighteen. I still preferred cigarettes over the fussiness of the pipe when I indulged in the bad habit of smoking in bed, or when I went out. However, it seems that once a new habit installs itself, the old one becomes somehow modified, and after a while I discovered I'd run out of my store of cigarettes. This was brought home to me when I went to bed. What's more, the light cigarettes I had smoked for many years until my illness suddenly no longer suited my taste, and I took to smoking a stronger brand. It was quite widely advertised at one time, but in the last few years it had begun to disappear from cigarette machines in my neighborhood, and now the only place I could be sure of getting it was a twenty-four–hour convenience store a quick five minutes' walk west along the highway from my house.

This is how I came to start going to the convenience store more frequently than simply to pick up the newspaper for the weekend race meetings.

As I walked down the road to the store late at night in my scuffs, I added things up to myself. Yes, I thought, it's not simply the convenience of being open at night; there are times when you just don't feel up to going into the usual shops, or having to talk to people there, and these places answer the needs of this mildly depressive state of mind. Of course you exchange words with someone at a convenience store too, but only at the counter. You're

41

more a passerby than a customer in such places, and this makes things very simple for a person who's feeling low. If I became aware of some alteration in my physical or psychological wellbeing, I told myself, I might easily become one of those people who find that the only place they can face going into is a late-night convenience store.

That night when I went to bed I remembered that I had run out of cigarettes. I was tempted to resign myself to a pipe for my bedtime smoke this evening, but I was feeling wakeful, so I got up, drew a pair of trousers and a shirt on over my pajamas, and left the house. Softly turning the front door key on my sleeping family within, and starting down the road, umbrella in hand, I was aware of the slight aura of danger that hung over the scene, of a man stepping out of his house late at night like this. Though I had been wide awake in bed, once I was outside my steps seemed those of a sleepwalker.

I went to the counter with the three packs of cigarettes, together with an evening paper whose unusual headlines had caught my eye. The young shop assistant was about to slip them into a plastic bag, and I was on the point of waving my hand to indicate that this wasn't necessary, when I became aware that while he was ringing up my items, he kept glancing out the front window beyond. Then he looked back at me as if to say, *Do something*, and I finally turned to look. Fujisato was standing facing me beyond the window where the magazine rack stood by the entrance, tapping lightly on the glass and signaling to me. Despite his evident impatience, there was something extraordinarily slow and languid in the way his hands moved, a sense that they were heavy with the distance of dream.

As I recognized Fujisato's face, I was struck by something weird. Of course I had no idea why he would be in a place like this at this hour, and his face too registered surprise at having seen me as he happened to pass by. What startled me, however, was that even though I recognized him, my own expression didn't change—I felt myself simply staring unresponsively at him, as if I had turned back to look with impassive gaze from some shadowy region beyond.

I have never liked leaving a gap of any length between someone's speech or action and my own response. Recently I've developed the habit of listening to people in complete silence, but only to the point where it doesn't bewilder the other person. I am particularly careful in cases where someone acts abruptly; even if it surprises me, I do my best to convey by my expression that I don't find it odd. So to find myself simply staring like this and offering no help to Fujisato, whose face was already registering perplexity, to feel my gaze instead growing darker, produced precisely the sensation of some ghost suddenly having manifested itself inside the store. For an instant or two I stood frozen, unable to move. There was even a moment when I saw myself from outside.

"Well, well. We meet again!" I said, raising my hand and walking out to greet him.

"Hey, you've forgotten your umbrella," Fujisato responded with a laugh.

Fujisato told me that he'd been in the city that night—not something he did much these days—and had quite a lot to drink, so he'd hailed a cab to go home. He left the driver to find his own way there, and fell asleep for some time in the back seat, and when he opened his eyes, he found they were driving through an area he felt he both knew and did not know. Then they drove past this store, and it suddenly came back to him. He'd thought the driver had misunderstood and gone too far, but now he realized it wasn't so out of the way, in fact. But when he leaned forward to give the driver instructions, suddenly everything went white. He couldn't even say the name of the station nearest his house. The cab crossed Kanbachi Expressway while he sat there stunned. Then, fearful of where he might end up, he decided to get out. He retraced the way to the store, ten minutes away, struggling as he walked with the impossible suspicion that he might have misdirected the driver in the first place. Eventually he found himself approaching the hospital diagonally opposite the store, realized he had passed this way before, and seemed at last to awaken. He turned the corner by the store and was about to take the short way home, when he noticed someone who looked like me inside the shop, and paused.

"It's lucky I ran into you. I'll walk home from here."

"You found out just in time, didn't you? If you'd gone past here, you would have ended up who-knows-where. But all convenience stores look pretty much the same from the outside, after all."

"That's true. I didn't so much recognize it as realize when I saw it that there'd been a mistake."

"Sure, that happens sometimes."

"I also thought at first it was some extraordinary mistake when I first saw a figure that looked like you. But you were picking something up from the shelf and looking at it with such concentration, I came around to the front to have a closer look."

We walked along the highway in the direction of my house. The area where he lived was not too far down the road. I couldn't have appeared as Fujisato had seen me through the window, in fact. I had scooped up the evening paper as soon as I entered the store, on my way to the counter, where I ordered the cigarettes. That was all I had done. But then I rebuked myself with the reminder that it had indeed been me he had seen. We were soon approaching the three-way intersection immediately to the right of my house, and Fujisato looked around slowly.

"This is right about where I woke up. If I'd noticed before we got to this point, there wouldn't have been any problem."

"That apartment block is where I live. I'll be there twenty-five years this autumn."

"Oh, I remember seeing this place when it was going up, and thinking how huge it was. It was just when a typhoon was approaching. It still had its scaffolding on, and I was amazed at the fantastic strength of this towering thing in the fierce wind, I remember."

"Come on inside for a bit. The family's asleep, so you won't get a real reception, I'm afraid."

"No, I'll stop by some other time, thanks. But now that you mention it, would you mind walking a bit further with me? Give me an inch, as they say, and I'll take an ell."

"I haven't heard that expression in a long time. How about going for the mile?" I joked.

"Oh no, a mile would be going too far," he shot back.

"Now you're the one who's going too far!"

Laughing together, we set off along the twisting road that followed the old canal, heading north.

4

Quiet Place

Once again I found myself spending time with Fujisato without having learned anything about his present situation. I knew nothing about his profession or his family, and I had also missed the chance to ask him more about his mysterious connection with Sugaike. Fujisato remained silent as we walked together along the old canal road, and I found myself saying the first thing that came to mind. It was this idle question that led to the following extraordinary conversation.

"You remember," I said, "how when we parted last time you asked if I'd been transferred from another school? It's true, I started at our school halfway through the first year. But how does that relate to the fact that students stopped dying of TB in our year?"

"Yes, I'm sorry," Fujisato replied. "You were quite prepared to listen, and I didn't bother explaining, did I?" His voice was full of sadness. He kept his eyes fixed on the distance ahead as he spoke, and a nervous little private smile played over his mouth. "We were doing differential calculus or integral calculus, so it must have been second year, right? I was aware that you'd joined the class in the fall of the previous year, actually. That's why I didn't really mind when I was aware of you watching me from the back corner. I was remembering all this forty years later, and that's why I spoke as I did the other day. But of course you couldn't have understood what I meant."

"Had you been ill before I came, then? Is that why you stopped talking at that point?"

"No, you'd mentioned the tuberculosis. It wasn't so much from our year that it stopped; the cut-off point was actually the year we started high school, apparently. 1953. It was when streptomycin was first developed, or when it became more readily available. There'd been a lot of sad stories at the school up until then. I remember hearing of one girl who couldn't get up the hill to the gate—you know, what we always called Running Late Hill—without constantly stopping and gasping for breath. But still she came to school every day. The homeroom teacher couldn't bear to see it, and she finally arranged for each of the students to write up their class notes and send them to her, so the girl could stay home. But then three months later she died. Even while we were at school, you could still feel the atmosphere of those times, couldn't you?"

His next words struck me. "It was suicide that was on my mind then." The "then" was a puzzle. I couldn't figure out whether he meant forty years ago or the other day.

The last suicide at the school, he told me, had been in June 1953, before I had transferred in. A third year boy had climbed up on the roof above the schoolyard and jumped one morning, before anyone was about. The security guard had gotten up particularly early that morning, and just as he was about to come around the corner onto the grounds, he saw the still figure of the boy up there. He had climbed over the protective wire fence and was standing on the narrow ledge beyond the parapet, his back pressed to the wall, arms spread clutching the wire netting on either side of him. He was at the diagonally opposite end of the grounds from the guard, so quite a distance away, but the guard froze in front of the entrance lest he be noticed. The guard finally managed to collect himself and decided to act by taking a quiet step backwards, but although the boy would surely not have been able to see him, at that moment the shape slid from the ledge and fell. The guard said afterwards it was as if the wall itself had tilted forward. It remains a mystery why he had climbed onto the roof at that hour.

"You saw it too," I murmured, becoming aware of myself once more as a shaded figure peering out from the midst of its own shadows.

"No, that was five in the morning," Fujisato protested with a bitter smile. "The sun had started breaking through the clouds around dawn, they said. It was raining again by the time I got to school, and all I saw was his body lying on the ground like a little bundle of flowers that had been tossed there. It wasn't until that afternoon that we began to learn what had happened."

"So you must have known him?"

"No, I'd never spoken to him, actually. We'd passed each other three days before this happened, in the schoolyard. He came towards me, then stood still and looked up, sort of breathing out. Not at the roof. You remember the ginkgo tree in front of the lecture hall? Watching him made me look up at the tree too, but I couldn't see anything unusual. Classes had just finished for the day, and the rain clouds were breaking up. I walked on as far as the edge of the garden and turned to look, and he was still there staring up at that tree. That's the only connection I had with him."

"I remember hearing that the sight of him left a lingering impression that he'd somehow been standing in a bad place, at a bad time."

"That's not so," said Fujisato. His voice had now become dark and heavy. "I didn't even remember the event for a year or so afterwards. But when I did remember, I didn't do it very well. You think of the weirdest

46

things at that age. What I wondered was, would it be easier to do it in the morning or at night, on a clear day or on an overcast, rainy day? It's not the sort of question that thinking will answer. And I wasn't that serious at first. But once you start wondering, you find your imagination homing in on the details of the scene—climbing the netting, going over the parapet, standing on the ledge ..."

"That sounds tough."

"It takes courage. You go on till you feel the fear creep up your legs. Your hair starts to rise, like with static electricity. And then, suddenly, there's this figure before your eyes, gazing up at the tree. So quiet. The sense of urgency fuses with that image. That was the really scary thing for me."

"So you'd come to look at the place from the classroom window those mornings?"

"I felt better when I could actually see it. The room we had for math classes was quite close, but not too close—just the right distance. It was the rainy season then, I remember."

"Wasn't it winter? I seem to remember it being cold."

"That was just the rainy season chill. It rained a lot, as I recall. During the morning, light would keep breaking through the clouds. The classroom would suddenly feel dark when that happened. I was surprised when the door behind me opened and you came in."

"I'd come out of a much more mundane need."

"You must have sat down right near the door."

"I'd happened on someone in there who was incredibly good at math, that's why. It's the same reaction as the weaker animal going to the far corner of the cage."

"We were sitting more or less directly diagonally opposite, weren't we? I used to look at your back during the class, and now you were looking at mine."

"I remembered when we met the other day about how we sat those mornings. If you extended the line between us on out the window beyond you, it would follow your line of sight."

"So you were aware of that, eh? You must have thought there was something a bit unnerving about me. I can say this to you now: I was in a cold sweat with what was going through my head. I didn't really believe it would be a scary thing to do as long as no one was looking. But when two similar people are looking along the same line of sight ... the wall looked completely different then. The feeling that no one was there suddenly became overwhelmingly strong and began to draw me. And your eyes pushing from behind ..."

"It scares me to hear you talk about it now. Why didn't you turn around? You'd just have seen the face of an idiot trying to work on his math problems, you know."

47

"But it's not so surprising that I'd convinced myself you were the same sort of person. I didn't know anything about you except that we were in the same math class. And there was that way you got around the math problems you had to solve on the blackboard. As if you were coming up with an answer that was impossible. As if you were calculating a completely different solution, begging a completely different question. It made me wonder what was going on there."

"It was all on account of my shaky brain, you know. The levels of abstraction or categories of thought or whatever would get tangled and confused, that's all. I've been doing the same sort of thing ever since, too, for the last forty years."

"But I was relieved, you see, when I heard from someone at some point that you'd only arrived halfway through the previous year. I almost felt inclined to go over to you, slap you on the shoulder, and say, 'So that's the reason, eh?'"

"I wish you had. You could have helped out while you were at it by showing me how to solve a problem or two."

"No, the relief just allowed me to settle down and really gaze at that wall out there. I saw it differently now, too. There was no change in what I looked at, but a sense of completion seemed to suffuse it now. It spread over the surface of things, like some enveloping layer dropped from heaven. Not that my fear disappeared. I knew now how terrified I was. The figure of that boy slid past me at tremendous pressure, still looking up quietly at the tree. Till then, I'd been seeing the things out the window simply as shapes. Now those shapes were being maintained by force of pressure. They remained shapes, there was no change in them, but from moment to moment as I gazed they threatened to disintegrate. And inside me too, something utterly without shape, so alien and empty of human life that even I seemed absent there, swirled slowly around. It had an inertia so dense that the passage of time seemed almost to disappear, yet there was an urgency to it. And yet, over all this lay a single simple feeling of completion. That feeling encompassed you too, sitting there diagonally behind me in the far corner, the strangeness of the fact that you hadn't been at school when this happened, that for you it hadn't happened. From then on, the only words that presented themselves were *It's over*. It's been like a kind of recurring stutter inside me ever since, really."

"I guess *It's over* could amount to the same thing as *It didn't happen*," I murmured, drawn in by what I heard, though not really understanding it. And I thought how the sight of my figure gazing up at the hackberry tree must have slid down past Fujisato with a violent force as he stared, and how he would have felt encompassing this figure the same sensation, of a time when all was over. This thought seized me, yet did not hold me entirely in its grip, and I was still able to be astonished at the tale of what had gone on in Fujisato's head.

"I wasn't thinking anything," Fujisato replied. "I was simply gazing at the wall. I was absolutely passive. It's almost closer to the truth to say the wall was gazing at me."

"You're an intense sort of person, aren't you," I said, moved by him yet again, and I thought back to the boy I never knew, staring up at the ginkgo tree. "Is that where things ended?"

"What would have happened, I wonder, if that was all there was to it? But after that I continued to run into you in the classroom each morning, of course. Each time, the sense of completion deepened. I felt I myself was complete. I just gazed at the wall, thinking nothing. It may all have been thanks to you there, knowing nothing as you did."

"Who knows what things may turn out to be of help, to people or to the world, after all? You endured a lot, didn't you, although that's over now, speaking of completion. But I suppose that wall must have seared itself into your eyes."

"It's stayed with me all my life."

"A terrible story."

"No, it's good."

After I had watched Fujisato cross at the lights and seen his back turn the corner, heading due north, I set off to return alone down the old canal road, and now I heard again at my ear the echo of Fujisato's voice: "It's stayed with me all my life—no, it's good."

Every time he found himself in some predicament, he told me, he would call up that feeling of completion and huddle up against it. Until his forties he felt somehow driven to cling to it, but once he had passed fifty the feeling began to relax into a more gentle attachment, and recently he had arrived at a point where he could almost see everything as completed. As I listened I could vaguely sense that for Fujisato, "completed" was not simply "finished" or "past," but held the deep peace of a place in which nothing more could come into being. But for whatever reason, whether because of the shadow I had unwittingly cast over him from behind some forty years earlier, or because he had seen me the other day gazing up at the tree, the connection to me seemed to keep me from being able to think any further about what it might all mean.

Fujisato's voice, quiet though it was, had still penetrated deep along that dark road. Were this not so, I could not have heard and grasped so fully this strange tale of his. Though it was past midnight, cars continually skimmed past us. We weren't walking shoulder to shoulder, and for the most part Fujisato spoke with his head bent. But only once did his voice grow dark as he spoke—indeed, the more the tale sank towards what should have been gloom, the brighter his voice became. Was it the passage of time that resonated there? Perhaps his tone grew brighter as the emptiness within

49

him increased.

Or perhaps, I thought later, looking back on the experience, it was rather that my hearing had grown unusually clear and sharp during that time. And if it had, what did this suggest? This feeling resembled the sudden attack of doubts and fears that accompanies the first apprehension of a physical change. I stepped in and tried to tell myself that it was perfectly natural to listen attentively to a tale like the one Fujisato had told, yet something in me could not accept this answer so simply. On the whole, in recent years I had grown into the habit of giving people less than my full attention. Even when I was listening, voices tended to sound somehow distant. Gradually I was coming to experience a kind of abstractedness that seemed to spread out endlessly from whatever I heard. It would be safe to interpret it as my hearing beginning to lose their keenness. But the hearing of one approaching old age also contains a hidden acuteness, and a kind of paranoia. If you listen with attention, you find yourself earnestly trying to hear all you can, in a way that seems to tip you in the direction of an almost self-destructive urge.

"Have I been imposing on you?"

"What do you mean ...?"

"By telling you all this now."

"I was the one who sat diagonally behind you then. Listening to your story has helped me get a little closer to my own salvation."

"'My own salvation,' eh? That's a good one!" Fujisato said with a cheerful laugh. He stepped briskly across the road at the green light, then as he reached the other side he turned to look back at me. His face was youthful, although his white hair shone under the streetlight. He gave another happy laugh.

"I'll be the one to visit you next time," he called, hands cupped around his mouth, just before the brief green light turned to red again, and then his form was momentarily hidden by three trucks that took off at the change of light.

What temporary confusion could this be, I thought. He was mistaken. I was the one who had been playing the role of host this evening.

· · · · ·

As it turned out, it was Yamagoe who came to see me not long after.

Two weeks or so had passed since I ran into Fujisato at the late-night store, and it was now mid-July. This time too, the hour was late. The phone in the study rang when it was well past ten, and I lifted the receiver with a feeling that this would be Sugaike, getting back in touch at last after five years, but instead a youthful voice gave the name of Yamagoe. He told me hesitantly that he was in a family restaurant close by, and asked if I'd care to join him there, if I had the time. I turned the invitation around and said,

"Why don't you come here? You know the place, don't you?" He replied in a small voice, "Yes, I do."

As I put down the receiver, I recalled that I had gone off to Germany three days after meeting with Fujisato. It felt like a long time ago, but in fact I had only been back a day from the two-week trip. The night I arrived home, I forced myself to stay up late, and the following morning I was awoken just after nine by the din of political campaign vans broadcasting on the street nearby. I had gotten into the habit of early rising while I was away, and now I couldn't get back to sleep, so though I generally didn't rise until about eleven, I was forced to get up, and spent a long day in the house. I found that the sedentary desk work that I had pursued for decades had suddenly become difficult after a mere two weeks away. My muscles had grown accustomed to activity during the trip, and now they stiffened painfully, while a stinging pain shot through the outsides of my little fingers and my knees felt weak. When I stood up from hours spent sitting, my legs were as stiff as a pair of stilts, although I had no problem once I started walking. It reminded me of the symptoms of my illness that I'd felt two-and-a-half years earlier. It seemed funny to think that all this might be an aftereffect of having spent the trip craning my neck, looking up at cathedrals and museums and crucifixions and so forth, but the same thing had happened on a previous trip that had been a month long. The inexplicable paralysis that appeared in my limbs about two months after my return at that time turned out to be a symptom of the spinal injury in my neck. I decided I should keep an eye on myself for a while. But, as always seems to happen after a vacation, I soon found myself swept up by the pressures of the work that had been on hold while I was away, and forgot the problem.

I had been busy for days before the trip too, anxious to compensate in advance for at least some of the blank days ahead. Forcing my increasingly tired body along from one day to the next, I began to feel it grow lighter, and while my hands dealt with the various tasks, I slipped into a state in which my spirit was somewhere else. After the day's work was over, I would sense my soul as being slightly separate from my body, while my face retained the locked mask of concentration with which I had sat down at my desk. Perhaps it was because Fujisato had caught sight of me in this same state from outside the store, and been unconsciously drawn by it, that he was able to speak as he did, protected by the abstractedness he felt in me.

I finally completed my work sometime after nine on the evening before my departure and had just set about packing my bags when the phone rang at about ten-thirty. It was a long-distance call from Gifu, from the widow of a relative on my dead mother's side, whose husband had died that spring at the age of fifty, informing me that my uncle had passed away. I sat down at the desk once more to write a condolence letter, and by the time I had settled on sending a funeral offering by registered mail, it was past midnight, and I

51

couldn't recall the next day's schedule.

"I called in at the hospital on the way home from work, to visit an old college friend," Yamagoe explained when he had settled himself on a chair in my room. He was referring to the large, sprawling hospital right across from the store where I had recently met Fujisato. The friend had apparently been taken there with a bad stomach ulcer, but no surgery was necessary, and he had simply cooled his heels in the hospital, feeling bored.

"We've got some kind of karmic connection with hospitals, you and me, huh?" he said.

I laughed and thought of the way my eldest daughter had spent two weeks in that same hospital with her injury that spring, although I didn't mention this to him. "I'll bet you went there late without eating properly beforehand, and stayed until lights-out," I said. "I bet when we had visitors back then, they would have gone straight to a nearby restaurant when they left the hospital."

Yamagoe didn't smile in response. Instead he said, "Did I sound a bit strange on the phone just now?"

"I didn't notice anything unusual."

"I didn't speak for a moment, remember?"

"Is that so? If the call's from a public phone it often happens that the other person's voice takes a moment to come through after you pick up the receiver."

"No, it wasn't that. For a second before I spoke, my hand was poised on the point of hanging up."

"You were worried that it was too late to call?"

"That may have been it, but anyway, though I was the one to call, as soon as your voice came on the other end I had a strong urge to hide. I guess I'd be capable of being one of those types who make silent calls."

"I gather that when I pick up the phone and say who I am, I can sometimes sound so abrupt that the other party flinches. But has anything happened?"

"Well, not exactly," Yamagoe said hesitantly. Then he began, "I can kind of understand it when I remember how I was in the hospital, but this friend of mine won't speak."

Though he refused to say a word, if Yamagoe rose to leave he would restrain him, and in this way he kept him there until lights-out. When Yamagoe arrived, the evening meal had been cleared away, and his friend was sitting cross-legged on his bed by the window of the six-person ward, glaring fiercely at any visitor who peered in round the door. He gave no signs of responding to anything, and his guest was beginning to grow rather miserable. Then, with his eyes still narrowed, he twisted up his mouth like a child getting ready to cry, and broke into a silly grin. He sprang down from the bed and came towards his visitor. But as Yamagoe was about to address

52

him, he walked straight past. He paused a few steps away, then went into the corridor and on into the common room. Yamagoe followed and sat down opposite. "You can smoke," his friend said. Looking back on it, Yamagoe said, these were the only words his friend ever addressed to him.

In the beginning, Yamagoe hadn't felt anything particularly odd. He talked about how well his friend was looking, and how at this rate he would probably be going home soon. To all this his friend responded only with grunts and nods. Some patients who are in the hospital for some time and are beginning to recover will become fearfully talkative when a guest arrives, while others can find it difficult to speak, despite the gratitude they may feel. But his friend had stopped talking completely, and would only nod slowly in response, so his visitor soon found himself at a loss for words.

Yamagoe was aware, of course, that something was not right with his friend. He turned his eyes to the window, looking out to the cloudy sky still visible in the darkness, and changed the subject to the weather, remarking that the rainy season looked set to drag on late this year. He was just deciding to leave when his friend stood up and went to the corner of the room, took from the communal refrigerator a can of oolong tea, placed it silently in front of his guest, and stood there with his arms folded.

Being quite thirsty, Yamagoe happily reached for it. He was grateful that his friend had made this gesture of detaining him, despite the fact that he was apparently feeling that day that it was burdensome to have to spend time with a visitor. He sipped his tea comfortably, chatting harmlessly about this and that without seeking any response, and finished by remarking that his friend would soon be getting tired—whereupon the friend, detecting signs that he was about to leave, rose to his feet again and, this time a little more hastily, carried back from the refrigerator another can of tea and again placed it before Yamagoe. Looking at the two cans lined up before him, Yamagoe noticed that the patient's name was carefully written on each can with a felt-tip pen.

"Well, just let me know when you get tired," said Yamagoe, resigning himself to staying until the patient was ready to see him go. He was no stranger to the need for patience of this sort, and his relationship with his friend was close enough to make it no real sacrifice. It was about seven-thirty, and Yamagoe wound up staying till nine. The time was not simply spent in silence. Once he was settled, Yamagoe stopped feeling too much pressure, and he managed to keep the talk going at a leisurely pace by relaying whatever news came into his head about mutual friends from their college days. As he spoke, he came up with things he hadn't really noticed at the time, or had forgotten, and he found that topic after topic occurred to him. He was aware that his friend was hanging on his every word. He was somewhat disconcerted at the way his friend kept on glaring and nodding. Still, as these responses eventually became closer in sync with the words he spoke, he found himself recalling the time when he was weak from his own second surgery. He remembered how, though what people said was quite audible to him and he could understand the words, he couldn't quite grasp their meaning, couldn't quite come to terms with it, though really there was nothing there he had to come to terms with, and how this made everything begin to buzz and disintegrate, the other's voice running rapidly on, so that he felt he'd be left behind if he didn't nod fervently now and then while the other spoke.

He could only think now that his friend wasn't talking because he couldn't. Less and less did he feel that he was remaining silent on purpose. A faint smile hovered in the grim, taut expression of his eyes, as each nod coincided precisely with Yamagoe's pause for breath. No, he wasn't choosing to be silent, he simply couldn't speak. It was clear that there was no malice or contrariness in his friend's silence, and Yamagoe was the sort of person who could therefore simply accept the situation, without for the moment becoming preoccupied with possible reasons. He felt that although his friend was sitting there before him he was in fact in some distant place—how distant he couldn't tell, but a distant and painful place. And now it began to seem to him that since his friend was continuing to listen from this distance, nodding from time to time, the content mattered little. The voice was getting through, and this in any case was for both of them a precious thing.

"You're a fine person," I blurted out, astonished at his maturity. Almost a saint, I added silently to myself.

"No, as soon as I left the hospital I felt stunned. So much so that when I came to my senses I discovered I'd passed the three-way intersection and was standing beneath an avenue of trees in the darkness gazing in through a brightly lit window, thinking it must be the hospital cafeteria, and amazed at what a fine place it seemed."

"Perhaps I shouldn't ask, but if this friend is in hospital with a stomach ulcer, he'd be in the internal medicine department, wouldn't he? Do the doctors know what's going on, do you think?"

"Yes, I think they do. While I was talking to him, a nurse came along twice, and the doctor on duty also came by casually, just to keep an eye on him. 'Seems okay,' the doctor said as he was leaving."

"You didn't know anything when you came, did you?"

"Actually, the first I heard was when my friend called from the hospital on Saturday night and said he was there. Then he called again on Sunday morning and on Sunday night. I had work commitments the next day, so I promised I'd visit on Tuesday night. But when I came home after nine last night, Torizuka told me that he'd just telephoned. It was only to tell me not to bring anything when I visited. I must have been feeling a little stressed this evening when I was heading towards the hospital. When I got off at the usual station and started hurrying in the opposite direction from home, I had a strange sensation—it seemed such a long way. You can feel somehow lost and forlorn even in a place you've lived in all your life, you know? But when I came out of a back street right in front of the hospital, I saw that it had been rebuilt."

"I wonder when that happened?" I said, distracted by the idea. "I seem to remember now that after I came out of the hospital before you that spring, and would take walks around that area, I did register the fact that it looked new."

"Really?" Yamagoe seemed deeply moved. He turned and gazed out the closed window, as if listening for something.

"When was this building put up?" he then asked.

"In 1968, so it would have been twenty-five years ago."

"When I was five. Things must have changed a lot around here since then."

"No, I think actually most of the change had already happened by that time. The Kanbachi Expressway was already here. The only roads still not connected when I moved here were the Tokyo-Nagoya and city expressways. The road out there used to be crammed with heavy-duty trucks heading into the city."

"It was two years earlier that my brother got killed by a car. No, they wouldn't have taken him to that hospital. He'd gone off quite some distance on his bicycle, but it wasn't in this direction. My parents didn't tell me precisely where it happened till quite a long time later. Apparently they were afraid I'd be drawn to the place if I knew where it was. In fact no one ever really told me the details. My sister maintained to the end that she hadn't been told either, that she wasn't interested in asking, but I'm not so sure. Anyway, neither she nor I had any connection to that hospital."

The young man's voice had taken on that same keening, singsong quality I'd noticed before, and I waited silently to hear more.

"This friend in the hospital lost his father the same year that my father died. It was in that famous 1982 plane crash, you remember the one, when the mad pilot plunged the plane into the sea just before landing, while shouting, 'Everyone exit! Everyone exit!' His father was sitting in the front of the plane. Ever since we were students, my friend could say things to me he couldn't to anyone else, because of this special connection we had. That Sunday night when he phoned me, this is what he said. He was still under orders to stay resting in bed. As he woke in the middle of the night, he felt the world under his bed hurtling down towards the ground with a fearful roar. He was held fast to the bed as it fell, and it was somehow his own doing. For the crime of not having warned people sufficiently, he was now condemned to lie here motionless on the bed, his hair on end with terror. He was never one to confide or talk very openly, you know, but once in a while he did remark wanly that we two had a right to yell out loud against

55

the world. But he was telling me this now as something that had happened just recently, while he'd been really ill, and I judged from his voice that it was only now that it was really bothering him. I said something sympathetic, sensing that loneliness behind his voice, you remember, the atmosphere of those Sunday evenings in the hospital corridors around lights-out time, when you could hear the soft occasional whoosh of the elevator rising. I checked when I visited him in hospital, and sure enough, the telephone is near the elevator."

Twenty-two years ago, my mother's body had been temporarily laid out in the underground morgue of that hospital. The hospital she had died in was a little further south along Kanbachi Expressway, at the edge of a low hill. The doctor who had looked after her for her three months of hospitalization had requested an autopsy, and although it was clearly lung cancer that killed her, there were some unanswered questions about the progress of the disease, so the family consented. However, that hospital was not equipped to carry out autopsies. Her body was put into an ambulance with only myself in attendance, and driven behind the doctor's car to this hospital. We turned east off Kanbachi and passed quite close to my house on our way. After she was carried from the morgue, I sat down on the cold bench and settled in for a long wait, until the doctor appeared again and urged me to go home. I walked back to the house, and then fell into a deep sleep for exactly half an hour.

"It's quiet here," Yamagoe remarked.

"No, we're the ones who have gone quiet," I replied.

5

A ROAD THE SOFT PINK OF A CRESTED IBIS

As I read, I was struck by the expression "the woods rang." I'd barely begun to browse through the *Samyutta nikaya*, a translation of the dialogues between the Buddha and the gods, when I came across these words.

There is a large wood. The sun is at its height, and birds sit quietly among the branches. It would be one of those fiercely hot days when birds do not fly. In the scene before me, the wind has grown quiet.

For me this is a fearful thing, says the god.

For me it is happiness, replies the Buddha.

Anyone who has had an experience of the great jungles of India and southeast Asia will recognize the scene. One can imagine how the faintest breath of wind brushes the countless leaves so that they tremble and rustle, with a resonance only amplified by the slight time lag, until the whole forest slowly swells to a mysterious roar. Yet this ringing is soundlessness itself, it seemed to me. That was how I felt it.

Soundlessness surely is almost never found in the natural world. Deep quiet is in fact made up of various small sounds and voices. But perhaps it can happen that this profound hush will through some chance occurrence—maybe a tiny sound or voice—suddenly veer toward the infinite boundary of soundlessness, those countless minute sounds canceling one another into nothing.

The ringing reverberation, then, must be the forest's own being, a thing contained for a brief moment outside the realm of natural sound. Or perhaps, if this is merely a ghost image, what reverberates is the fact of the forest, visible here and now, all around. Perhaps an illusory image will, at its purest moment just before becoming extinct, ring with its very soundlessness.

A fearful thing or a happy thing—two very different ways of seeing it.

Such rambling, leisurely contemplations that leave the normal self far behind only occur on summer afternoons when the exhausted body rebels against its duties. But in fact this day was not one when the summer heat was intense, such as would suit the picture in my mind of a ringing forest in the fierce midday sun. Even at the end of July, the rainy season had

57

shown no sign of lifting, the weather had stayed overcast and drizzly and the temperature remained low. Towards the middle of August a typhoon had passed through, but even then a chill still lingered in the air, and only towards the end of the month had the days become hot and truly summery. Then another typhoon had approached, twisting itself through the trees and lashing them with a gale that was somehow chill, and now at last the summer cicadas, which had remained silent until that moment, burst into mad song. As I lay sprawled there, their song throbbing in my ears, my state of mind was invaded by that shrill agitation, a sensation deeply at odds with the hush I was contemplating.

Just a few days earlier, waiting for the arrival of this late summer heat, I had set off into the city on business in the middle of the day. Walking back in the wind that evening from the station closest to my house, the scenery of the streets I passed along struck me suddenly with an unusual intensity of detail. Even when I entered the shopping street close to home, my remarkable clarity of vision continued. The familiar buildings appeared extraordinary. Perhaps it was partly due to the quality of the rays of the evening sun, or to the unusual purity of the air. Of course, there is also the fact that in everyday life you never really pause to take in the details of the scenery in your own neighborhood. But now, as I went by the shops I had been passing for over twenty years and looked up at their oddly old-fashioned names, I realized that this was not just a sensation of seeing more clearly—what I was experiencing was true visual clarity itself. With increasing age, my eyes had developed a tendency to weakness, exacerbated by the fatigue of summer. I had been told that it would be sensible to put up with the condition for the moment, and wait until the cool weather began and I had recovered from the summer before going for an eye exam. But now my frail summer eyesight seemed to have turned right around and become instead a bizarre, almost crazy clear-sightedness. The memory of it now suddenly returned to me.

It was a summer three years earlier. The season had been a particularly hot one. As usual, I got off at the terminal station that evening and walked down the stairs. While riding the train I had been aware that my vision seemed a little odd—not exactly blurred, but when I looked at something I had to gaze hard through my tiredness to see it. Approaching the stairs, my feet tended to stumble. I kept my eyes on the steps as I descended, and from time to time I had difficulty judging their height. There was a moment when three steps seemed to run together into a flat plane. Nevertheless, I didn't slacken my pace. If I slowed, it would obstruct the flow of people around me. As I went on, the thought crossed my mind that even if I were to feel a heart attack coming on, I would no doubt keep going down these steps, and only at the bottom would I quietly separate myself from the flow and go to crouch somewhere at its edge. I reached the bottom and moved on with the flow of people around to the right, looking with surprised attention at the subway station I had seen so many times over the years—and at that moment, I felt that a headache that had long tormented me without my noticing, suddenly fell away, and I stepped suddenly into a world of clear-sightedness.

This was only a momentary experience, in fact. Each person in the vast jostling crowd around me stood out clearly, somewhat distant, yet quite distinct. The air was stretched tight. This is just like a scene on a stage, I thought in wonder. I turned my eyes from one face to the next. Each seemed like some Buddhist saint. As my eyes moved, each face in turn became the center of all that surrounded it. Innumerable centers of the universe seethed before my eyes. Everything leaned just slightly to the right. My own center of gravity seemed slightly askew, perhaps owing to some muscular spasm. I felt both deaf and dumb, but this appeared to be an effect of the extraordinary light flooding my eyes, since I was able to hear people's footsteps perfectly well. "How quiet the day," I murmured experimentally to myself. My voice felt close.

On hearing this feeble attempt to say something poetic, I assumed my visions hadn't been anything too bizarre. From the moment when I heard my own voice, the clarity of sight disintegrated, and what had just occurred felt like a scene I had witnessed at some point in the distant past. But when I looked back on it, wondering if it had all in fact been an experience of *déjà vu*, I suddenly felt the word "premonition" present itself.

The point at which premonitions manifest themselves, I thought to myself, is perhaps the exact point at which the present moment becomes the past before your eyes. But I hastily brushed the thought away and assured myself that this had nothing to do with me. Yet my mind continued to run along this uncharacteristic track, and I found myself wondering whether it was the future pushing in on the present that forced the present back into the past, or rather the vacuum created when the present moved backwards that drew the future into its place.

"This isn't actually about me," said a voice within me. "I'm just pondering the phenomenon of the seer, that's all. What's wrong with that?" and I found that in my bewilderment I was retreating to internal dialogue. Although I was talking to myself, the face that hovered before me was that of Sugaike, who surely must telephone soon.

"Be that as it may," I continued, "from the seer's perspective, whether he calls it the providence of the Lord or whatever, the future has invaded the present, so that the people and indeed the world of the present moment are being thrust into the past, and he's left standing in the place where the present has been. But from the point of view of some other, unrelated observer, this could be seen as the seer thrusting the present back toward the past and creating by sheer force a vacuum in the present, the reality of the lived moment, into which he summons the future. Yes, in fact, in order to produce a premonition, it's essential to make everything that exists from moment to moment into a matter of past history, and thereby to recreate the present as emptiness. And the reason is ..."

Here my words suddenly came to a halt, and I realized disconcertingly that my interlocutor had long since disappeared. This feeling was then overwhelmed by loneliness, as I stepped out through the station's ticket gate, and set off down the road. As I did so, I observed my own strange gait with considerable wonder. Good heavens, it's amazing that I've been able to get around as well as I have all these years, considering what an odd walk this is, I thought, observing how my steps gradually shortened as I proceeded, until every so often I would give a strange little double step and resume my former pace.

This was around four months before the first symptoms of paralysis of the limbs appeared.

.　.　.　.　.

I had this dream—

There is a small Japanese-style room where evening is at last drawing in, casting blue shadows over the tightly closed sliding paper doors. Everything has been beautifully tidied and set to rights. No one has come back home for half a day now, and no one looks in.

I myself am not present either. The evening deepens.

So who is it seeing this? I mutter, and at this point I begin to surface as if from a normal dream … The person who lay there, puzzled to discover that although the room was familiar, the house itself was strange, had by now become myself again. The last person to leave seemed to have been a woman, I thought, finally awake, and I tasted a residual sensation of something akin to sadness. Then a slow astonishment grew in me—I really had not been present. The room was clearly there, I could watch the passage of time and see the absence of people, so there must have been some point from which it was visible, but there was absolutely no sense of my own existence as the subject of the dream. Could such a thing be?

My bewilderment about the dream stayed with me through half a day's work. It was not a room I had ever seen before, and yet I was more keenly aware than ever of its atmosphere of long years of familiarity. Still, this sort of thing often happened in dreams. Perhaps, I thought, in the dream I was an infant waking from a nap to look around at a room from which my mother was absent. But the viewpoint had not been from a very low angle, nor did the tidiness of the room suggest that someone had, for instance, just stepped out to the shops for a while. Furthermore, the room was completely sealed, its sliding doors shut tight on both sides, one wall lined with chests of drawers, the other with a small closed window. I was not peering in through some opening. The room was simply there, unlooked at. Even in the process of waking, the thought occurred to me that the room's being so absolutely there and its being observed by someone were in fact mutually exclusive.

After days of cloudy weather, it was at last clear again, a hot day in late summer. The day before, a typhoon had approached Boso Peninsula, crossing land at Kujukurihama. In Tokyo, a strong westerly wind had been blowing since morning, with occasional heavy rain, but in the western suburbs where I lived the weather had grown no worse than this. By evening, although rain was still falling, the black clouds to the west were lit from beneath by the setting sun, which brightened the falling rain into swaying fiery columns. However, the evening news reported that around the Otemachi area of the city, the rainwater had overwhelmed several manholes in the center of the main road; water was gushing from them and threatening to flood into the nearby moat. Floodwaters had risen to the level of the subway platform at Akasaka Mitsuke Station.

Reports since yesterday had stated that a large typhoon of about the same size as Typhoon Kitty of forty-four years earlier was approaching the Kanto region, along the same course that the previous typhoon had taken. The name "Kitty" provoked in me a deeply unpleasant sensation. A quick calculation revealed that forty-four years ago was 1949, when I was still at elementary school, a year in which, quite aside from the typhoon, the summer had been unusually wet. There had also been a series of train-related incidents that were not simply gruesome but also somehow ominous, beginning with the discovery during the July rains of a dismembered body, hit by a train and flung onto the embankment along the railway tracks. I remember overhearing the adults muttering that it might all be the result of a curse laid by the war criminals who had recently been hanged. It may have been around the same time that a murder was committed in our neighborhood. Word had it that the girl whose body was found buried in the woods was a waitress at one of the restaurants right near my house. Apparently a bucket had been placed over her face. I think it was a few years later that the incident occurred in which body parts floated one by one to the shore of the Arakawa canal, but in my memory this too had been drawn in to become part of that year of great rain. I remember the body parts were said to be wrapped in oiled paper, and whenever I recall the smell of oiled paper it seems to bring back with it the memory of flood rains.

There was a parliamentary election in the middle of July. I expected to read that the government had gotten back in with a smaller majority, but owing to a factional alliance that amounted almost to electoral rigging, the long-time administration conceded and a new government was formed. People talked up this turn of events, proclaiming it as the end of the single-party reign that had continued since 1955. In my opinion, however, it would make more sense to compare it to another situation in which a long-standing government at last reached an impasse and was forced to accept change, in about 1949. I believe this was the period when the economy, on the verge of bankruptcy after the war, first gained a measure of stability, and the course was set for the "new economism." It was then, I believe, that people's habits of mind became more or less fixed in their present mode—there has since been lip service paid to ideas of change and reform, but at heart I feel nothing has really changed. It seems to me that the present system in fact perfectly represents the aggregate of all the vested interests that were first attained by people at that time.

These and similar thoughts filled my mind during the few weeks after the election, as I listened with gloom to the word "reform" being bandied about. But it wasn't until I heard talk of the present typhoon and its earlier counterpart that I was prompted to count up the years and realize the double coincidence involving the year 1949.

Another memory, that occurred at night:

"This town is kind of scary."

"Why do you say that?"

"It hasn't been burned at all."

"That's true."

It was Sugaike who had suddenly produced this statement, and I was quick to agree. This was thirty years ago, back in 1963, right in the middle of the great snowfall that occurred in the Hokuriku area that year. He and I were walking down the main street of the provincial city of Kanazawa, late at night.

The snow had brought traffic to a standstill some days before, and people were walking wherever they needed to go, wearing rubber boots with straw rope bound around the instep to give added purchase on the slippery snow. Small neighborhood bars welcoming weary customers on their homeward route were suddenly flourishing. Attendance had been so sparse over the last week that I had canceled most of my university classes and spent my time at my lodgings, keeping the snow from piling too high on the roof. It took a full day, working till dusk, to clear the snow from the main roof and another day to remove it from the subsidiary eave roofs and a third full day for the barn, by which time new snow had accumulated on the main roof and I needed to start over again. After I'd done all the roofs for a second time, I got up the next morning, heaved open the heavy window, and gazed up at the fog-shrouded sky. Large flakes were still tumbling down with the same relentless force as the day before. The landlord came to stare with me in astonishment, then we both burst into crazy laughter.

My landlord and I made preparations to go up onto the roof again that day, but in fact we found ourselves ensnared in listless chat, and wound up spending the whole day sitting and talking. Once during the afternoon I let myself out through the wooden door by the toilet, to see what was happening; I climbed the large pile of snow that had built up in the courtyard garden, jumped from there onto the eave, and put a ladder up to the main roof. Just before I reached the top of the ladder, I steadied myself, reversed the thin-bladed shovel I carried, and began to wield it to break the wall of snow that rose like a parapet before my face along the edge of the roof. As I dug, the shovel registered different textures of snow, from the various softnesses of the early powder snow, through the ice and sleet layers, to the layer formed by large heavy flakes. As I thrust each shovelful of snow from the edge of the roof up towards my chest, the snow surface before my eyes seemed to tilt up toward the grey sky, and for a moment these two alone filled the whole of existence. When I moved on to the main roof, the boundary between earth and sky had blurred. In preparation for the next day's work, I stamped down the snow around me to make a small area to stand on, then set off to climb up to the angled ridge of the roof.

I stood for a while at the top, watching the fog of snow grow now denser, now lighter around me, and the houses and mountains beyond the river coming in and out of view. Although the snow fell thicker than before, no human form could be seen today on other roofs, unlike on previous days, nor was there any human sound from within the houses. I stood still, taking in the silence.

So much snow had fallen, I thought, that there was no sign of anyone having gone outdoors for the past day or more. Then I suddenly caught, amid the snow, the wafted scent of a woman's hair and skin.

When I ventured out early that evening to visit the bar, there was Sugaike's voice greeting me from the far end of the deserted room, as if he had been waiting for my arrival.

"What have you been up to? You have the look of someone who's been inside with a woman all day," he called, and then, without waiting for a reply, he seemed to pick up on the word "woman," and continued, "Apparently there are only women in this house, and they haven't been able to get the snow off the roof, so if it keeps on like this they say the first floor rafters are likely to collapse."

While he spoke, he tenderly stroked the old wall beside him, as if it were a woman. It was no laughing matter, however. The little lanes in this area were filled with the snow that had been shoveled off the roofs on both sides. It lay in great mounds in front of every house, so that passersby were forced to clamber over it, stamping down a path through as they went. At about eye level here and there above these snow mountains, the remains of a second floor whose rafters had collapsed were visible. The doors and windows were twisted and broken, and through the resultant gaps the insides of the rooms could be seen—a chest of drawers half-buried in dirty snow, a glimpse of red bedding, were mercilessly displayed there amid the ever more thickly falling snow, beyond reach of help. Sugaike remarked on one occasion that the sight of this upset him, rather like the sight of a violated woman. That hand stroking the wall was also a habit of my own at the moment. In this way did one test doors and windows for the beginnings of warping, and calculate the curve under the weight of the roof's snow. In severe cases, you could feel this from the surface of a pillar or a wall.

"You should come along when you have some spare time at night and help them with the snow," I replied. "This place doesn't have a separate wing, so it's much easier to do than mine. You just have to throw it onto the street. The daughters can stand outside on a snowbank watching for passersby, and shout 'Okay!' or 'Stop!'"

Both Sugaike and the woman behind the bar, who was in her forties, had a twinkle in their eyes as they listened, but they didn't speak. Whenever a customer brought up the problem of the snow on the roof of this house, she would reply simply that there was no one there who could deal with it. She shared the first floor with her two working daughters, but they were apparently both quite nonchalant about the problem and asserted with a shrug that fate could take whatever course it chose. Once, when the subject of the snow had come up, the woman said, half-joking but quite sharply, "If young fellows like you would marry into some of the houses around here, there'd be less places being destroyed." Evidently this memory was what prevented Sugaike from speaking now, but after a short while he rebuked me with a low laugh.

"Do you really imagine none of the women here has thought about all this?" he began. "An old house has its own balance and stability, you know. The heavier the snow on the roof, the more fragile it becomes, but as long as you don't interfere with the balance, an old wooden house is fairly strong. There are certain strategic points. From what I can feel, this shop part is outside the structural bounds, and I'd say the equilibrium sets in at the staircase. I can tell from the way the footsteps sound, you see. They're very quiet. The women in this house have a natural sense of where the strategic points in the building are. They're aware that they must step gently on the points of balance. As the snow up there gets heavier and heavier, the balancing joints lock in more firmly together. The inhabitants are shifting about on the strategic points of the building's balances while they're sitting and standing, sleeping and waking, crouching and stretching, going about their business—at least when they're upstairs. Even when they get dressed and undressed. There's nothing more erotic to me than a woman protecting a house against imminent collapse. If some blunderer like you or me is asked to step in and help at this point, and rushes cheerfully upstairs to have a look around, thinking he knows what he's doing, this will be enough to bring the rafters crashing down right then and there."

"Dear me, you must have been peeping!" the woman shot back teasingly, but she looked bashful and pleased.

"Don't make us laugh too much or the rafters really will come down," I interjected. I was quite aware that the young girls upstairs walked about very quietly.

No more was said. The three of us fell into a drowsy silence. From time to time there would be a roll of thunder, and a gust of small hail would beat fiercely down on the road outside the door, then the sound would grow gentler as we listened, and the hush of falling snow reigned once more. A long thin cry could be heard in the distance, like the wail of some water bird—a bulldozer at work, pushing down onto the riverbank the mountain of snow deposited beside the bridge.

. . . . .

A few days later, I had exactly the same dream again. All was deeply quiet, as if to bring home the fact that no matter how many times the experience was repeated there was no possibility of change. I marveled over it as I awoke—it was a dream that denied the existence of the dreamer, yet there was a distinct sense in it of the passage of roughly half a day. For some reason, this slow tilt of time sent a brief shudder through me just as I crossed the boundary between dream and waking.

"This town is kind of scary"— thirty years later I recalled Sugaike's words. We were treading a narrow path along the middle of the road, now empty of traffic, the tracks of previous walkers disappearing into the snow fog directly in front of us. It was very late, and no one was about. Fresh powder snow filled the hardened snow hollows of the footsteps made by those who had passed there on foot earlier in the evening, but they remained as shallow indentations in the white surface, and some trick of light cast a line of shadow along one side that brought to mind the soft pink of a crested ibis.

I think I had walked ten steps before I asked, "Why do you say that?"

The snow fell endlessly. Neither of us was carrying an umbrella; we were dressed only in thin mountaineering clothing, our feet protected by light hiking boots with metal under the instep. The powdery snow that poured endlessly down as if filtered through the air's dense moisture was pleasant to crunch underfoot. As we walked on, the evening's alcohol rose to our heads, and a white ecstasy enveloped us.

"It hasn't been burned at all." Sugaike's answer seemed to come after a short pause, its context by now erased in the falling snow, the atmosphere of the surrounding buildings already different.

"That's true." My own response was immediate, with only a moment's pause to listen through the snow.

Seventeen years earlier, late in May of the final year of the war, both our houses had been burned in the same air raid—mine in Tokyo's western suburbs, Sugaike's in Shiba, closer to the city. My own experience was only

65

my mother dragging me along by the hand as we ran out through a burning wall that was beginning to topple. Sugaike, however, had become separated from his mother as they were escaping. His father, like mine, was away at the war. He had run along beside his mother, clinging onto the large cloth bundle she held in both hands, but some time later he discovered that the bundle his hand now grasped was held by a woman quite unknown to him. What's more, he told me, he realized the mistake must have happened early on, in the midst of the swirling confusion when everyone was running chaotically here and there in front of the wall of flames.

His mother had been instructing him for some time that if that kind of emergency ever occurred and they got separated, he wasn't to wait around, but must run straight on in the direction everyone else was going and be careful not to fall. And so, a child of eight, he simply ran. He hoped to catch up to his mother, but he found himself instead passing numerous other adults who were staggering along with their bundles. Falling in with this flowing throng, he fled with them into the communal air raid shelter in the park, a tunnel carved into the side of a hill.

How long did they all crouch there, crammed together into the darkness of the air raid shelter, holding their breath at the moan of enemy planes that reverberated even there in the earth above their heads? Then suddenly a man's form appeared, clearly outlined at the entrance, a little way above the heads of the huddled people within. For an indeterminate span of time, he stood still, hung there as though considering, then a blue flash lit the tunnel, revealing something almost like a smile on the myriad faces of those men and women, and the place was suddenly flooded with the fierce stench of sooty smoke.

The tunnel would have been transformed into a scene from hell, but Sugaike said all memory of those moments was erased for him. All he remembered was a deep hush within himself and his mind moving with a terrifying languor. When he came to his senses, people were shouting 'Stay calm! Stay calm!' as everyone pressed desperately towards the entrance. To keep from being pushed over, he clung with both hands to the back of the trousers of the woman who happened to be in front of him. She kept trying to push him away, mad with terror, but he gripped desperately, digging in his nails, till locked together they went tumbling out of the tunnel, where she finally beat him away from her. As he leapt to his feet and hurtled off, he glanced quickly back and saw mad dancing flames pouring up the timbers of the tunnel entrance and the wooden retaining walls.

He wandered then for three hours on his own. By the time the sky was at last quiet again, he no longer moved faster than a walk, even when he saw flames. He didn't necessarily follow where the adults were going. Here and there the occasional new fire still flared up, but almost everything was burned by now, so people's movements had lost purpose and become scat-

66

tered and incoherent. His mother had instructed him that if he became lost he should either return to the house or go to a certain relative's house, and so he set out towards them. There was nothing to see but burned ruins, yet he had a general sense of the direction. Every time he set off to walk, however, he would come upon some area now strangely peaceful in its desertedness, with flames flickering beyond it. As he skirted one fire after another, he found himself back again in front of the park. He didn't go in, deterred by a sense that as he fled he had seen people fallen in front of the tunnel.

The sky began to pale into dawn through the smoke, and a huge sun, dull red like the sun at evening, rose suddenly in the sky. He was now heading towards home. Most of the town was burned, but here and there some neighborhood would still be standing freakishly intact, and this was enough to show him the way. He had long since lost any fear of the flames. Nevertheless, judging from the passage of time, he had been going far out of his way en route. He seemed to have been continually avoiding the intact areas, and choosing to walk through the open spaces.

Noticing a burst pipe from which water gushed, he joined the line of people there and washed his eyes and moistened his throat. Later, his route took him past a gathering where emergency food was being distributed. He merely glanced at it as he walked, but a woman came running over and gently pressed into his hand a rice ball wrapped in newspaper, and when he had gone a little further he set about eating it as he walked.

Still further along the road, he went past a house standing alone in a burned neighborhood. He paused on a casual impulse and gripped the windowsill to pull himself up and look in, and there he saw his mother, sitting in an unfamiliar room, talking and sobbing. Much later, after his mother was dead, this scene came back to him in dreams, he said. Recently, the scene had shifted to an area near the edge of the city upstream in Kanazawa.

In fact, when he finally found his way back to the ruins of his home, his mother was actually crouched among the wreckage, earnestly writing something with the end of a burned stick on a bit of board that had survived the fire. He learned later that she had been unable simply to stay waiting by the burned house, and had kept roaming about vaguely in search of him. Then, worried that he might return while she was away, she decided to leave a message saying that she was all right and he was to wait there. However, the point of the stick kept breaking, and when she tried to write she discovered in growing panic that she could hardly recall how to form even the simplest letters.

When he arrived, the boy paused there for a while gazing at his mother, who was oblivious to his presence. He simply stood there blankly, he told me, with the wind around him.

6

AT THE CROATIAN CORNER

This is not my own dream but one I learned of from someone else and which I recalled as I lay on the boundary between sleep and waking.

I myself find it pitiful, the dreamer had remarked unhappily, that I keep on having this dream. He was a man about my age, and this happened when he was in his early fifties.

In the dream, he is a college student again. It's the end of summer vacation in his final year, and he is counting up the credits he still needs for graduation. He has barely been to class since school began in the spring. Still, if he makes a point of going from now on, he may be able to scrape by. However, he has for some time been entangled in other matters besides study, which show no sign of being resolved soon, no matter how hard he may try, and he feels utterly listless in both mind and body. As the dream goes on, however, he begins to realize that these other matters are not some affair of the heart, nor some artistic endeavor, nor some vague work he's engaged in, nor any kind of addiction—they are none other than his present professional work. He has a wife and children. The children are still small, so he guesses he must be in his early forties, when a man enters his "unlucky years," according to the old belief. The dream has a double structure, in which his fifty-year-old self dreams of himself in his forties dreaming of himself in his twenties. However, it is twenty or more years since the man in his forties left university and began his working life. He is living with his wife and children in the home of his dead parents. Even setting aside the fact that this house has long since been gone, he is aware in the dream that it's illogical, as it ignores all the effort he and his wife have put in over the years to deal with the mortgage on their own home; nevertheless, there he is, suffering in the dream from the exhaustion of the unfinished business of both schoolwork and his profession.

It was a dark morning. From the moment he had awakened, his mood was black. He didn't speak roughly to his wife and children, but his grimness never lifted, and when they timidly saw him off on his way to work he avoided their eyes; unintentionally, a cruel strength in his hand slammed

68

the door behind him, distressing them further. He was struck with sudden pity for them as he walked along, a middle-aged man in a business suit, from his parents' house to the train station. He was planning to go to college for the first time in a long time. He also planned to drop in at work on his way. The idea was to make a certain amount of headway on both fronts. However, he couldn't decide what this would entail. His mind continued to obsess over whether he should pull himself together and start afresh, and, if so, whether this applied to both his studies and his work, or whether it was better simply to put a clean end to both. His knees grew weak. The familiar road felt long. It was lengthening further, he felt, with each passing day. When at last he reached the corner from which the railway crossing was visible, his feet came to a halt, and he muttered to himself, "Maybe I'll drop in at my friend's lodging house."

At this point in the story, the man burst out laughing. He laughed here in the dream too, he said. His only connection with this fellow was that someone had casually introduced them that day, and they had happened to sit next to one another again that evening in the hotel bar.

"This may be the dream of an old man, but the fact is, even when I was a student I didn't live a life that would have allowed me to take things easy like that. Later on, when I was working, it was the same—I guess you could say I wasn't in a position to have the luxury of getting tired of work. The only possible logic to the dream might be that I lost both my parents in quick succession before I was twenty, and at the time I had this idea that if I kept working this hard, I might very well die young myself. Maybe this is what produced the dream's lassitude. I was quite strong and healthy as a youth, actually, but of course it's natural for a young man to feel this way."

Just a few days earlier, I heard the news that the man who had gaily told me all this had died last year of heart failure.

I recalled the words of another man who had since died, who said that the hearts of the living are a kind of repository to receive and hold the words that have drifted like falling leaves from the mouths of others now dead. Perhaps he meant that these "fallen leaves" could nevertheless sometimes dance and swirl with a strange power more alive than the hearts of the living. For all that, it was almost a month after I heard of this man's death before his words recounting the dream, which were almost my sole memory of him, began to come swirling gently in to fill the vacuum between sleep and waking each morning. This too was a long journey, you could say.

"A dark morning." These words lingered in my mind. Even when he had spoken them as he related the dream to me, I had registered that it was a long time since I had heard anyone speak those words. When he was forty, it was already many years since people had begun turning on a bright fluorescent light on dark and rainy mornings, but no doubt in his dream the room felt dark as of old. A household may be inclined to economize, and dislike turning on the lights in the morning, with the idea that lights would make the neighbors think that there must be some trouble in the household. But as they all wander about in the dark house getting ready for the day, husband, wife, and sleepy children at their breakfast table would all be likely to grow increasingly silent and morose. Even their behavior will take on an air of gravity. The atmosphere of a sudden departure for some distant place settles over the household. And it is on those mornings that shadows of the past creep in more easily, even when not intentionally summoned by memory. Under circumstances like these, it would not be so surprising if a man in his "unlucky forties" began to merge with a young man not much older than twenty. It may well have been the darkness of the morning that provoked the man's dream.

The pale light that seeped in around the edge of the curtain suggested that it was another cloudy morning. All that day, although the sun occasionally shone briefly, it was generally rainy. This was no doubt typical October weather for this area. I guessed we would be farther north than the latitude of Hokkaido. I'd heard that German people had such strong eyesight that they didn't feel the need to turn on lights in the morning or as evening drew in. This was natural enough when you considered the shortness of winter days, and indeed, Japanese in the old days did the same.

The alarm clock at my pillow, set for eight, was about to go off. Whatever time I set it for, I always woke just before it rang, and I had brought this habit with me on my trip. It was something I had acquired because of the pressure of work deadlines. I wasn't in a profession that meant I had to leap up and rush out the door, and indeed I would lie about in bed for a while after the alarm clock had startled me awake. Yet though the alarm apparently didn't have much of a real effect on the situation, I did seem to need some particular encouraging voice to get me up once I had woken of my own accord. It was four days since I had booked into this room. The purpose of the trip had been attended to two days earlier, but I had stayed on, and spent yesterday with a friend from the area on an expedition out of the city. I came back late and finished my packing before going to bed, so today all that remained for me was to leave. I had in mind to go in to the city center not far away, but I had made no plans of how to fill my time after that.

The time of the alarm had been set by the previous guest. I would normally have been asleep at this hour. The night I arrived, I first thought when I saw the alarm clock that it would be too early for me, but then I began to feel an easy inclination to follow the choice made by my predecessor. Yesterday morning I had had to leap up and leave at six to catch the early train, so the night before I had pulled my own alarm clock out of the case and relied on that. I saw nothing strange in this. Perhaps there was somewhere in me an urge to leave no trace of my existence in the room. Two hours from now, I would leave the room forever.

70

But did I perhaps have an irrational urge to position myself within an absence of self? Indeed, come to think of it, don't other people also do something very much like this from time to time, in one way or another? It is at moments of change that this happens. Perhaps, I thought, at such transitional moments you stop aging, or the past and the future are both drawn into the moment and spill over it, or you might age quite suddenly, and as these thoughts went through my head, my earlier sleepiness abruptly came washing back over me. I was looking at an empty room, gazing and gazing until my own self disappeared, and though even the shadow of self had faded, yet the sense of time passing was constant, and as I was drawn down into this blank place inside me, suddenly a horrible voice seemed to speak, and the alarm was ringing. I sat up in a panic, losing for a moment all sense of where my own limbs were, until I managed to put out a hand and turn off the switch. I was just heaving a sigh of relief at having emerged from something like temporary paralysis, when from beside the pillow the muted telephone began flashing.

I grabbed the receiver and barked out my name, so confused for a moment about time that I wondered if someone might be calling from the front desk, worried about me because I was still in my room so late. There was a short silence at the other end, then a voice said, "So you're there?" and burst out laughing.

Then the voice went on, "It's Sugaike. You're not there with a woman, are you?"

．　．　．　．　．

I had come to take part in a large book fair being held here, at which publishers from throughout the world came to display their books. Sugaike happened to be in the same country on business, and he said he had decided to drop in to the book fair in a spare moment, and there noticed someone who looked like me. Apparently this had happened two days earlier, a little before noon, at the Balkan countries counter, and when I heard this, I was able to recall just when it must have been. An Asian man had been standing in front of a Croatian publisher's stand, Sugaike said, looking at a book of monochrome photographs; Sugaike had passed directly behind and gone a considerable distance when he paused, struck by the way the man had been staring intently at a photo of a dark landscape. He quickly retraced his steps, but the man had disappeared. A swift instinct led him to run past the Slovenia to the Hungary stand, and when he looked left from the next lane over, he caught sight of what appeared to be this same man, heading towards the exit from the end of the aisle. He followed, weaving his way through the crowd, but there was a large crush of people on the bridgeway across to the main building, and he lost sight of the man.

He was wiping the sweat from his forehead, with a private grimace at all the fuss he was putting himself through, when his eyes lit on a public telephone. He checked the time difference with Japan. "I'm probably wrong about it," he thought, "but it will be fun to try and see," and he rang my home in Tokyo. He said if my voice had come on the phone he would have concocted some excuse about his being in Frankfurt and wondering if I'd ever been here. However, when my wife came on and told him I had gone to Frankfurt, the coincidence of having his slightly delusional guess being answered so neatly by reality gave him an eerie feeling. Nevertheless, he asked for my schedule and the phone number of my hotel. My wife told him the name of the Japanese publisher I was with, and he set off immediately. After some confusion, he located the stand. At that moment I had finally managed to make my way to a German publisher's stand upstairs, where I proceeded to stay for a considerable time being plied with wine. I didn't get back to my room till late that night, and it was also after ten when I returned the following evening.

"Well here we are—not exactly 'fellow travelers,' precisely, but at least we can meet as two people both on the point of leaving," he suggested, and hung up, having established that I didn't have much luggage to carry. He apparently had business talks that morning and would be flying to Berlin in the evening, so we arranged to meet at twelve-thirty. After some consultation, we decided to meet at the wine cellar where apparently we had just missed each other two nights earlier.

"Well, that's a strange coincidence," I said to myself as I got up, drew back the curtains, and sat down on the chair by the still dully lit window. Then I added to myself, "But perhaps it isn't really." A month earlier, at the beginning of September, I had telephoned the company where Sugaike worked. He happened to be away at the time, but I was relieved to learn that he was in fact still at the "previous company," a term he always joked about when he ruefully spoke of how often he changed jobs. He would at least have received a message telling him I had called, and would probably remember this when he saw someone who might be me in the crowd at the book fair. And then, he did have a bit of time to spare. Still, I was puzzled at why it was that I had suddenly decided to call his company, after five years of estrangement and despite the fact that it had never been me who initiated contact.

It had been about three in the afternoon on a quiet, clear day. It was the sort of hour when I would have completed a block of working hours, and might feel inclined to wonder about the welfare of a distant friend. There had also been the chance event that a few nights earlier, tired and disinclined to read, I had been flipping through my collection of old business cards when I came across the last card Sugaike had given me, had recalled his phrase "my previous company," and had laughed to think that I was still in "my previous house." However, since my illness two springs ago I had gotten lazy in regard to people and the world in general. Though I wouldn't go so far as to say I was withdrawn, I had developed the habit of not bothering to call others except when it was really necessary—even stopping myself at the times I reached for the phone without thinking—although I didn't mind if they called me. Any reckless connection I made with others, of any kind, filled me with a feeling that was not quite fear, but more like momentary timidity based in a superstitious sense of a vague threat, and this timidity then seemed to shift slightly, to a reluctance to be bothered. This entire response was no doubt related to my physical condition. Even now, when I was disgustingly healthy again, I still had buried within me the habit of convalescence that believed that my body's well-being was maintained only by a fine balance, and this was evidently projected outward in the form of a premonition of personal harm. Or perhaps there was a simpler reason for all this. It may just be that all those whom I would be inclined to telephone on impulse are the sorts of people who are only fleetingly present for me, on the boundary between being acquaintances and being unknown or forgotten—people quite removed from my daily life, like Sugaike, or Fujisato, or Yamagoe.

After all, I said to myself, Sugaike is an acquaintance of thirty years, but he was the one who said those words when we last parted five years ago, to the effect that he and I both are somewhere between the living and the dead.

The room grew darker. I stood to look out the window, and saw that a cold rain was falling over the distant hills, which still preserved the outline of their edge against the sky, while below me the river shone leaden. A four-oared boat was gliding along with smooth strokes, leaving a faint purple trail in its wake.

A faint worry crossed my mind that I may not have left my name when I telephoned Sugike at the company, but instead hung up as soon as I heard he was absent. In that case, Sugaike would have known nothing of this when he saw the person he thought was me at the fair, chased after that person despite knowing he might be mistaken, and telephoned my Tokyo home on a mere guess.

Perhaps if I had picked up the phone in Tokyo, he would have said, "So you're there after all."

.   .   .   .   .

A number of times I have happened to see a couple of elderly Japanese men meeting up in a café or restaurant in a foreign country. Their minimal glance of greeting always suggests that they see each other every day, but then you hear one say, "How many years has it been, eh? How are you?" The ensuing conversation maintains the same laconic tone, interspersed with long pauses. They give their orders. An air of exhaustion seems to cling to them.

73

Since Sugaike was the one who had had to give chase two days earlier, I decided that I should be the one to arrive first this time, so I set off early. As I went down the stairs to enter the basement restaurant, a back in an overcoat ahead of me twisted around in my direction, and we exchanged a look of greeting. He looked just the same as when we used to meet at the entrance to that bar in Kanazawa thirty years ago.

"Ho ho, here's a scene of two Japanese standing around together."

These were Sugaike's first words. Sure enough, there we stood side by side, the epitome of the Japanese traveler—floppy travel bags slung from our shoulders, the front of our all-weather coats lolling open on account of the sudden touch of warmth in the breeze, gazing once more at the ceiling of the old wine cellar where we'd both been two nights earlier.

"Wherever we go, I always get the feeling it's not your sort of place, you know. It's just the same in Japan. It's been that way for thirty years. Right, I'll leave the German to you." So saying, Sugaike put down his bag, and asked the waiter in good English about a cloakroom.

"I see you're still at the 'previous place,'" I remarked after I had ordered wine and food in bad German.

"Still and even more so the 'previous place,'" he replied, looking deeply serious.

"What have you come over here for?"

"Business, what else? I gather your work on this trip is to go to parties. That's what your wife said. She told me you won't be back till the end of the month. How will you get by, with so little luggage?"

"I phoned you."

"Ah. Good thing to do."

"No, I mean I phoned your company. Around this time last month. They said you were away on business."

"I got a phone call … ?" Sugaike paused and frowned. "Oh yes, so I did. I got a message."

Apparently it had slipped his mind. But at least he'd only forgotten, which is better than not having known at all, I told myself, a little bewildered at how things didn't seem to add up. I sensed there was more to the story, but I didn't feel I could ask. Just as our conversation had reached a pause, the wine arrived.

The moody look that had momentarily settled on his face relaxed again. He raised his glass to his lips and said with a sudden warm smile. "You seem to have gotten taller. That must be why I couldn't track you down at the book fair. With that added height, you looked like a different person."

"How's the wine?"

"Mm, not bad at all. You choose well. But listen, I really did think when we were standing there shoulder-to-shoulder just now at the entrance that you're taller these days."

74

This was something that numerous acquaintances had half-teasingly said to me in the two-and-a-half years since my illness. It was a result of the aftereffects of the paralysis, which meant that these days my knees began to give unless I tried my best to keep my back and neck straight and stretched. Perhaps, in fact, I had developed a habit of lengthening my back and straightening my spine even before the symptoms appeared, to try to ward off the encroaching paralysis. There was no doubt that the plates between the vertebrae in my neck had grown brittle with the years. I wondered how things were when I'd met Sugaike five years earlier. As I explained this to him, I felt as if I were having to justify and explain an unforgivable slip of decorum in becoming taller at my advanced age.

Sugaike gazed intently at me as he listened. When I began to lose interest in the story and tried to cut it short, he would drive in a well-aimed question. Inevitably, this spurred me to greater verbal clarity, so that I settled in and was able to give a straightforward and coherent explanation of it all. When I thought about it, the sight filled me with amusement. Here we sat, two friends met over a midday drink, sunk in fervent conversation, our mutual nods and the rhythm of our hands as they lifted and set down the wine glasses expressing an ease and a certain tension at once. Puzzled to note how exceptionally expressive our gesturing hands had become as we talked, I remarked, "Funny, isn't it. The moment elderly Japanese men launch into talk of illness, they become so eloquent and impressive they almost represent the country at its best." I tried to pass it off as a joke, but Sugaike stuck his elbows on the table and looked embarrassed.

When lunch arrived, we checked that neither of us had any obligations that day besides travel, and ordered another bottle of wine. Now it was my turn to ask how Sugaike had been.

"Actually, I had a fall on the station stairs," he replied.

He had apparently been heading down the stairs toward the platform, having finished his business at Suidobashi. That particular staircase, a rather narrow one, was never crowded, and at a little past two in the afternoon, with no train coming or going just then, it was particularly quiet. He strode rapidly down, to a point four steps from the bottom where the staircase turned a corner. Here, he almost lost his footing, and to save himself he made an impulsive leap. He'd intended to jump lightly down, but he misjudged the distance and landed with a surprising degree of force, then staggered to regain his footing, and in the process slammed up against the far wall of the little landing.

He just managed to avoid hitting the wall face-on, and instead struck it with his right shoulder, with a sudden blow that felt like an open-handed slap. He may have lost consciousness for two or three seconds. Next thing he knew, he was kneeling, almost ceremoniously, beside the wall on the hard concrete. Anyone climbing the stairs at just that moment would have found themselves unexpectedly face-to-face with him as he knelt there. Luckily, by the time the next train's passengers were approaching, he had managed to stand and pretend to be looking for something he'd dropped.

"You'll laugh, but the instant I leaped towards that cramped little concrete landing, all I could see before my eyes was a great stretch of pale blue."

"Were you flying through the air? Had you turned into a bird?"

"It was water. And on the far shore stretched a field of delicate flowers—you know, like one of those scenes of heaven."

"What? Come on! I've never heard of anybody flying there. And surely you weren't being beckoned from beyond. Not to mention that this isn't really the right territory for discussing these things."

"No, it isn't the right territory."

"But is it true nobody saw you?"

"Well, just as I got to my feet I caught a sudden waft of fragrance, and a young girl went past. She looked about sixteen or seventeen. She went calmly on down, and I was just thinking to myself that young people these days aren't very sensitive in this kind of situation when she turned around after a few more steps and gave me a faint smile. Her face was very pale."

"There you are, that's the field of flowers."

"Fine by me," said Sugaike, indulging in a little private smile.

We were having a relaxed lunch as we talked. Sugaike had left the ordering to me, and I apparently had managed to choose something that suited our digestions, since we both kept our forks moving continually. An onlooker would have assumed that we were simply having an enjoyable conversation together.

After his fall, Sugaike had made his way to the office and worked till evening. Once night set in, he found himself oddly invigorated, and took a few friends off drinking till well into the night, coming home late in a fine mood. The next morning when he awoke, his whole body felt rigid and immobile. When he tried to get up, the area from his shoulders down his side all the way to his thigh thrummed with pain. Even so, he decided to go to the office. But when he stood in front of the bathroom mirror, he discovered that his face was black and blue and swollen, and looked as if he had spent the night in violence and debauchery. He called the office, reported that he was running a fever, and spent the day in bed, but as he lay there his stiffened body continued to swell, and the next morning he hurried to the nearest hospital, feeling like death.

After careful examination and numerous X-rays, he received the unsurprising diagnosis of bruising. "Bruises, eh?" he repeated stupidly. Thanks to the doctor's probings and manipulations, the stiffness was already somewhat alleviated. After checking his blood pressure again and peering into his face, the doctor tilted his head to one side and looked quizzically at him.

"I thought perhaps it was high because you were nervous when you first arrived," he said, "but it isn't any better now, even with you lying down." He'd assumed, when he was left resting on the examination table, that the doctor was preparing to put him through some kind of physical therapy. But the doctor informed him that he would need further treatment.

"So to the next day—my first time taking a hypotensive drug, in my fifty years of life. I woke up to a fine morning, but the world around me was suddenly dark. When I tried to stand, I felt like some ghoul staggering up out of a coffin. Apparently I stood in my pajamas at the kitchen doorway staring in solemn astonishment at my wife—though we've been married heaven knows how long. It was just luck that it was on a weekend when this happened."

"I've heard the medication can make you depressed, but I never knew it was as bad as that. So you rested, I suppose?"

"Yes. I spent all Saturday in bed feeling as though the earth was sucking me under. I slept through half of Sunday too, then in the afternoon I had some rice broth and began to feel a little more human, so I went out for a walk around the local neighborhood."

"Ghouls aren't supposed to go outside, you know."

"You're not kidding. It felt like either I was a ghost, or the town was an apparition. It had absolutely no feel of familiarity to me. And I know the area incredibly well, you know. I've lived there for over twenty years. There's not a single street I don't know. But every time I arrived at a corner, I'd come to a stop and look vaguely around, although I ought to have known the place perfectly well. It was a bit like losing one's way in the dark, but it was also like that *déjà vu* that you used to carry on about in the old Kanazawa days, remember, where you feel sure you've seen the exact same scene pass before your eyes at some time in the past. Maybe a long long time ago, before you were born …

"Before you were born, or maybe after you've died … You did well not to get lost. I wonder if you might have spent the last ten years or so walking around the neighborhood without really taking it in."

"Yes, that's right. When I came to one particular corner, I remembered having taken my kids to play nearby when they were little, and my feet set off of their own accord in that direction. But the funny thing is, there I was, more or less lost, but on that day and only that day no less than three old people asked me the way. They had all lost their way home. And each one was actually very close to home, I discovered. I took my time and told each one the way as painstakingly as I could. And my instructions were fine, despite the state I was in. Actually, those old folk probably saved me. I think in fact they were bodhisattvas, you know."

"You met three bodhisattvas! You must have felt so grateful you decided you could go to work the following day, is that it?"

"Yes, I refused to listen to the family's anxiety, and decided that just so long as I could get there without getting lost, I'd go, even if my shadow was still pale on the ground and my legs giving way under me."

"So the medicine didn't work?"

"No, that's not exactly it. I was able to stand a few centimeters, or anyway millimeters, back from myself and laugh at the sight of me there wrapped in depression."

"Saying 'serves you right'?"

"No, I wasn't simply being judgmental. I was also impressed at how well I was holding together."

"You must have been in pretty bad shape, then."

"I'll tell you something, I've never behaved as competently and impressively as I did then. I was seeing myself from the outside, you see. Doing that, of course, has its pros and cons."

"From the outside, eh? ... I haven't ever felt that, except at odd moments. How long did it go on for?"

"About a month and a half, all told, I think."

"A month and a half? That's a long time!"

"Yeah."

Sugaike glanced up at the ceiling, and appeared to be listening for something. I started listening as well, recalling that we were in a basement room, but the thick domed roof did not seem to hold within it even the slightest sound. I was reminded once more of how long I had known and been friends with this man. Though I had no idea what had startled Sugaike just now, the impulse that moved us had been almost simultaneous.

We sank into silence. Naturally enough, having started on our second bottle of wine, we were beginning to feel a little drunk. When the meal had been cleared away and the coffee arrived, Sugaike took up the conversation again, but in a tone that suggested he was recalling something now grown distant.

"After a while, I stopped taking the medicine."

"I thought I heard you had to take that stuff for the rest of your life."

"I'm okay again."

"Was it because you were exhausted?"

"The doctor said it was probably the aftereffects of the shock from my fall. I don't know about that, but it makes me sound rather pathetic, doesn't it?"

"So this was a while ago?"

"About when you were in the hospital, I guess."

I had started to feel rather sleepy. I knew it was sensible to always do things at a leisurely pace when traveling in foreign lands, for fear of doing something silly, so I decided it would soon be time to make a move. Though I'd gone out of my way to try to contact him the month before, it was only by chance that we had met now, so we hadn't gotten around to inquiring about each other's recent lives. Now we were about to go our separate ways again without a thought, and perhaps by the next time we met we would both be over sixty. But this is how the relationship had always been. We had never had any inclination to talk about our present circumstances.

The question that had been haunting me for the past six months suddenly emerged.

"I gather you know a man called Fujisato?"

"You know him too, huh?"

"We were together in high school. But he knew that we both know each other."

"Now, where would he have found that out?"

"This spring, near where I live, he came up out of the blue and started talking to me. I don't think we had seen each other for thirty-seven years, since we left high school. It turns out we'd been living quite close to each other for years. He came right over to me, and the first name he spoke was yours, not mine."

"My name? Ah yes, I remember now. When we first met, I asked him about you. He'd mentioned the name of the high school, and that reminded me of you. There wasn't much else to talk about, you see. But this would be going on ten years ago."

"What does he do?"

"Same as me. He's in a telegraphics company. His place is much bigger than mine, of course. He's probably gone quite high up the ladder, I'd say."

"Telegraphics" was the word Sugaike used back in Kanazawa long ago, when he first told me his profession. Kanazawa was a small city, so I could guess the place he was referring to. The next time we met, in Tokyo, he said he was in a computer company, something that even I could understand when I read it on his business card. But the next time he changed jobs he told me he was back in the old telegraphics company again, and then although the company would change after that, it remained telegraphics, and I basically lost any real idea of what sort of field he might be in. I wasn't even sure whether this was a word that was commonly understood, or whether he was just using it out of habit when he was with me.

"It's only natural I'd forgotten," Sugaike declared, and burst out laughing. "We were talking about you together in English!"

"In English?" I repeated, startled.

"It was pretty dumb—a bunch of middle-aged men playing at speaking English the way students used to do in the English Speaking Society at college, remember?" Sugaike's grin was now rueful. "You might have heard of it at the time; a scheme to put the fear of God into some fat, complacent businessmen in their fifties, get them together from various companies and give them training in how to be 'international.' My company was pretty tight-fisted, but it chose to send me along to this thing. A month of being holed up in a hotel together, with lectures and debates from morning to evening, all in English. And at night we had to write reports. There was time for free talking in the middle of it all, where we were paired off with someone we didn't know and had to make conversation, but talking about business was forbidden. And I got paired with Fujisato. He was on a different level from me, in career terms as well. He was there as an observer. His English was excellent. This was tougher for me than being raked over the coals by the young foreign female teacher, I can tell you that. There was no way I could talk in English the way they expected. When were you born, where were you born, those sorts of things. And when it came to questions about experiences during the war and so on, I barely had the words to even attempt an answer. So I managed to scrape through by asking what school he went to and what he studied. That's where you came in. Wow, that did it! 'HE IS MY FRIEND,' says he in very slow, careful English. 'MANY YEARS,' says he. We'd finally hit a raft we could cling to there."

"It may have been quite unintentional on your part, but that really was territory you should have stayed clear of, you know. Why didn't you tell me earlier? So what did he say?"

"I can't remember a thing. It was in English, you see. I just remember him chattering on about 'MATHEMATICS.' There was no way I could understand it all."

"Yes, he was amazingly good at math."

"He was pretty good at English too. And then various experiences later in life brought that home to me. Whereas mine stays creaky, unfortunately. His just went rolling smoothly on."

"Did you meet again after that?"

"Yes, just once, three years later. I ran into him one summer evening in town, and he invited me for a drink. I'm not fond of geniuses, you know, but still, it was nice to get together again. The place he took me to was actually an amazingly run-down bar. He's a quiet type, isn't he? But later it struck me that he'd said quite a lot of heavy stuff, in his very calm way. When I praised his English, he said that in fact he couldn't really communicate with it, and indeed he constantly felt aphasic. Then he said this nation's got no way of communicating with other nations. We do our best to sound plausible, he said, but in fact the real stuff doesn't get through at all."

"Aha, I guess it's just as well that I'm no good at foreign languages, then."

"I understand you made a speech at the party the night before last."

"Just a three-minute one."

"Yes, I heard it was short."

"Where'd you hear that?"

"This German guy started talking to me in English at the party last night, and asked if I knew your name. It was the 'HE IS MY FRIEND' scenario all over again. But this time it wasn't so completely unexpected. He said you did the speech in English. He told me what you said, too."

"That's ridiculous. I spoke in Japanese, and someone translated into English for me."

"But he seemed to suggest he'd heard it from your own mouth."

"Probably because I paused after each sentence. My head went completely blank while I was speaking, so the translation didn't go very smoothly."

"Well well, so it was Japanese, eh?" Sugaike tilted his head and glanced down at his watch. He paused, straightened himself and went on after a moment. "Actually it wouldn't matter what language it was, you have this unmistakable way of speaking. You know, that ghostly thing, the 'spirit of language'? By the way, you say you're going by train as far as Mainz? I'm going to the airport by train too. I don't imagine you're in a hurry, if it's Mainz you're off to, and I have some time. Your bag doesn't look too heavy. How about walking to the station, just to clear our heads? Like we used to do in Kanazawa. We've even got the same kind of sky."

Smiling, he seemed to be listening again for a sound from above. "Apparently the air raids were terrible here too," he said finally.

Then he added, "Oh yes, and Fujisato. I recently heard a rumor that he went a bit peculiar and took a leave from his work for half a year."

7

WHITE SONG ON A NIGHT ROAD

I must already have been hearing the sound for some time before I became fully aware of it.

Each footfall on the stone floor grew heavier. Again and again those feet would move off toward the staircase that led up from the room, seeming on the point of climbing straight on out, only to move around the pillar instead and return to the spot in front of the chapel again. This chapel was like a cellar within a cellar. Under a round cap set oddly high, the altar consisted simply of an assemblage of square-cut stones, with a smallish, slender, red cross set there. The crucified Christ hung low from the crossbeam, head inclined to the right, as if lamenting the blood that ran from the wound in his side. There was no other offering or decoration on the altar. The wall behind it was pierced with a single, very lightly tinted stained glass window, through which seeped the pale light of a rainy day that found its way in through a skylight at ground level.

I was deep inside a crypt, which was simultaneously a kind of graveyard; stone tombs of medieval emperors were set into cavities in the walls. The place had a tepid atmosphere that emanated from the reddish sandstone—almost the rufus color of the crested ibis—that was used for the walls and pillars and arches, and the stone was imbued with a lingering sweetness from the hundreds of years of incense that had burned there. It was a little like the scent of a body wracked with fever. And indeed, considering that outside was a rainy October evening, the air in here did hold a slight warmth. No one had entered or left for some time, but it seemed as if the stone had absorbed a certain amount of warmth from each of the bodies that had passed it.

Only my own footsteps were audible. This hush was no place to linger for long. People are constructed in a way that apparently enables them to constantly distract their ears from the sound they themselves make, I thought, as I walked off, following the clear ring of my own footsteps. Momentarily pausing a little earlier, I had been brushed by a fearful sense that I was hearing all around the faint echo of other voices, and this uncanny apprehension had impelled my feet into now unstoppable movement. Yet though I was clearly bent on escape, I found myself reluctant to leave, and I moved with the reverence of one quietly awaiting some imminent arrival. And now my footsteps grew hushed and slow, as I again approached the altar. I thought of choral voices raised discordantly, and as I did so a low moan reverberated through the ceiling, the pillars and the walls around me.

Simultaneously, I raised my eyes to the round vaulted ceiling, and felt the cavern seething with a black mass of darting eyes.

The roar of a distant plane passed slowly overhead.

The cross on the altar glowed ruddily.

· · · · ·

Whenever I return from an extended trip abroad, the various problems that have accumulated in my absence keep me frantically on the run until finally I awake one day with a feeling of exhausted peace. No doubt I have managed at last to readjust from the jetlag and altered seasons, and the excitement of the trip has dissipated.

So it was that one morning when I awoke, because it was fine, and as a gesture to the fact that things felt a little better, I found myself leaving my accustomed walking path on a whim and made my way to the park with the old hackberry tree where I had met Fujisato that spring. The park was full of noise, though there was no sign of children. In one corner, a thin old man in a jumper was walking energetically round and round the enclosure fence of a zelkova tree that was in its full flush of yellow autumn leaf. In one hand he had a walking stick, while the other, thrust skyward from the elbow, held a transistor radio that was playing at full volume a young people's disc jockey program. He paced with an exasperated fury, waving his stick high and bringing it down as if beating the air about him.

Despite the swift walk, however, his jerky movements made him appear to be engaged in some form of rehabilitation, as if he was recovering from an illness or accident. Yet surely it would be risky for such a person to be doing his exercises so furiously. No, it must be that he'd become enraged and was now attempting to relieve his feelings. Even if the loudness of the radio, the wild swings of his stick and the ferocity of his walk, not to mention the boredom, only served to inflame his rage, no doubt this was better than staying quiet.

I watched in admiration. Still, today I obviously wouldn't find here the peace I sought for thinking about Fujisato. That spring day, the park had been suspended in a deep pre-noon calm, out of which he had seemed to emerge. He had come towards me then looking almost accusing, I thought—and turning now just as I had done that day to look at the spot where Fujisato had stood, I saw a tramp lying face up on a nearby bench in a brightly colored sleeping bag, his hair long but quite clean, intently reading a comic book in the sunlight. He was about forty, and his considerable girth, combined with the bulky sleeping bag he was so warmly wrapped in, gave the impression of a baby's body. Under the bench was neatly stowed a blue and purple climber's rucksack, together with shopping bag and a little shopping cart. Gazing around the periphery of the park, I registered that there was indeed no house with stone wall and stone steps....

"So it was madness, eh?" I inquired, after a considerable pause. The voice that emerged was hoarse, somehow sad—the wind that blew across an earth whose season was tilting sharply into late autumn struck my face full force, chilling its drunken flush.

Sugaike immediately understood that I was speaking of Fujisato. "There's some dispute about that," he replied. "It may sound rather old-fashioned to use the term 'feigned madness' ..." We were approaching a busy crossroad, and he was gazing at the nearby subway station. When we left the restaurant in drunken spirits he had declared we should walk to Central Station, but now perhaps he was realizing that it would be over-reaching ourselves for two men in our fifties to carry our luggage so far. However, he then averted his eyes, and took the road that led on to Central Station after all.

We walked on in silence again. Perhaps, I thought vaguely, he would be at a loss to know how to give a simple rendition of things to someone completely outside his line of work, even though on this occasion the subject was a third person, and overall exhaustion may also be making him disinclined to talk. Deciding I would leave the subject at that, I remarked, "Even though we were intending to take it easy, you set a good brisk pace, don't you? Do you remember that time we came down from the mountains and walked that extra six miles out to the bus route? We didn't even glance at the fields we were passing through as the evening came down." Sugaike gave a wry grin, but the question he answered was the earlier one.

"Apparently he made out he was crazy in order to avoid people's resentment. The company he was in was praised because it was already quietly practicing reductions back there in the heady days of the boom economy five years ago. While other places were expanding, this one was busy transferring a number of its staff, and quite a few among them were in fact dropped altogether. The opinion at the time was that the director saw the writing on the wall, and took the responsibility for some preemptive action. He quit just when everyone round him was beginning to praise him. That may be the way it goes. I heard tell he said something about the old emperor having died, so this was his last gesture of service to him. He was a fine, gentle person by all accounts. I seem to recall he died recently. But what of Fujisato, you say? Well, he was in a pretty high position, but I didn't hear he was on the board. It's a big company, after all. But there are rumors that he was one of the brains behind it. So the story goes he bore the brunt of everyone's grudges and it sent him round the bend, or that maybe he faked it in order to leave—it doesn't seem at all likely to me now, but rumors have a life of their own, don't they? It's all too remote for me to really know, anyway."

We walked on again in silence for a while, then he gave an embarrassed grin and asked, "What do you think? Just say, say I was driven into a real corner, so tight there was no way out of it. All my own doing, of course, but nevertheless. And I went off my rocker, or half off my rocker, and left. If a rumor began later in that little world that it happened on account of being the sole scapegoat for everyone's resentments, would that seem like divine providence?"

"It's the sacrificial myth, isn't it? Generally when people disappear they leave behind them some tiny myth."

"It would be unbearable to have left so pointlessly, don't you think? If you got to hear later what people said you'd be overwhelmed with shame. Rumors are deadly serious things, especially rumors about what happens to people in life. Even the stupidest ones are somehow sacred and unalterable. Ignorance is the bliss of Buddha."

"That's true. We're all buddhas."

My words were not the result of any personal revelation, they simply sprang from my lips in natural response, part of the pleasure of our enjoyable repartee—but the instant I spoke, every face in the crowd of people advancing toward us across the street suddenly seemed to me to be holy. The sun had long since set, leaving behind only a trace of red in the sky, and the sole illumination came from the dim lights inside the shops that lined the street. The faint light falling to earth seemed to be gathered into those pale, unknown foreign faces brushing past me. At a certain point as they approached through the evening's darkness, each stood out in sharp relief for an instant, their alienation from me vividly conspicuous—yet from the depth of this alienation I felt an emanation of some strong preknowledge, some incomprehensible recognition that was the stronger for being utterly unrecognizable. At length, like one descended from a floating feverishness, I felt myself drawn into a state of clarity of vision, though it was vision empty of all content.

"You're walking along looking happy," remarked Sugaike. Then he asked, "Do you ever have the experience these days of being swept up in a kind of incomprehensible ecstasy?"

"I do, yes, I do."

Again I felt pleasure in my smooth responsiveness to his words. After I had spoken, I did indeed have a sudden sense of being perpetually harassed by a faint but inescapable ecstasy.

"It's a fine line between that and desolation, though," Sugaike murmured. "It's like the feeling of rocking your body to and fro, to and fro, singing some song you don't know."

"In a drawn-out, hollow voice."

The station was visible not far ahead.

After Sugaike had jumped onto the train bound for the airport, I sat down on a bench on the platform. As soon as I lowered my bag to the ground, my whole body registered the weight of it and my eyes momentarily clouded, and when I opened them again there was Sugaike at the window of the already departing train, smiling and bobbing his head.

About half an hour after he had left, I thought I caught sight of his figure again.

I had walked about the station after his departure till I found the train for Mainz, scrambled on board just in time, and settled down by a window. Watching the strange bewitchment of darkened field and forest that spread around us from the moment we left the city limits, I seem to have drifted off. When I returned to my senses the train was running underground, and in no time it surprised me by arriving at the airport station. I had been assuming that the airport was in the opposite direction to that in which I was traveling. It seemed Sugaike, accustomed though he was to travel, had also mistaken the direction. Our parting had been foolish. Somehow this sort of thing had happened every time we met for the last thirty years, yet the three-minute stop at the airport irritated my nerves unduly. The smattering of descending passengers disappeared, leaving behind them the empty and stationary platform,.

It must have been a case of mistaken identity. Given the time difference, Sugaike surely wouldn't still have been loitering on the platform. Yet when the train finally set off again, my eye fell on a coated back standing at the far end of the platform. The man was repeatedly mopping his forehead with a handkerchief, and as he wiped and wiped, his back gave off an air of increasing astonishment. But though I was intent on catching a glimpse of his face to identify him, embarrassment made me avert my eyes for an instant when the time came, and the corner of the platform flicked by and was left behind as the train rushed on into the darkness of the tunnel.

I had the impression his overcoat was wide open, the buttons of his suit coat were undone, and his tie was loosened.

· · · · ·

It has become usual in the last four or five years, at around the time when the local zelkova trees are past the height of their autumn gold and the leaves of the oaks are withering, for me to be constantly beset by a vague drowsiness. At the same time, my working hours grow fuller.

Enveloped in drowsiness and constantly astonished by my stupid blunders, my work in fact progresses all the better for it. The faster I work, the sleepier I become. The sleepier I become, the more I persevere. I wonder if others in the outside world who reach my age also find themselves working like this, conscious of the year's end looming closer day by day. And do they ever feel that this way of working is in fact rather dreamlike?

As the days press in, so too the pressure of each day's hours increase, but once engaged in work, I can forget time for a while. It's not that I am focusing so very intently. Rather, it's the opposite; my brain becomes a kind of semi-transparent free-floating creature, through which passes a great variety of idle thoughts. Thoughts not your own attract your eyes to them, slipping into the midst of your busy concentration, rather like the experience of lying idly in bed, hearing the sounds and voices inside and outside the house. Good heavens, what was that I was just thinking? you say as you pull yourself together after the bewildering abstractedness has passed, and in its wake you register, though faintly, an incomprehensible flush of ecstasy.

—Still, I said to myself, that time between autumn and winter three years ago, when quite unbeknownst to you the nervous paralysis was slowly progressing, you did well to experience a sense of ecstasy, I must say. If you don't speak for a long time, even the very silence grows vague....

That form I had glimpsed on the airport station platform continued to worry me during my trip, recalling Sugaike's mention of his high blood pressure as I did, but I was forced to put it down to mistaken identity. Some days after I arrived home, I rang his company, but he was away on work again. If I told him the story, he would likely respond, "If that had been me, the lawyers would be tidying up my estate by now."

Three weeks later, when I found myself yet again wandering about feeling lost and purposeless in a foreign country, like some callow youth on his first trip abroad, it was myself I was more worried about. A few days after that, Sugaike phoned again during the day. He told me with a laugh that he'd discovered once he was in the train that he'd mistaken the time of the flight, and had to run like crazy through the airport to catch it. These were his own words, and so it was now clear that it had indeed been a case of mistaken identity. But away from him, that figure on the station platform continued to hover at the edge of my mind as I worked....

He was wiping away the sweat with his handkerchief. Shoulders heaving at each breath, he mopped and mopped as the greasy sweat poured ceaselessly from his brow. Until a moment earlier, he had been crouched over his bag, blocking people's path, searching desperately inside it for something. When he descended from the train and set off to walk with the flow of those around, he was suddenly struck with doubt about whether he could recall putting the thing in his bag that morning in the hotel, though in fact it wasn't anything whose loss would matter greatly. Of course it was unreasonable to expect that he should remember every little detail of events, yet the blank in his memory somehow swelled in importance. He thrust it away with a little frown, deciding that if he walked smartly on till he reached the stairs, his feet would find it easier to continue on down than to stop, and there he would be, inside the plane—but no, it was a mistake to think of how bad he would feel once arrived there. In the end, he returned to this present version of the self, crouching at the feet of the passersby, clearly a soul obsessed. What does it matter? he thought to himself, but his hands were scrabbling in the bag independently, and when the footsteps around him had faded, his body stilled into rage. Then, when his eye fell on the missing object, he suddenly remembered carefully saying aloud to himself as he packed that morning, "You've put it here, remember."

As he closed the bag and stood up, sweat suddenly sprang from his face. He felt it run chill from around his neck down his back. There was still plenty of time before boarding, he realized when he glanced at his watch. Now that he had found the missing object, the thing felt still more irrelevant. It wasn't as though he couldn't have replaced it if it hadn't been found. He'd left such things behind in hotel rooms a number of times before, after all. He ought to take into account the fact that these little attacks of nerves were likely to happen sometimes on occasions such as these, when he was traveling on a tight work schedule. But there had been a space of time, while he was scrabbling desperately in his bag, when all idea of departure times had deserted his mind. Nor had he had any thought of work, or indeed of why he was here. Nor of his life, his family, or the passage of the years. It wasn't that he had forgotten, but that his whole body had closed itself against such thoughts. The only image in his mind was of a cat he must have noticed somewhere, asleep in a scant little patch of sunlight.

Perhaps it was all quite irretrievable …

. . . . .

It was a cold, windless afternoon in early December, cloudy since morning. In the midst of work, I was astonished to hear a voice that suddenly remarked, If Fujisato really did go mad, that's unbearable. The oaks in the nearby park were long since past the height of their autumn colors, and on a fine day they presented a scene of dried brown wintry leaves, but in the half-light of a cloudy day such as this, they seemed to blaze forth again in their autumn richness. Even with all the firm intentions of my drowsy state, my heavy workload had carried inexorably through into December without a break.

Just when are you talking about? I asked myself sternly. Even if it was true that this had happened, Sugaike had indicated that it would have been around the time when the economic crisis was becoming evident to all, and that would be two or more years ago at the latest, long before the shadow of his existence had fallen across my path. If he had indeed gone mad, I could have had no idea of it while still in the midst of our nearly forty years of estrangement. Even if I'd heard such a rumor from some classmate, I would have responded blankly by checking the name, quite unable to connect it

88

with a face. It would have been the same if he'd died. There would be no difference from the countless deaths of unknown others.

—Still, Fujisato couldn't have gone mad.

—What are you talking about? How can you make such statements, when you've only seen him twice recently? Can you really come out with pronouncements like this about such a perfect stranger? Or are you trying to make an issue out of whether he's still crazy now, perhaps?

Thus did Fujisato continue to haunt me—in words, and yet before those hovering words could emerge, in image also, a sense of a warm hand groping in empty air; and this image separated itself from that of Fujisato and became something I had witnessed somewhere, then words dropped away, and from the midst of a bewildered smile there emerged the memory of an old man's hand waving as he slowly began to dance. In place of reply, it was that gesturing hand, brushing the very edge of the ridiculous and grotesque, dancing on and on, half in jest and half serious, that would not leave my head as I sat there till evening at my desk.

Later that night, when the print began to blur in the book spread open before me on the desk, and I raised my eyes from the page, astonished to realize I had just misread something, the memory of Fujisato's face calling me through the store window came back to me. It was not his fault that that face, popping up so suddenly above the iridescent stripes set into the glass, appeared so weird. There was also nothing inherently strange about the fact that he had lost his way in the night, retreated until he found a place he could clearly recall, then seen in the deserted brightness of the corner store a face he had come across again only recently after almost forty years, and gone round to the store front to check, amazed to see me again and at such an hour. Such a series of unlikely coincidences would probably make me too go first to the window rather than walking in through the door, and hammer like a moth at the glass and call out. I seem to recall he shouted for quite a while before I turned round. Rather than irritation, that beckoning hand waving at me revealed a dull hopelessness, as if he was gradually retreating into the distance while his hand continued to gesture.

When our eyes met, Fujisato looked more surprised than I. No, rather, his expression was one of innocence. I recalled now that in the instant before I recognized him, it was that innocence that struck me. He wasn't smiling. His brow was smooth, and it was if anything the questioning face of one who has heard his name suddenly called, that looked expressionlessly in, passive to the other's gaze. I in turn for a moment did not smile or give any answering nod of recognition, but simply looked. Perhaps it was because I was drawn by that innocence that I was nevertheless held, despite my flicker of fear at the grimness of my own unacknowledging gaze, a grimness that made me sense in myself the look of one who scuttles into shadow to glance warily back.

Yet how could he have looked at me with so smooth and inexpressive a face, when he had called through the window, and I had turned to him? Had he perhaps if only for a moment disconcertingly found himself thrust deep into my unresponsive and stolid gaze? Into a gaze that, while drawn inside the other, yet trembled with fear at the eeriness of my own reaction … An accusing voice rose in me against Fujisato, a voice at once tinged with reactive resentment, yet with an edge of anguish in it. Ever since you were young, the voice declared, whenever you were cornered you always clung to that serene sense that it's all over, didn't you. As you've grown older, you have moved in closer and closer to this state of serenity. Such a person must not go mad! an anguished mutter added. What of that time in your youth when the peace of completion descended over everything? That peace that descended over all the urgency, over the dulled loss of time, over what was and what was not, over the absence of anyone then in that place, over the fact that someone was right there diagonally behind you, the peace that descended equally over all …

—It's over. There's no need to fear madness.

The words were audible to me. It seemed to be Fujisato's voice, but he had not spoken such words. Still, some of what he said late that night six months earlier as we walked together along the old canal path did seem to have dropped from my memory.

—So you've been ill too, eh? Come to think of it, you do look younger,

—I wasn't able to age for a while there.

—But if it comes to that, just what is this growing younger?

—Comes to what, exactly?

—I've been ill too, you know. It all went white.

Then he told me he'd grown younger day by day. But no, we couldn't have had this conversation. I didn't tell Fujisato about my illness. And of course I hadn't grown younger in the two months since I'd met him again back in April after all those years. We may, however, have exchanged a few brief words laughingly lamenting the awkwardness of feeling somehow younger these days.

Yes, I do believe now that Fujisato actually said, "I've gotten younger." I think he spoke with a sudden brightness, in a voice somehow lit up. Even without knowing anything of the intervening decades before we met, my impression of him from that time makes this seem quite possible. But I didn't reply. In fact a momentary fear passed through me that he might have gone a little strange, though I quickly brushed this away as absurd....

Now I think of it, though, it was I who was a little odd that night. After I parted from Fujisato, I was humming softly to myself as I made my way home through the streets. It was a halting, artless, wandering little tune. It wasn't particularly sad, however. It was a song that spontaneously sang my satisfied acceptance at having re-met Fujisato that evening and heard some-

90

thing of his story, a white song that wound its way along the night road.

That night my sleep was quite peculiar. Once home, I slipped back into the bed I had left an hour or so earlier, that still held the shape and warmth of the moment when I had slid out of it. As I lay there, playing out in my mind once more a loose version of the conversation we had just had, I slid down into sleep without my thoughts hardening around the facts, and after a considerable period of deep sleep, I found myself saying with a suppressed laugh …

—So your idea is that this fellow slowly went strange in the head from the curse of all those years of stress and effort. That he actually kept it under control for quite a while, but finally it began to get the better of him. Then one evening, after midnight it is, his wife senses something odd, and when she comes out of the bedroom there he is in the living room with only the small light on, not on the sofa but sitting on the little cane chair with his legs apart as though he's on the toilet, deep in thought.

It seems she's been keeping an eye on him for some time, and she tells him to quit trying to hang on, they'll go to the hospital the next morning. Her husband gazes round the room, then slowly points a firm finger at something on the shelf and asks when it was bought. When our eldest child began middle school, replies his wife. So how much did it cost? he asks. She has a wife's memory for such things, so can tell him more or less what the price was. She goes on to relate how the family had gone out and bought it together. She's pleased that he's trying to recall the past. But all he says is, Is that so? and he retreats to his thoughts again.

After a while he looks up once more, points to something else, and asks when it was bought and how much it cost. His wife does her best to remember, and answers him in as much detail as possible. Interspersed with long silences, he proceeds to ask about one object after another. He points with increasing desperation as the list goes on. But the more scrupulously she answers each question, the further he sinks into amazed thought, till at last he cradles his head and remains silent. Can't you remember? she asks tremulously. A man doesn't need to have such a detailed memory about such things, you know, she goes on soothingly. However, it seems he replies that he can remember it all. But, he goes on, it's just that I can't finish thinking. About what? she asks. I don't know! he exclaims, I don't know what it is, no matter how I think. And then he goes on, But I'm not going to go mad. I've lived my life that way. And apparently it's true, he didn't go mad in fact.

He didn't go mad in fact—the voice had rushed eagerly through its story in order to say this, the very eagerness spinning the story out. A repressed laugh burst out now, but when I opened my eyes, there was no sense of laughter on my face or in my throat. I drew a breath, and wondered what the joke had been. Then I fell asleep again, and when I next began to surface, I was in the midst of making a declaration …

—Yes, my father died eleven years ago. My mother died twenty-two years ago. We lived in a small house full of old things. After the war, we sold all we could, and the worthless things that we eventually found we couldn't sell, mostly clothes, we carried about with us every time we failed to throw them out when we moved. They were like a household affliction. My mother would often sit for half a day at a time in front of a drawer full of moldy clothing, patiently taking out and putting back all the things that hadn't been dealt with in an effort to keep it all tidy. It may have been breathing in all that dust from the cotton fiber that gave her lung cancer when she was past sixty.

Then, when my father died ten years later in his mid-eighties, they had to clean out the house where the old man and my unmarried sister had lived together. My sister declared that this was the great post-war clean-out, and threw away all she could, but in the end she was still left with more than two big wicker trunks' worth of things we didn't know what to do with. She rang begging me to help, so I went round, and when I opened the trunks on the sunny veranda, there were all the clothes that must have been the cause of my sister's dilemma, women's kimonos, so gaudy that people would be astonished to see someone going about in them now.

They'd been left to us by my grandmother on my father's side when she died at over ninety, some thirty years earlier. The wrapping paper showed that they had been ordered from department stores in Tokyo and Nagoya when she was in her sixties, in the mid-nineteen thirties, just after her husband had died. She had scarcely worn any of them. I remembered having read somewhere that the patterns on the kimono of respectable women of the period appeared to older folk at the time as shamelessly bold. Still, I found it depressing even to begin to imagine how my thoroughly austere grandmother could have craved all these things, even given the female fascination for clothes, and I closed the lid of the trunk before I'd looked at even half of its contents.

My sister was bewailing that even second hand shops wouldn't accept these things, so I agreed to take one of the trunks home with me. I remember the trouble of hauling home in a taxi that weighty-looking trunk with its leather corners and sturdy leather belt, but this memory is mistaken in fact. My sister called a delivery service to take it to my house. My job was simply to load the unopened trunk onto a hand cart, frowning at the thought of all those gaudy colors locked up inside it, take it down from our second floor dwelling to the basement of the apartment block, and toss it into one of the storage spaces there, a place like a cross between a locker room and a charnel house.

For the next ten years or so, I would occasionally think of the old lady's fantasies rotting down there in the damp underground concrete room. Meanwhile, my sister married late, then died soon after. My elder brother, who had had nothing to do with decisions about the trunks' contents, also died. Then, this spring, a friend who heard about my grandmother's legacy took an interest in it. His wife was a serious doll-maker, and the idea was that the kimono material might do for dolls' clothing. I was delighted that they would see the light of day again, even as cut up pieces of cloth, and we arranged a date for the couple to come round. I decided to take this opportunity to also deal with the heaps of old books that had been piled on top of the trunk. I solicited my wife's help, since my back was still a little weak from the illness, and after a number of trips we finally carried them all upstairs, where I packed them up and sold them to a second hand book dealer.

Two days before the appointed date, I wiped the dust carefully off the trunk and took it up to our apartment, but when I opened the lid, I discovered that it contained nothing but men's clothing. It seemed that my sister had carefully picked out and sent my grandfather's clothes. I don't remember my brother-in-law saying after her death six years ago that he had inherited any such trunk of things, so she must have dealt with them herself somehow. I regretted now that I hadn't checked the trunk's contents when I received it, and rung to thank her. I had shrugged off the thought of showing the contents to my wife, since the revelation of this unlikely coquettishness in my grandmother didn't show her in a very flattering light. The odd thought did cross my mind that if, when I died, the trunk was still there where I'd tossed it, the three women of the house would be puzzled and perhaps a little disturbed to find this collection of flashy women's clothing rotting away down in the cellar without any possible explanation. But the time for regret was past now, so I quickly rang my friend and shamefacedly confessed that all the clothing had in fact turned out to be men's. However, he said that was fine. They duly came round together on the evening of the appointed day, and we spread out my grandfather's clothes one by one on top of the wrapping paper and gazed at them under the fluorescent light.

In fact, I never knew my father's father. He died the year I was born, in his mid-seventies, but I don't know the details. His photograph was there in the altar at home when I was a child, and frequent prayers were made before it. I'd heard from my parents that he was a well-built man, and there had been no mention of his being small. I had a general sense that he was probably of middling height from the full round face in the photograph.

His clothing fit this physical image of him. Almost all the items were everyday wear, but among them we were intrigued to discover something like a traveling outfit. My friend and I remarked admiringly on how men in those days were apparently so dandyish, for all the somberness of their taste. He had run one of the provincial banks, and served a term or two in the Congress. He threw himself into the rationalization and integration of provincial banks, but he just about lost the family fortune several times over in the stock market, and apparently he also spent quite a lot of time out on the town.

This must be for going to the red light district, remarked my friend with laugh, as he spread out a jaunty set of kimono underwear extravagantly decorated with ukiyoe scenes of courtesans. The other three were meanwhile busy exchanging and comparing kimonos, pondering their relative merits. I have absolutely no understanding of kimonos, so their doubts and indecisions made no sense to me. Eventually, my friend held up what looked like an everyday-wear kimono, and urged me to try it on. Laughing, I wrapped it clumsily round me, and as I straightened my back and adjusted it, a strange feeling came over me.

I'm around five foot eight, on the tall side by earlier standards. But though the length of this kimono fitted me nicely, indeed was a trifle long, the sleeves only came down to around my elbows. It turned out that both the body and the shoulder width of the garment were considerably sized down in relation to the length.

We've got someone else here, my friend commented. The women muttered that whoever it was had a rather odd shape. That's all that was made of it at time. The sake came out, and dinner was produced. Late that night my friend and his wife loaded into the trunk of a taxi the bulk of the kimonos, together with the old case they were packed in, and took them home,

To my relief, it turned out that my father had had a relative who was tall and lean, and very narrow-shouldered. Neither my father nor my sole uncle had this build. They were shorter, and quite stocky. This heirloom had come down to my father through the hands of first my grandfather and then my grandmother, so the relative must have been an important one, but I never heard of the existence of any such person from my father. Even if he had died early, the fine quality and sober tone of the cloth suggested that he would have been approaching middle age. He seemed to have been of quiet demeanor; though it was an item of everyday clothing, there was virtually no sign of wear. Furthermore, it had been carefully washed and starched before being put away.

Standing bolt upright in this kimono, I must have looked very strange to the other three, rather like a kimono stand, or the ghost of one. But, aside from the chill of my forearms sticking so nakedly from the sleeves, and the alien sensation of wearing a kimono, it fitted itself perfectly around my body.

My shoulders have always been on the broad side, in fact.

8
MAUVE SKIN

Little yellow daisy flowers dotted the dry grass. Up in the sky, the light had already taken on a feel of spring. Men were standing on top of the mountain of composted straw that was piled high at the edge of the barnyard, breaking it up with shovels, a dense white cloud rising around their feet as they worked. This fertilizer would no doubt be transported to some racetrack, but meanwhile the cloud that rose from it drifted across to the nearby exercise yard, misting the pale figures of the horses that were walking around and around inside the netting fence, as in a revolving door. It was sometime before noon.

We were seven days into the coldest period of winter by the old calendar, but in recent years I had grown increasingly sensitive to the first signs of spring. With the fierce cold that set in at the turn of the year, my convalescent circulation grew sluggish in my limbs and my joints stiffened, so that I found myself longing for the spring. Or perhaps, as the winter solstice was left behind and the sun's rays grew stronger, my body responded with a slight but increasing dilation in the capillaries, and I mistook this minute commotion beneath the skin as a disturbing sign of incipient numbness.

As I sat in the stuffy atmosphere of the crowded evening train going home, the arms of my coat folded over my knees, I found myself recalling the chill of my forearms protruding so awkwardly from the kimono sleeves. I felt now that those exceptionally narrow shoulders relative to the hem length were in fact very odd. Perhaps after all it was a woman's kimono? My maternal grandmother was a small woman, even by the standards of the day. Still, a hem of that length would probably have been adjusted with a fold under the *obi* belt, and the kimono's brown-and-black striped pattern would work well as an elderly lady's everyday wear. True, I had felt at the time that it had fitted itself perfectly around my five-foot-eight frame, but then I had been so amazed at my nakedly protruding arms that I hadn't bothered to tie the kimono firmly around me. Nor had I checked the width of the sleeve openings carefully.

I recalled my grandmother moving restlessly about the house, obsessively tidying rooms already ordered with a precision severe enough to chill even a summer day. Her look never softened, even for a little child like me, and when she was angry she would sometimes tremble all over, and subject me to long lectures in her thin, shrill voice. She evidently hated her clothing to be the least bit disheveled, for on occasion she would undo her *obi* belt in front of us, open up her kimono and rearrange her clothes, beginning with the undergarments. Until he began to grow old himself, my father held his old mother in respectful fear. Could it be that her now-elderly grandson had casually wrapped himself in the kimono of this fierce old woman, shuddering a little as he did so at the thought of an unknown male relative whose body had been somehow misshapen by illness?

Yet there should really be nothing particularly weird in the merging of relatives of two sexes, after the passage of all these years. From the point of the view of the dead, at least, the physical features of the grandchild who has inherited equally from both the male and the female line must look like some strange hybrid sex, and perhaps still more so as that body moves into old age....

The train was filled with the scent of plum blossom. I had yet to see a plum in flower this year, but for some reason I have been sensitive to the scent of night plum blossom since I was young. Sometimes in a closed room, a meeting hall perhaps, or a bar, I will suddenly catch a whiff of this scent and doubt my senses, but later when I leave the building I will come upon a stand of plum trees in blossom in some quite unexpected nearby place. When I first smell the scent, what I register rather than its sweetness is a sudden feeling of something like unease. I have sometimes wondered whether this was an association from days spent crouched in the darkness of the air raid shelter in the terrifying Tokyo air raids at the end of winter. But on this occasion, in the moment just before I registered the scent as plum blossom, I murmured to myself, It's the smell of camphor, that's what I hate. There seemed to be some association between camphor and plum blossom. Perhaps there had been a smell of camphor deep in the air raid shelter.

The train pulled into a large station where many passengers would transfer to other trains, and as people were moving towards the door, through a sudden gap in the bodies I caught sight of Yamagoe sitting opposite. For a moment his features betrayed the drawn appearance of a young man racked with love, and I felt I had witnessed some rare and special sight. He had the tired, glazed look of one lost deep in thought, and when he became aware of me watching him from across the way, he gave an embarrassed nod before he was lost to sight again among the passengers crowding on.

·　·　·　·　·

This was no chance encounter. We were on our way home from an evening out drinking together. We had got on at the first station, and though the

96

seats were already almost all taken, we managed to find places directly op-posite. However, for the last ten minutes or more the intervening crowds had hidden us from each other's view. I seemed to have fallen asleep for a little while after the train began to move.

We had met up in Shinjuku for a drink that evening, and found our-selves fellow-residents on the same line who shared a local station.

"Your father would be two years older than me—he died before he was fifty, didn't he?"

"He was forty-seven."

"That's young."

These are the brief words we exchanged as we were preparing to stand and leave the bar. To a youngster of thirty, it would have sounded like the repetitions of an old man with a poor memory.

"The year you were born, I was renting a room above a carver of sig-nature seals off in the provinces, in Kanazawa. It was the year of the huge snowfall. No, that was January through February, so you wouldn't actually have been born yet."

"I was born in November."

I frowned inwardly at having revealed my inattention again, but my words were drawing me into a widening memory of the quietness of those snowy nights—I recalled the longing I had felt during that time for a wom-an's body, and then the next instant the quietness became one with the qui-etness of the time before someone is born. Yamagoe gave no sign that he was inclined to continue the conversation. If he did speak, the talk would quickly become detailed, even perhaps broaching secrets. There was nowhere in the city where we could have such a conversation, I thought, and then, return-ing to my earlier sensation, I looked around at the bar, which would surely provide a quieter place than elsewhere.

At the end of the previous year, I had received from Yamagoe the formal card one sends at this time when a family member has died that year to an-nounce the death in lieu of sending a New Year's card. When I had written my other New Year's cards, I used an undecorated postcard to return my greetings to him. Recalling my own experience of the New Year after a rela-tive had died, these days I do my best to answer before the end of the year any cards I receive from old friends who are currently in mourning. I re-member, again around the busy year-end period, receiving a postcard sent from a distant hospital by someone in my neighborhood, and then a few days afterwards coming home late and noticing a sign announcing a death on the door of their house. I went back and checked the postcard again, and noticed now that it was written on a Sunday, and New Year's greetings were added at the end. It made me call to mind the chill loneliness of hospitals on Sundays, as evening sinks into night.

"Let's go out for a drink sometime soon," I added along the edge of my card to Yamagoe. Twenty or so days after the New Year, two days earlier, again on a Sunday evening, Yamagoe had telephoned. He began rather reticently, saying that if I ever had reason to go into the city, perhaps we could meet up while I was there. We discussed possible dates, then began to warm to the idea that we both set off now and meet up at a bar at the end of the shopping mall near our local station, which would be open even on a Sunday evening, but for one reason and another this didn't work out. In the end it was decided that we should meet, anyhow, in a coffee shop two days later, between eight-thirty and nine at night, after a meeting I had scheduled until evening that day. After we hung up, I began to think about a suitable place to go on to from there to have a few drinks.

"It reminds me somehow of that common room where we used to meet at night in the hospital," said Yamagoe, after he had looked around the place I'd brought him to, and praised the fact that it was quiet. It was a bar with a considerable collection of bottles of wine from Eastern Europe; the long room, which seemed to have been added on to the building's original layout, had in addition to its counter a bland row of table and chairs, with no attempt made to soften the bleakness. When you sat at a table there, you felt as if you were eating and drinking in a corridor behind a partition.

"This is the first time I've met you dressed up like this, so let me take this occasion," Yamagoe continued, and he drew a business card from the inner pocket of his suit and placed it before me. It was true that since we'd been in the hospital together, I had never asked him about his work. Even I knew enough to recognize that the name was of a major textile company that had been an object of envy for my generation of students looking for employment, but that had run into difficulties long ago, only a few years after Yamagoe was born, and barely managed to save itself by diversifying. But I had no clue about the job description under the name of the planning office.

"I'm afraid I haven't any idea of the meaning of people's business cards," I said in rueful apology as I tucked the card into my pocket. A memory flashed through my mind of the remark made to me some time earlier by a contemporary who had evidently forgotten that I left employment early in life, that though there had been much to astonish him over the years, he was still puzzled at how we could have had the idea, thirty-odd years ago, that we could stay working in the same company till retirement. We outstayed our welcome, he added with a laugh.

"It's almost three years we've known each other now, isn't it?" I said, changing the subject.

"Yes, in just a few more days it will be three years," Yamagoe replied. Clearly he was referring to the night his motorcycle was struck by a car.

"That was just when I was beginning to have walking difficulties, but I didn't realize yet that I was ill. I flew to Kanazawa on business, and I remem-

98

ber staggering along in the falling snow. And here I now am wondering if I'm going to die."

"The person who hit me ran away, you know. It was a hit-and-run."

I hadn't heard this before.

"Good heavens, you certainly don't talk about your grudges, do you?" I sighed, gazing into his face.

"It was my own fault. And that was the least of it, after all. I got through it alive. But later I began to get scared, when I remembered that all three of us had met with traffic accidents. I didn't feel as though the story was over and done with yet, somehow."

I counted up the facts again, as I did every time I thought of Yamagoe—his brother's death at age six, his sister's at twenty-three, and his own accident at twenty-seven—and I too felt a shudder at the terrifying press of calamity upon them.

"That worry about my mother ..." he continued, as if his mother were still alive.

"I remember you said your only concern was for your mother, while you were in the ambulance."

"She'd been saying her body was beginning to weaken, and she didn't feel she'd last much longer. I wondered if it ever crossed her mind that a child of hers might be saved in her stead if she died. She was the kind who might easily make some such pact with the gods, you know. I used to worry about her going outside on a freezing night—she had high blood pressure, see. My sister died in early summer, but six months or so later, in the coldest time of the new year, when I came home late I would find that my mother wasn't there, and I'd have to go off to the ancient shrine down the road and bring her back. She'd be performing the hundred circumambulations ritual there. It was only when this happened that she seemed a bit deranged, and kept talking about how my sister was in hospital. I didn't like to think of her doing this on my behalf as well."

I began to say that in fact she probably was doing it for him, but when my eyes met his I closed my mouth.

"I guess this makes me sound as if I'm fixated on my mother," he went on with a laugh. "Some kind of mother complex, maybe. But while I was stuck there in my hospital bed all that time, I began to realize that in fact some other idea was in my mind. I somehow felt that even though this event seemed to be over, in the end my mother would probably be the last one left alive. I couldn't anticipate when this would come about. Even when I was told that I needed another operation, it didn't cross my mind that something might happen to me. If my mother was the last one left, of course that meant that I'd be dead, but somehow I didn't grasp this aspect of it at all. I never thought about my own death. Contradictions aside, my only idea was that she would be the sole survivor. When I woke at night, suddenly an image of my mother living on alone would pop into my head, quite as if it had all happened already. What it meant was, I was already dead. But I didn't feel the least fear. Nor did I feel bad at the thought that my mother would have no one to turn to. Rather than any distress or tears, the feeling I had was a deep acceptance that this was right."

"Right?" I asked, simply out of a conditioned tendency to question the word.

"All I can say is 'right,'" he replied. Then his gaze slackened again as he returned to his recollections. "Speaking from the way I felt then, at any rate."

"This sense of rightness," he went on, "was a heavier thing than simple fear. It virtually paralyzed me." He paused a moment, then added with a laugh, "Of course, it turned out that my mother died first."

He's avoided the word "fate," I realized belatedly. In fact, I thought, at this stage it's an excellent word to have avoided. The memory of a woman's laugh reverberated in my ears again. He had told me how he found himself saying to the girl who had so devotedly looked after his ailing mother while he was hospitalized that if anything happened to both of them she should stay on alone in the house. No doubt this was a desire for her to be there to see his mother through to the end, which would not be long away, and then to stay on in the house after her death. When he had whispered this to her, she laughed in a trembling voice akin to a sob. But the laugh that began as a kind of spasm quickly extended into a clearer peal, and with each deep breath it took on a growing overtone of eroticism, as though a sense of physical intimacy inadvertently had led to inappropriate touch.

"No children yet?" I asked. I was horrified to hear the repulsive tone of a meddlesome crone in my voice, but I reflected that this role was probably quite appropriate for me, in fact. If Yamagoe chose to spurn me with horror, that would be that. "Or perhaps you're thinking of closing up the house," I went on.

This was apparently rather a brutal thrust for him, and he frowned sharply.

I expected to hear him say, as his forehead cleared, "Well, I'm not the childbearer, you know." But instead he replied, "Torizuka isn't against it, actually." He spoke in a composed, even carefully clear tone of voice, yet for all that the tone expressed utter helplessness. Apparently it was not only me who registered this, for he also looked surprised to hear his voice.

"Is she well?" I asked.

"Yes, fine thank you," he responded. "She almost seems to have lived there longer than me—she can draw my attention to things I haven't noticed all these years. Things like the odd position of a closet, and so on." Then he suddenly grew formal, bowed his head, and thanked me. I was momentarily nonplussed, but he went on, "for spending the evening with me."

At that stage, we moved on to drink a rough, full-bodied liquor, and the two of us, though we were in age difference like father and son, fell into fascinated talk together of the finer subtleties of the experience of convalescence.

I had assumed that someone of Yamagoe's youth would have no further problems once he had made his way through to the end of hospitalization. However, he told me that after he left the hospital, still in a cast and on crutches, he had at first spent some days back at work, but though his strength was slowly returning, he was losing weight steadily, and his face was that of an emaciated old man. He therefore decided that in this state he was no doubt an unpleasant sight for those around him at work, and he took further sick leave until the cast came off. Even after he did return, he commuted to work for some time with his bad knee still in a metal support, and he needed to avoid the rush hour. One leg was shorter than the other, and at first he was extremely worried that the resulting loss of balance might be a hindrance for those trying to walk with him, but as he grew used to it he began to have the odd illusion that he was moving along quite lightly, though still far slower than the crowd around him. Even now he sometimes found himself limping about the house as if his leg was still in a cast. The woman he lived with would watch, and at some point when he moved clumsily she would give a painful smile and say, "I hate that!" Then he would realize what a depressing sight he made. He had sometimes wondered how she must have felt, when he had embraced her in that state. "You smelled," she told him.

He should have been completely healed by the time his mother went into the hospital again, yet as he walked there to visit her he realized he was still dragging his right leg a little. He felt his shoulder slumped to the right, even his eyebrow. Still, it seemed he could keep going longer if he walked this way. Once as he walked down the corridor late at night carrying her dirty washing, sliding his foot along, he found himself momentarily drifting off to sleep. The sound of his own sleeping breath woke him. One night he couldn't bear to sit beside her, and he rose and wandered in and out of the room, but his footsteps evidently roused her, for her eyes flickered half-open, and when he paused, aware of her gaze, her eyes stayed quietly on him, as if to follow his movements once he began again.

"You went on looking like an invalid for a long time," Torizuka told him. When he left the hospital, the doctor instructed her to stand behind him and watch how he walked, and this habit stayed with her. It sometimes happened that they met on their way to or from the hospital to visit his mother; they would exchange brief words and go their separate ways, but even when she was in a hurry, she paused and looked back. She told him that the further he receded, the sicker he appeared.

Even now his right knee would sometimes throb dully on cold nights as he lay in bed. It wasn't a fierce pain, just a tingling ache like soft breathing, and thoughts emerged from this ache, though what thoughts he could not tell. His mind was a blank whiteness, into which seeped the hush of night. Even the nearby expressway's roar of traffic sounded quiet.

. . . . .

"Is this what's here now?" Yamagoe exclaimed, pausing at the corner to look sternly at the new children's playground that spread out to his left. It was true—until a few years earlier, this had been a residence with a garden of fine leafy trees. The house had been pulled down, leaving the trees standing, and a low fence erected on the two sides facing the road. I expected them either to pack the block with small condominiums, or to cut down all the trees and turn it into a parking lot. In fact, however, the land was left untouched for some time, slowly filling with the trash thrown over the fence, until the vegetation began to grow quite dense again. I had very rarely been this way at all in recent years, so I had no idea of how long it had remained like this. It had certainly been several years, however. I felt I had noticed only recently that the trees had been either cut or removed and the area had been cleaned up and made into a cheerful children's playground, but then again it also felt as if this could have been several years ago too.

"They've fixed it up nicely, haven't they," he said as he averted his eyes and walked quickly on, and there was a morose tinge to his voice. I hastened after him, impressed by the realization that even a thirty-year-old, if he has grown up in the area, will have a stronger reaction to such change than someone who moved here to live the same amount of time ago. The road we followed led away from Yamagoe's house and toward mine.

When we were about to part outside the station, Yamagoe had instead silently set off walking beside me. I wondered whether he would go into the nearby store, but after we crossed the railway tracks he said, "I feel inclined for a walk to clear my head, so I'll come partway home with you." There was something a little angry in his voice then too, and I recalled the face of the man I had seen just now as we were about to leave the ticket gate. He was a man somewhere in his mid-forties. He was ahead of us as we approached the gate, obviously a little drunk, ambling along at his own pace quite unhurriedly, and when he joined the flow of people going through the gate someone happened to momentarily block him off, then several more moved in ahead of him. His back stiffened, and he came instantly to a halt. There he stood, stubbornly holding his ground, heedless of the obstruction he was causing to those behind. I glanced at him as I went past, and his expression was one of indignant rage. Apparently it only lasted for a brief moment, for when I turned and looked back after we had passed through the gate, there was no sign of this grim figure—but I was astonished to realize that my own step had taken on some of the fury of this man. At this point

Yamagoe casually joined me.

We came out onto the road that followed the old canal route, and his pace grew gentler as we set off in the direction of my house. The road led directly away from his house. It had been between 1950 and 1952 that the canal became a garbage dump and was finally buried, which would place the event more than ten years before Yamagoe's birth, I calculated. It would be hard for him, though he was born in the area, to imagine the old scene of the embankment winding through fields. At this stage in my thoughts, Yamagoe, silent until then, suddenly said, "I heard something awful."

"About whom?" I found myself asking. I already felt tired, as one does when another introduces in a roundabout way some subject that you know will turn out to be about yourself.

"Actually, it's about a friend of a friend of a friend—someone I can't in any way recall, which I grant you is irresponsible of me."

The story seemed to fade out at this point, but then he took fresh breath and began to speak.

"A friend told me about it just the other day when he called to talk about something else—just idle chat really, but afterwards I began to think that if we hadn't been talking on the telephone, and if this man had been one of the people involved, or if it had been about a direct friend of mine, I might have punched him. I wondered why he had to tell me. Was it just that he wanted to get it off his chest?"

He was silent for a moment, choked by his own rage.

Then he laughed. "But in fact it might have happened a hundred years ago, who knows?" And he proceeded to relate the story.

A couple just three months married asked three men to dinner at their house one evening. All the men, the host included, were around thirty years old.

The meal began calmly. The husband did his best to relax his guests, his wife was quietly attentive to their needs, and the talk and laughter flowed. After a while, in fact, the guests began to feel that the jollity was getting a little out of hand. The husband was now drunk, and his high spirits began to become somewhat uncontrolled, though he didn't get quarrelsome with his guests or force drink on them. He simply grew more and more exuberantly happy, exclaiming what a wonderful evening it was, and his wife nervously began to reprove him. Then his wife went into the kitchen, and after a while she called her husband in there, so he casually stood up and left the room. They could be heard for some time talking softly together. The guests reverted to making each other's acquaintance, and set about exchanging information about their respective jobs, keeping the conversation going in an effort not to listen to what was going on next door.

Then footsteps were heard softly ascending the stairs, and the voices ceased. The guests breathed a sigh of relief, and began to exchange tales of unusual experiences abroad. But time passed, and there was still silence above. Inevitably, the talk began to falter, and then one of them muttered, "Perhaps our host has been overly polite, and has decided to go upstairs and sleep off the drink." The three of them burst out laughing at this. Suddenly from the staircase they heard the thunder of two people hurtling down the stairs, apparently locked together. There was a crash as they fell into the entrance hall, then the sound of fiercely whispered argument approached down the corridor, the door slid open with an eerie slowness, and there in front of the guests cowered the wife, stark naked. Resisting all the while, she was gradually and relentlessly forced into the room.

She staggered in face forward, with a shove from behind, then twisted her body away and rushed to a far corner, where she huddled with her back to the guests. Eventually she sank into a formal seated position on her knees by the wall, where she sat with bowed head. Her hands covered her face and she seemed to be crying, but she made no sound.

The demonic face of the husband now peered round the edge of the door, then suddenly withdrew, and he appeared to slip immediately around to the kitchen. There was the sound of running water, then in no time he came out with his head lowered. "I do apologize," he said. He appeared quite unruffled. He returned to his seat, straightened his back, lifted the cold pot of saké, and solemnly offered his guests another drink.

At this point, of course, you imagine that the guests, stunned into appalled silence, will stand one by one and quietly move off towards the door—but no. One mute guest, taking his cue from the host's polite solemnity, in fact declined with a formal bow, stood up, removed his coat and draped it over the woman's shoulders, and only then went out; the other two followed.

They put on their shoes in the entryway, and when it was time for the man who had covered the woman with his coat to put his overcoat on, the husband appeared courteously holding the coat, and offered it for him to wear. "Do put this on, it will be cold out there," he urged solicitously. The guest silently took it and draped it over his arm.

"I shall take good care of my wife," the husband said as they left. There was nothing barbed or sarcastic in his tone. But behind him, scattered up the staircase, they could see a tumble of women's underwear. It looked as if she had clutched to her breast the clothes he had pulled from her, in an effort to cover herself.

Year after year, a New Year's greeting card would arrive with both their names on it, and brief news of their doings. The following year, a child had been born, and soon there was another.

· · · · ·

"All three of them had had a previous relationship with her, hadn't they?"

I asked, after the story finished. I was loath to say it, but felt this was better than forcing the words from him.

"Apparently the event prompted them all to confess to each other after they'd left the house," said Yamagoe, and then he fell silent.

I was intrigued by the question of why they had all accepted the invitation, but I sensed a danger that if I voiced my amazement about this it would reinforce Yamagoe's mood, and in the end I kept my mouth shut. Our pace had quickened again, and we were by this point quite close to my house. "Let's walk a little longer," I suggested. "Your house will be somewhat closer if we take this route," and I steered him across the street in a gap between the traffic. Here I hesitated a moment, but the only natural road to follow at this point was the one that led towards the park where I had met Fujisato the previous spring, so I set off along it. Yamagoe followed me round the corner, eyes still lowered.

"Whose story would that be?" I asked after a while.

"I guess it was one of the men involved who originally told the story, but I have the impression there were a number of people who handed it on before someone told my friend and he passed it on to me over the phone. I said earlier that it was an awful story, but actually when I heard it it came across as too oddly neat to strike me as unpleasant. When I thought about it later, I realized my friend had told it very well—and he's not usually particularly good at telling stories. He was laughing as he told it, but it wasn't a crude kind of laughter. The story had nothing to do with him, that's why. It must have become more and more polished and impersonal as it passed from one man to another. But I have a strong feeling that one of those men along the way was so struck by its unpleasantness that he constructed it into the impersonal story it became. I mean, I didn't feel particularly revolted hearing it over the telephone—it just came across as a funny story—but when I thought about it later on my own, I began to wonder why it was told like that. I don't mean the events themselves. I mean the order they were told in. What I decided was that someone had gone out of his way to get around the awfulness of the event by telling it this way. But then a few days later, I found I couldn't really remember how my friend had told the story that night. When I tried to recreate it, I came up with various ways of ordering it, and all of them revolted me. In the train back there, that was what I was thinking about—how could I tell the story to someone so that it would not be disgusting?"

As he continued these difficult ruminations, his voice once again took on the keening, singsong quality I had heard before. In this state, he didn't wait for any response, but simply talked on. I felt now as I listened that perhaps it wasn't so much that his talk gathered strength into a monologue, as that he was gently forbidding any premature response to it, and also that in this way he was feeling for a moment of natural opportunity to make some revelation. There were evidently matters here that could twist and swell into the truly repulsive, if spoken with a certain trick of timing; yet on the other hand, by simply missing that moment's timing, they could as easily remain unspoken.

The road dipped gently downhill, and now hanging over us on either side were the sturdy leafless branches of cherry trees. Masses of tight buds, swelled to an almost unnatural size, were visible in the gentle glow of the streetlights. The bark glistened mauve in the sunset. I found myself gazing at the glossy skin of the branches swaying in the chill wind, somehow sensing them as part of a body slowly stiffening, but not yet manifesting the signs of the onset of terrible disease. They looked as if a scent would emanate from that coldness.

"Ah, this is a middle school, isn't it? Schools seen late at night are always kind of creepy, aren't they?"

"Yes, as if you might suddenly see someone at one of the windows."

"You feel that too, do you? I sometimes feel as if it's me there. I had a scary dream like that when I was a child. I'm suddenly in there, alone."

"Was this your school?"

"No, I went to the one across the tracks." Then he added, "But I once slept with a girl who went to this school."

As we went on beside the elementary school, he muttered, "She didn't like me."

It was only after he'd spoken that the thought occurred to me, as if I suddenly had registered a certain tone of voice, that this was perhaps the first time this young man had ever spoken in terms of "sleeping with" someone. The word "slept" evoked associations of the texture and scent of the skin of a woman with whom he had almost no connection, a woman he had known for a single, cold night together; it slid into the distance, leaving in its wake an aftertaste of regret at her revulsion from him, and a sense of ending with a failure to touch or be lost in any deeper relationship. But it also ended in the hush of a local school building in the night, and would be hidden too in this road that led to and from the school.

"Well then, shall we part here?" I was the one who first came to a halt and spoke. We were going along a narrow lane. If we turned left at the corner, we would soon find ourselves at the park with its hackberry tree. The white of a CLOSED signboard that dangled from the door of a dingy nearby restaurant struck my eye with a painful vividness. The wind seemed to be rising.

"I presume you'd know the way home from here, being brought up in the area?" I asked. Yamagoe looked around him wonderingly, then his eyes lifted to the straggly little bare-branched tree on the corner, covered like the cherry with thick buds. His long soft hair glinted in the faint light, looking for a moment like a luxuriance of fine white hair, just as it had done that

106

night in the common room when I first spoke to him. But his youthful body suddenly seemed younger still, as he stood gazing up at the tree as though it were blossoming above him.

"I know the way," he finally responded. "If I go down that hill, any road will take me to the railway tracks." He peered down the road in the direction of the shadowy shape of the hackberry, which now, no longer transformed by the dazzle of sunshine, was visibly just a broken and rotted tree. Then he slowly turned back and looked me in the eye.

"It was in that house, you know—the first time it happened between my mother and father. There in that chilly, unheated guest room he lectured and harangued her, and she just went on pleading and begging forgiveness till suddenly he turned pale and began to rip off her jewelry and even her clothes. In a kind of abject abasement, she flung herself weeping on him, crying, 'Oh please, do something!'—this is what Torizuka told me."

He set off walking, but then turned halfway back around, and in that same singsong voice he added, "The eldest son was called Sakae, the daughter was Megumi, and the second son's Hitoshi." His finger wrote the *kanji* for the names wildly in the air, then he waved the hand to me and turned back, and as he strode off his shoulders shook with sudden laughter.

Reaching the hackberry, the lone figure suddenly swerved left.

9

THE DREAM OF THE BUSH WARBLER

Against the outer wall of the store near my house, right next to the entrance, stands a little prefabricated shack, three sides of glass that form a kind of hot-house despite the fact that the sun never strikes this northern wall. It contains a flower shop, something like a street-side stall. It hasn't changed since I first moved to this area more than twenty-five years ago. In the old days, a small, thin, plainly dressed girl of seventeen or eighteen used to bustle energetically about serving customers in her slightly husky voice. She looked like a girl whose only ambition was to make the business thrive. People of my generation would assume that her plan would be to stay firmly wedded to this shop for the time being, and in due course open her own business somewhere. All these years later, however, the same woman is still running the shop by herself. Whenever I pass it I am struck by the fact that the same lass has stayed on there all this time, and I pause to review the years. She looks her age, but I always see in my mind's eye the young girl who worked there with such fervent energy in the old days. She is essentially quite unchanged. Seeing her, it sometimes strikes me that the passage of twenty-five years is in fact nothing at all. The only change is that the flowers in her shop have grown more various and colorful; they are there in just the same quantity, however.

Long-term residents too have aged through the years, now recalling and now forgetting this little flower shop. I also sometimes find myself wondering whether the fact that people constantly pause there to look at her shop and suddenly feel an urge to buy some flowers is a sign of ease of lifestyle, or rather one of times of stress and difficulty.

From the mid-point of the pedestrian crossing that takes you across the main road to the shopping arcade, on fine winter mornings you can see, at the far end of the two lanes that run almost directly due west, the perfect shape of Mt. Fuji. It is astonishingly large, and depending on the clarity of the air it can seem very close; the jumble of buildings that line the street on either side of it have about them the dark air of the original street buildings in the old post-town under Mt. Fuji, that I once traveled through in my youth. When you cross to the other side and turn again to look from the pavement, Fuji has disappeared. There is not even a sense of this being a place that could contain it in the view. I am aware, however, of some scent that always lingers in the back of my nose here —not the exhaust fumes of the traffic, but a smell of oil and iron, fats and rust. It was over ten years ago I first realized that this had its origins in a very early memory.

One winter back when I was fifteen, every fine morning I used to gaze at the imposing sight of Mt. Fuji, standing there just like this, in the middle of a townscape. It was a view from the midst of a wild patch of dried grass, at the site of the burned remains of an old house left standing on that particular block since the war. The place was in Shinagawa, at the very tip of the southern edge of a plateau area called Gotenyama. I can calculate that it would have been the winter of 1952 to '53, because we had only just moved to the area. I used to go to school from there by heading down the hill from Gotenyama to Yatsuyama Street, walking as far as Gotanda Station, then catching a tram to the middle school at the foot of Takanawadai, part of the hilly area that was an extension of where I lived.

I had found a shortcut from the point where I left the house, and I would go into the burned out block of land and gaze up at Mt. Fuji. An industrial area spread off along the Meguro River towards Fuji. It would have all been burned to the ground during the bombing, but already a tight jumble of small and medium-sized factories had sprung up again there. Though it was a drab and colorless landscape, when I stood there before the sounds of factory work had started up, looking at the white mountain in the clear early morning air already thick with the smell of oils and iron, I registered the hushed activity of the scene as beautiful, just as the mountain was.

In fact, my own father was involved with one of those factories. Even as a youth I was aware of what lay beneath their corrugated iron and slate roofs, the cheerless conditions and wasted labors that accompanied the new prosperity. Whenever I came in contact with that atmosphere it depressed me deeply, and this feeling was not something I could manage to throw off —I bore its weight with shoulders hunched against it.

Whenever I felt myself drawn by that scene of Mt Fuji and the industrial area, I would also be thinking of the girls at school who came from the same sort of environment as this, and when I recall this now I realize now that in fact this would have been one of those moments that are part of sexual awakening. Now, decades later, whenever this country attains yet further dizzying heights of economic growth, and whenever I turn to look back down the bleak road that has led to this point, I find myself protesting: No, the same bleakness has always hidden inside our prosperity, and it's a kind of lust that reacts to this that is driving us in this way. We are as we are today because we're urged on by a chill work ethic, diligence built over a sense of wasted labor. And when the day comes that this suddenly stumbles and fails, how desolate a place we will then find ourselves in.... When these thoughts fill my mind, it is that landscape that rises before me like a powerful vision.

This is the landscape in which Yamagoe's mother, still barely twenty, was living. How hard, and with what fervent energy, she must have worked there. The man who embraced her would have smelt, mingled with the scent of her skin, a whiff of oils and iron.

This spring, I often hear the song of the bush warbler.

It was at the end of February that I first heard it. I had sat myself down at my desk after lunch, and not long after that I heard its brief ringing call outside the eastern window. A strange feeling came over me. I recalled the words "The sun was at its height, and birds sat in branches, when the woods rang," and I wondered whether what I had just witnessed was the opposite of that description, or in fact the same. A long while later, the bird called again, a half call, then twice more, and then it stopped. I stood up from the desk, went out into a room my family had left empty that day, and walked round it once, as if searching for that birdsong.

This was just about the time when the previous summer's unseasonal cold was beginning to have its effects on the rice stocks available in shops, and our family was slowly getting accustomed to the taste of imported rice. My daughter, a girl in her twenties, asserted that it didn't taste too different from the home-grown variety. My wife and I had undergone the experience of eating imported rice in our youth, and since the local product had lost much of its taste since it was first harvested, we too had no problem with the foreign rice. We knew that it was immensely better than the imported rice we had eaten just after the war. Still, it did have the same scent. That scent had plagued me in the old days of hunger. Now, it was simply a different taste, which provoked a different appetite depending on how it was cooked, suggesting that in the old days my body had been quite weakened. People say that if you're hungry you'll eat anything, but malnourishment in fact leads to a diminished appetite. You're particularly sensitive to unfamiliar tastes and smells. The starving body rejects them. You even vomit. Perhaps in fact these last fifty years of eating habits have changed my physical constitution. Whatever the reason may be, at all events I was puzzled by the assertions of people in middle age and older that they couldn't eat this rice that had been mixed with the imported stuff.

Once March had begun, the bush warbler frequently sang near our house; sometimes it called repeatedly, between long intervals of silence. When this happened, I took to leaving my desk and wandering about the house. I also enjoyed alerting the others to the song if they hadn't noticed it. If someone cocks a dubious ear to hear it, the bird will respond by singing with astonishingly splendid timing and delivery. Always, just as your attention begins to sag disappointedly, it suddenly sings out. It's a sharp, clear

110

call, but people don't really register it fully till they hear it twice.

It wasn't for these elegantly poetic pursuits, however, that I prowled the house —it was on account of the fact that whenever the bird called and called like this, even in the midst of my busy work schedule I grew oppressed by a sense that time hung heavy. I paced up and down as I waited for the song to cease....

Perhaps the variegated leaves of the wood's thick understory of dwarf bamboo were daily intensifying in color, for my eyes were struck by a whiteness to the green there. That day, I heard only a single call.

It was just when I was beginning work on a translation I had completed after immense and painful efforts twenty-seven years earlier, that was now to be published as part of a complete collection of the author's works.

Quite apart from the laborious working and reworking I did on the original translation with all the dogged energy of my early thirties, I had gone over it again quite thoroughly seven years ago when it was being brought out as a paperback volume. The present publisher probably wasn't hoping for a whole retranslation of the work from me. He had simply sent along the galley proofs to show me. But the deadline for returning them was a long way off, and as chance would have it I was between jobs and had time on my hands.

I had no urge at this stage to expend my nervous energy on searching out the unavoidable translation problems. After a certain point, it was useless to wrack my brains over phrasing. If I was going to play around now with a translation I had done in my youth, I would be surprised to find myself from time to time slapped in the face quite painfully by my present ignorance. I decided that I must rid myself of my obsessive way with prose, if I were to do this job. I began to think that it might be fun to take this happy opportunity of a distant deadline and no press of necessity to spend time with a labor of my youth without any urgent sense of simply getting it out of the way. But though I set off with the intention of a leisurely approach to the project, my work slowly took on an obsessive quality. The first ten pages had become a mess of red ink, further scrawled over with revisions in an angry hand, and after this I found I couldn't finish. No one was forcing me to do this, yet though I hadn't intended to throw myself into the task in this way, it had turned out that as long as I was engaged in this piece of work, my labors as a writer were blocked. And then the bush warbler came and sang at my window. Again and again it sang, between long intervals of silence.

It also sang at the edge of a wood one fine day just before noon. It was just two days before I was due for surgery, three years earlier. That too was a beautiful day, and a long one. Only one more day or so of the ten-day wait for the surgery now remained; the time inched by, and in the afternoon felt almost as if it had altogether ceased to pass. I clung to the thought that once tomorrow came I would know that the surgery would be tomorrow, and time would flow easily once more. It had felt as if "tomorrow" was the day when everything would be over.

Some time after four thirty in the afternoon some days later, on a day of continuous rain, I thought I heard one brief call of the bush warbler beyond the window, and then the song came again and again, sometimes far and sometimes near, a song sung to the dying day as the rain began to lift and the skies cleared.

I didn't get up from the desk that day, but doggedly pursued my work, resisting the urge to let myself be drawn into the silences between one call and the next.

There had been an occasion, over ten years earlier, when I recall listening intently to the call of the bush warbler in amongst the mountains on just such a day during the rainy season. In fact, the song filled all the mountains; the birds called and answered incessantly through the rainy mist, from the mountainsides and the valleys, in a great clamor. I was waiting to hear among them the call of the little cuckoo, that never came. The low opening notes of the little cuckoo's call for that first brief moment can be confused with the bush warbler. Then, where the bush warbler's call lifts fluidly up in its long arc, the little cuckoo's song instead flattens out into a squat, almost syllabic cry, that seems almost to contain tentative human words, as if it is indeed calling to someone, a stumbling, beseeching sentence. I once had the experience of being called to ceaselessly by that voice, and finding myself struck silent, my ears straining to catch the message. On the other hand, when each bush warbler's call catches me by surprise, my hearing becomes from hour to hour alert to hear it again; and when my expectation is not answered, it only increases my hypersensitivity, until in the end I can no longer tell for a moment, when I hear it again, if it is real or a hallucination. Held suspended in this state somehow akin to deafness, hearing the bush warblers calling continuously, the mountains seemed to quieten to the opening of the little cuckoo's song.

Half a day passed as I listened thus. When night began to draw on and I was back in the mountain lodge, the song still rose clearly in the distance. It continued intermittently for close to an hour, and even late into the night I would still from time to time lie straining my ears in bed, wracked with the promise of an imminent and utter clarity. For two or three days after I returned home, a weak exhaustion continued to haunt mind and body. That summer, my father, who had shown signs of difficulty with his movements since early spring, suffered a stroke on a day of fierce heat.

· · · · ·

The dream occurred, apparently, on the night of the twenty second of December in 1819. I had to flip back and forth through the pages quite some way before I could discover that he had died in 1824 on the seventeenth of August, at the age of forty-four. My eyes were tired. It took me some time to make the simple calculation that the dream was about three years and eight months before his death. Recently, I have been having difficulty again with calculating dates and times, though not as badly as when I was ill.

Three years and eight months, eh? I said to myself thoughtfully. But in fact I wasn't thinking anything. I was simply gazing at the remaining years of life.

I had been reading one of the novelist Mori Ogai's historical biographies, only late at night, and a little at a time. I hadn't intended to read such a thing until one evening my hand had chanced on his biography of Izawa Ranken on the shelves, and I had pulled it down for a look. I'd never read it all the way through, nor did I imagine I would this time. But as I made my way through the difficult quotations of Chinese poetry and other documents that littered the text, as carefully as I could without straining my endurance and eyesight, I recalled the earlier self who had impatiently skipped over these parts, and laughed wonderingly at how I could now have become so much more dedicated as a reader. This humorous interest in turn became a spur to read further. Also, settling down like this to what was an almost desultory, even dreary read, not forcing myself to concentrate particularly on any one place, proved a kind of physical and mental relaxation after what was becoming the day's grim battles with the translation work. Still, it was a sign of my having in fact relatively little to do that no sooner had I finished *Izawa Ranken* than I moved on to his biography of Hojo Katei.

> "Of a sudden, I find myself in dream in Hayashizaki Library in Ise. It is the day of the autumn moon-viewing party. I call on Baio, but he is not at home. I then visit Oko. He says regretfully that he is prevented from going to today's event. We talk for a while, and lament the death of Keiken. Rinya too has died. I then conceive the idea of visiting Kango, and my thoughts fly to Naniwa. However, my plans remain unfulfilled.
> Then I awoke. The light by my pillow was flickering, and wind and rain raged without."

It was getting towards the latter half of March. My initial reaction was only to register a pervasive forlornness in the dream. There was also a kind of embarrassment at having been witness to such a candid dream. Then I thought: But even if this weren't a dream, something very like this really did occur.

It was when I was very young. Bored and penniless, I decided in the afternoon to call on a friend, but he was out. This wasn't a time when people simply telephoned each other. At a loose end, I then dropped round on another friend. He was in, but he hastily slipped on his *geta* when he came to the door, and set off with me at a stroll while he explained that the house was in some confusion at the moment, so he couldn't really leave for long. Still, we stood on a street corner a little way from the house, talking on and on. I recalled the scene, which rose to my mind together with the scent of a cloudy day in early spring. We would have had at least two people in common who had died. The day was still far from over when we parted, and I didn't feel like going home, so I remember I caught a train to another friend's house quite some way off, though I was fairly sure he would be out.

Still, at that advanced age, and physically and mentally debilitated even in his dreams, though Katei might suddenly find himself transported from Edo to Ise, it would be beyond him to travel further than that. I imagine that as he set off to visit distant Naniwa, congratulating himself on the idea, already the dream world was beginning to grow vague, then incoherent, until he woke with a start. Unfulfilled —the entire gamut of feelings on waking seem contained within this one word.

Apparently there are those who declare Katei to be a boring person, on reading Ogai's biography, but he doesn't strike me this way. I can't judge whether the age he lived in was a boring one, but it does seem to me that he was constrained by the circumstances of his time. It's impossible to know from Ogai's biography whether his nature was determined from the moment of birth, or whether a sense of futility grew on him in his rebellious youth, or he was driven into a corner in the act of resistance, or whether there was some fault in his conduct. At all events, unlike in our present age, once the circumstances of his life had been determined there was little chance of changing them, and little opportunity to even develop the illusion that one could do so. Hence, once he had determined to set about refining his spirit, every resultant word and action would naturally have been defined in terms of the dictates of his age. No doubt this would make one boring as a person. These days, the twists and turns of a life formed in this way hold more fascination for me than the half-baked flash of genius.

Having thought this far, I moved on, before my eyes had time to grow blurry with reading.

I too had recently had a strange dream. Well, as a dream it was not so strange, in fact. I imagine this was so for Katei's dream too, but I feel it is often the case that in dreams, the more piercingly intense the accompanying emotion, the more ordinary the content of the dream can be. And in my dream, there was not even a sense of heightened emotion: simply, five or six old friends had gathered.

They were friends from my first years at university, and the place was the home of one of them. The scene began in an inner corridor of the house that glowed with a black, rather oily light. The house was beside a railway track. It would have been one of those built in the late twenties, after the big Tokyo earthquake, in the mixture of Western and Japanese architectural styles common at the time, and had survived the wartime fires. A banquet had already come to a close in the inner reception room and the guests had withdrawn to the drawing room, where they were taking a glass of whiskey before the party broke up.

At this point an old family photograph album was produced. Everyone gathered round to look, the album was opened, and there was a faded sepia photograph showing a number of Japanese military men standing among a stern line-up of foreign military and civilian gentlemen in the open air. Apparently it was a photograph commemorating a large military exercise that had taken place in some Eastern European country. My friends gazed at it eagerly. We were all humanities students, so no great adventures or achievements could be foreseen for us in life. We would have loved to stow away on a freighter and go to a foreign land. Many people had already made their way to America and Western Europe, so there was no thrill in that, but perhaps we could find a way in to somewhere such as Eastern Europe. Though we might be prepared for the difference in political systems, however, these countries had just undergone civil war—this was the whisper, and in this the dream reflected the reality of the time.

We had in fact as well as in dream met like this at this house, and gathered round the album with the son of the house, who had spent part of his childhood in Northern or Eastern Europe, gazing down at it with eyes full of longing. In the dream too, we were all young. But the young man who should have been shyly explaining the photograph was no longer there. The sense of his absence, unclouded by any doubt, was strong in the air, and together with it came the image of that dark inner corridor, with the cold night deepening. Eventually I realized that this man had died the year before. He had met his death in an accident —yes, that was it, caught in an avalanche in the Bayern Alps in early summer. I had been astonished that even after he became an ambassador he had continued with such dedicated mountaineering.

I had this dream at the end of February. That afternoon, I heard the first bush warbler of spring. For some reason, I remember that when I heard the song for the second time that day, I suddenly recalled that I had had a strange dream that morning. My next thought was that I was dreaming a lot about the dead.

In a dream the morning before, I had been having breakfast with my father. It was in the poorly lit room my father had rented some two years after the war, in an old, slightly leaning house deep in an alley. He was then in his forties and struggling to make ends meet, and had secured this room for his family of five thanks to an old college friend. The scene felt as if it belonged to a time around four years later, when we were even more hard up. We were at a cheap, round, red-lacquered low table that was propped on the old matting floor, hastily shoveling in a meal of cold rice and kelp. My second eldest brother, the one who was still alive, was also at the table.

There was no sign of my mother, sister, or oldest brother, nor did it feel as though they were in the house.

My father and brother were wearing worn old everyday clothes. I, however, was dressed in a suit and tie. It seemed there was something urgent to discuss, and I had been summoned during the breakfast hour. It felt as if I had left home before six, and I was dressed to go straight to work after the discussion was over. This struck me as rather odd, since I had given up work over twenty years earlier. But despite the fact that I had been called over so early in the morning, there was no sign of the important topic being broached. The three of us simply ate, with an urgent haste. I too seemed to have nothing in particular to say. Objectively, I found myself thinking that this was how it always was at home —we dealt with matters by avoiding talking about them. Yet when we finished eating and I stood up a little awkwardly and remarked, eyes averted, "Well then, I'll be off. I'll come again," a bleak feeling swept over me. Perhaps my father will start to talk about earthquakes now, I suddenly thought. If a quake of any real size struck this two-story house, with its leaning rafters, there would be no saving it. During the earthquake while we were in Imaichi in Nikko, the rafters had shrieked and swayed wildly, and the house seemed about to collapse from moment to moment. But what would be the use of discussing earthquakes now? I thought, perplexity and weariness flooding me. "What about moving house then?" I managed to say, despairingly, and I was astonished at my irresponsible words. When I awoke, I felt suspicious at how suddenly the thought of earthquakes had entered the dream, and wondered if perhaps there actually had been a small tremor while I slept.

For a month or more after that, however, I had no further dreams of the dead. It would be perfectly reasonable, after all, for a person of my age to have such dreams more frequently. Surely it's only a natural process of ageing to find the dead gently encroaching, at first in dreams, until they hold the primary place in one's mind. But my father never showed the least inclination to act like the dead in my dreams. As for my old school friends, it was only by absence that they revealed to me that they had died. Perhaps it was out of reserve, or a fastidious repugnance, but it seemed to me that this lack was anyway a measure of the dreamer's poverty of spirit.

There had in fact been an alumni gathering within the previous month, when my classmates from middle school had invited out our old homeroom teacher and his wife.

In their late fifties, people begin to gather again. At each meeting, you come across faces unseen for decades. Each time, though they may have aged astonishingly, the unchanging nature of the face makes you feel that even if you had happened to brush against them in some crowd recently you would have recognized them instantly —just as if meeting with the dead. At that recent gathering, everyone spoke in turn describing their circum-

116

stances, and at one point someone stood up and revealed that our classmate S had recently died. He seemed to be deeply moved, but unable to express himself on the subject; he began to speak, but simply sighed and lowered his head again and again, so the information was frustratingly vague. Everyone nodded, as if having more or less grasped the story. However, I was secretly astonished, since it seemed to me that this man had also reported S's death at a previous gathering.

This would have been at least two years earlier, when we all at our old teacher's house in early spring. It was our custom to meet every year at this season. I had been absent from the last gathering, because my younger cousin on my mother's side had died at the end of February. I had a feeling I may have missed the year before as well, but at any rate, assuming it was two years ago, what I remembered hearing was not that things were looking bad for S. It was that he had died. This may, of course, be a mistaken memory. But no, the unpleasant coincidence was surely too strong for any such mistake. Perhaps it was a mis-remembering that had occurred instantaneously on hearing the news just now that S had died, or something in the line of *deja vu* or *deja entendu*. Yet for at least the last two years, I had believed that S was dead. I waited for someone else to voice the same doubt, but no such question arose, and my own perplexity was soon dissipated in further pleasant talk.

There was no possibility of having misheard him; the man had definitely spoken of S's death as recent. In which case, this suggested that I had foreknowledge of S's death. But it was hardly a case of foreknowledge, when I had known he was dead for two years. These were perilous waters, even just from my own point of view, and days passed with my doing no more than vaguely wonder about it from time to time. I rather assumed that matters would end there, but on the fifth day the question began to bother me, and I pulled out my schedule books for the previous three years to have a look —I use my old schedule books as a kind of diary. There I discovered that I had in fact been present at the gathering at our teacher's house the previous year, and that it had been a month later than this year's gathering. In that case, S's death had occurred less than a year ago, and there would be nothing odd in this friend recalling it as a recent event, considering how long an association they had had. Even if a year had passed, it would be quite possible for emotion to overcome him anew when he stood there in front of his old friends. He had said "last year," but it would surely have been before March last year. Even granted it was the year before, given that the gathering was held in February, it would feel more like the previous year. From my point of view, there seemed a great distance from the event. But there was really nothing strange in either of our perspectives. Yet the sense of amazement stayed with me.

To be certain, I searched back to the previous year, and found that the gathering had been at the end of February, and I had again been present. I even recalled that on that occasion I had taken along some Armenian cognac as a gift, and that last year, since the upheaval in the old Soviet Union had interrupted supplies of the cognac, I had taken red wine instead. It was in fact the year before that that I had been absent, and whether it was February or March, I would have been in hospital.

· · · · ·

On the afternoon of the holiday, Sugaike telephoned. He told me that he had happened to meet Fujisato the week before, and they had spoken of me.

"Was he well?"

"Yes, he was."

"Ah, that's good."

What on earth am I saying? I thought in surprise, as I turned my eyes to the window of my study, now shrouded in afternoon shadow though the day was fine, recalling how that morning in the forest by the little Kannon shrine, the bush warbler had sung again and again, heedless of people's voices.

"Lovely weather, isn't it."

"It's the middle day of Higan."

I knew that the world out there was in holiday mode, but I was unaware of which day was the old spring equinox known as Higan, when memorial services for the dead are performed. It had been a long time since I'd heard the expression "the middle day of Higan."

"Your voice sounds a little odd."

"You can hear it, can you? I've gone and caught a dose of the flu this season."

He told me he had spent the weekend in bed. He had developed a fever on the Thursday, but it improved after a night's sleep. He went to work on Friday, but he was unsteady on his feet all day, and on his way home he suddenly felt as if he were dying. Arriving home, he checked his temperature and discovered that his fever was quite high.

"I tell you, I had nightmares all night long. Someplace that was sort of a deserted field, and running round like a demented fiend. Absolutely tireless."

"Who?"

"Well, it must have been myself, I suppose. And what's more, in my fever I was shouting. 'Leave me alone!' I yelled. 'I can't sleep for your noise!'"

"Things aren't too bad if someone can still yell. But really, are you okay? I hear quite a few people have died with this flu."

"Yes, apparently so many old folk died round the end of the year that the nation's average life expectancy dropped a little. I guess you could say I got a tiny share of it. Things are hard for the ones left behind."

When he heard the birdsong that morning, he felt as though he had wakened from a spell. He felt almost unpleasantly fresh and bright, but since he generally developed pains in the back if he slept in, he got out of bed, and discovered that all was well. In the afternoon, the day seemed to be dragging. Then he remembered that it was the middle day of Higan, and decided to telephone. He said he had originally intended to call on Thursday.

I silently counted back the days, and realized that Thursday evening had been when I had read that account of Katei's dream. I would probably have been surprised if Sugaike had telephoned just then. No, quite likely I would have forgotten all about the dream of someone far in the past, in fact.

"So Fujisato was well, was he?"

"Yes, he was."

After a moment, we both burst out laughing.

"You're asking if there was any trace of his having been crazy, aren't you?" he asked.

"That's right."

"No, I don't think there was."

I had an odd difficulty in grasping the meaning of this concise and apparently clear answer, and the incomprehension remained as we continued to talk.

"We spent the whole time talking about you, you see," Sugaike added. "There was nothing else we could talk about. We couldn't bring up the subject of work, after all."

"Did he say anything?" I asked.

"He just told me how you'd met after forty years."

"So he said the same thing, eh? It must really have been forty years, then."

"After forty years," Sugaike's voice repeated in a mutter, and then he fell silent.

"That's right," I responded, and then my own words trailed off, as though a thought had been interrupted. This quite often happened these days, for no obvious reason.

"Forty years," Sugaike then repeated again.

"Hullo, are you there ...?" I said, rather stupidly.

"Yes, sorry," the hoarse voice came back. "I was just holding back a cough. Actually, you know this business about forty years, well when I was having my fever dreams, after the fiend had stopped his hurtling about, that was what popped into my head. It wasn't to do with Fujisato, or with you. I simply felt amazed at the idea of forty years. Not in any particular way, just generally deeply amazed. That forty years began to turn into a sort of bag surrounding me, a semitransparent red sack, and it shrank and expanded as the waves of amazement passed through me. Finally, my body was floating and sinking and bobbing about upside down inside it, quite unbearably. I knew I should stop feeling amazed, but it was simply impossible."

"That sounds pretty dangerous to me."

"Then in the midst of this, suddenly, whoosh!"

"What was that?"

"I thought it was a great towering red wave, but in fact it was me yelling. Everyone in the house came running. I looked round and asked with a gasping laugh if this was a wake. Apparently sweat was pouring from my forehead. I got them to turn on the heater, and I got up, stripped off and put on fresh pajamas. They even had to change the sheets. Not long after that, dawn came."

"This wouldn't have been this morning early, would it?"

"No, yesterday morning. After that I fell into a deep sleep, and only got out of bed three times in twenty eight hours."

"You've made yourself warm before you rang me, I hope?"

"Yes, I've brought the telephone over to sit in a patch of sunshine. The rays are slowly moving towards the wall, mind you."

His voice broke off, and I heard a sigh. Several more followed, and still he did not speak. He wasn't one to make long phone calls, nor was he someone who would abandon his interlocutor and retreat into silence.

"Speaking of sweat," he finally began again, in a drowsy voice. "That man who was wiping the sweat from his face in the station at Frankfurt Airport, you know, the one you saw from the window as your train set off, who you thought might have been me. Apparently that was someone Fujisato knew. He was walking along the platform when suddenly he began to sweat. He had no idea why, he said. He wasn't in a hurry, there was nothing urgent happening. He didn't feel sick. He had no physical problems. He decided to make sure he was okay when he got back to Tokyo, and went for a thorough medical examination, but there was nothing wrong with him. But apparently when he arrived in Hamburg from Frankfurt and happened to pull out his handkerchief next morning at the hotel, he thought he could detect a faint red stain through it. He quickly changed his underwear, but there was nothing there. He decided that it must be his imagination, but still he was uneasy, so he went to the bathroom and washed the handkerchief. He hung it up in the bathroom, and it had dried by evening. But when he held it up to the light at the window next morning, it still looked faintly red. Still, he decided not to worry about it any more, and stuffed it into his bag. When he remembered it again days later, his wife had already put all the dirty clothes through the wash. I said to Fujisato that you sometimes saw some funny things, and told him your story at the airport, you see, and then he told me that he knew the man. The time didn't seem quite to fit when I asked the details, but it must be the same person, mustn't it?"

Sugaike spoke with a weary slowness, punctuated by sighs. I felt I could see him there as he talked, eyes squinting against the sunlight.

10
THREE ANCIENTS

A few blossoms had opened on the cherry tree.

There are two ponds in the park near my house, the smaller of which used to be overhung by the great gnarled branches of an old cherry. When spring came around, these branches would be heartstoppingly smothered in pale blossoms that filled both the sky and the pond beneath. Almost ten years ago, however, there was a great snowfall just at the height of the flowering, which snapped branches from trees all through the park; this old cherry by the little pond received the worst damage, and after that, year by year, it began to wither. When about half its branches were removed, the ancient tree took on an emaciated air, and there was something scant and pitiful in the way it bloomed. I used to avert my eyes from the tragic sight as I passed the pond each year at blossom time, but this year I stopped to look. Perhaps it was the frail beauty of the scattering of blossom, with barely a third of the flowers open, but those old branches, grown yet more ancient in recent years, seemed to have taken on once more all the jaunty gaiety of earlier days. Standing there bleak with rusty age in the faint chill of the cloudy day, they also held a whiteness that seemed to float outside time.

During this same period, plans were laid for Sugaike and Fujisato and myself to all meet in the near future. Then, on a sudden request from Fujisato, it was arranged instead that Sugaike and I should call on him at home.

· · · · ·

I double-checked with Sugaike about whether Fujisato had really claimed he knew the man, in that conversation we had on the middle day of Higan. "That's what he said," Sugaike replied leadenly, his voice acknowledging my doubt. He told me that Fujisato had been impassive and apparently indifferent as he listened to Sugaike's tale of my seeing that man on the railway platform at Frankfurt Airport six months earlier, then at the end he had said he knew him. "I suspect he may have a reckless and unpredictable side to him, for all his appearance of sedateness," he muttered. Then he went on with a chuckle, "You're a bit the same yourself, I must say, believing that man was me."

121

I couldn't manage to connect recklessness with Fujisato in my mind at all. Through a corner of my mind flashed the odd idea that if indeed Fujisato had such a quality, this would be real, serious recklessness, not some passing whimsy. But the man Fujisato talked about was not a direct acquaintance of his. When I heard this, the whole story disintegrated still further into vague and ambiguous territory. Surely there would be any number of Japanese businessmen these days coming and going at that airport station, either so accustomed to travel that they no longer used taxis, or constrained these days from using them by Japan's straitened circumstances. Everyone experiences much the same sort of exhaustion at their destination, so there was nothing unusual in seeing similar such figures in similar such places abroad. Wouldn't this man have been simply standing on the platform, wiping away his pouring sweat? And the fact that he later discovered a faint red tinge to his handkerchief could surely be put down to the aging person's tremulous tendency to find symptoms of some physical problem.

"One person's mistake can set off a chain of mistakes," remarked Sugaike, quite determined that this was a case of mistaken identity, and then he turned the conversation back to the subject of Higan. He said that the way things were, he had omitted the traditional visit to the family grave that spring equinox; he hoped the dead would understand that he went whenever possible, but that he couldn't always go. Still, on deliciously long warm days like this, even though it was clear that he couldn't visit the grave in his present condition, it was weird, the way a feeling of mourning would creep over him as the sun began to sink. Actually, though he was generally far from praiseworthy in this regard, he'd had it on his mind since the beginning of March to visit the grave. He'd spent a lot of time going over and over in his mind whether to make it a Saturday or a Sunday, and pondering the fact that he wouldn't be able to decide till just before the day. And yet he had had a premonition that this year for some reason he would end up not going. When he let the previous Saturday slip by without acting, this began to affirm his feeling. It was with relief that he found himself developing a fever on Thursday night. But then in the middle of Friday night, floating on the height of his fever, he found himself struggling in the rain to perform the purification of the grave by pouring water over the headstone. He was the more desperate because the stone seemed to have been scorched red. "Well," he finished, "it was a bit like the sort of dream you wake up from when you have a hangover; nothing admirable in it, I'm afraid. But on this lovely long, warm day, I just feel …"

And then he said, in a voice suddenly blurred, "When the sun has gone down so far, a chill does creep up my spine."

The usually brisk Sugaike had slipped towards incoherence, and I sensed that he was wandering in circles. Anxiously, I urged him to go back to bed.

"Yes, maybe I'll go and have a sleep till the sun's gone completely. Let's meet again," he said simply and hung up. When the line went dead I too put down the receiver and turned my eyes to the eastern window of my study, which was already darkening. It had been a fine day, yes, but I wondered whether the day had been as brilliant as Sugaike had been claiming. And I had omitted to ask him where the grave was, who was in it, and whether he was the one designated responsible for its upkeep. Indeed I hadn't even asked his address. Though we had been friends for more than thirty years, I still didn't know his address or his phone number.

Since those far-off days when we two young bachelors had gotten together from time to time in that provincial city to drink and make merry together, we had only once, when we happened almost twenty years ago to meet up in Tokyo, informed each other with rueful smiles of our families and two children; otherwise, neither of us had ever broached the subject of our domestic life. Of course, during those twenty years we could count the times that we had met on the fingers of one hand. Once every three or four years, Sugaike would suddenly call late at night; once we heard the other's voice, the distance would evaporate, and we would arrange to meet for a drink the next day or the day after; and then, when we met, the night would end before we had time to move on from our elated reminiscences and think to report on our present circumstances. This was quite the opposite of the usual course of events, but it happened every time we met. Once outside the bar, we would immediately part ways. Sugaike always seemed to be headed for another appointment, despite the lateness of the hour, though this might simply have been the habitual air of a busy man. Every time we parted, I would remember that I had yet again forgotten to ask his address, but for some reason I always brushed away the idea with the thought that he would telephone me again before too long, and so the years passed.

I now can no longer clearly remember what it was we always talked about so excitedly in the bar, though I think it could only have been recollections of our time together as bachelors in that city long ago.

While we spoke on the phone, I had a vague sense of the direction in which his house lay, though in fact I couldn't have known it. Perhaps people are constructed in such a way that they cannot bear not to know the whereabouts of the person to whom they're speaking. I seemed to remember that, when we had met in Tokyo that time, Sugaike mentioned that he lived near a line that runs to the north of my house. He may even have mentioned the name of his station, but I have no memory of it. On this particular occasion, we talked for several hours, excited by the unexpected reunion, but I don't believe either of us had any idea of reviving the old friendship beyond this point. In our mid-thirties, we were of an age for our interest in things to maintain a leisurely focus on what lay ahead of us. Also, though Sugaike remained as easy and magnanimous with me as he had been in our youth, this magnanimity had always had a certain nervous edge to it, and I was now aware that this had grown somewhat more prominent and inflexible with the years.

It was not simply the result of ten years' estrangement. It seems to me that people who find themselves in intimate relationships in life gradually develop a kind of shyness in relation to the outside world that keeps them at emotional arm's length from others. It wasn't as though he or indeed I had grown cold, but simply that we were now careful not to enter more private territory by inquiring about personal circumstances. For the same reason, I imagine I was quite content merely to be told the name of the line he lived along. This kind of distant answer was in fact better suited to the feeling evoked by our old experience of drinking together in the heavy snows of that northern town long ago. But since that chance meeting, when Sugaike would startle me by phoning suddenly in the night, as we talked I would find myself following in my mind the old canal road near my house, then turning north midway along it, crossing the railway track, and continuing on along the narrow road towards him, and when I hung up I was left wondering at the experience.

"He said the chill had crept over him from behind. But perhaps it was just a relapse from the fever." I found myself talking aloud, and when I raised my eyes from my work to the window, the world beyond had grown quite dark. The chilly air of early spring rose from around my feet. I saw before me the newly convalescent man, talking on and on to me, one arm hugging his knees as he huddled closer on the floor while the pool of sunlight slowly shifted away to the corner of the room. I heard my wife and daughters laughing in the living room, and as I did so, I suddenly wondered whether Sugaike's voice hadn't perhaps been that of a man alone in the house talking on the telephone.

Later that night, Sugaike began to worry me again. I wanted just to make a brief phone call to apologize for having talked so long without remembering that he was barely over his illness, and to make sure he was okay, and I was regretting having yet again failed to learn his telephone number, when it occurred to me to ask Fujisato. His home phone number would be in the high school alumni book. He may well know Sugaike's number. It would be an oddly roundabout route to it, via someone with whom I had had no connection since our high school years until a brief year ago, but it was all I could think of tonight as a solution to the problem.

I imagined I would start the conversation with the remark that I heard he had recently met up with Sugaike. This would imply that I was calling him on nostalgic impulse, having just heard the news from Sugaike that afternoon, and in fact I would probably feel something of the sort when I phoned. I'd probably go on to tell him that Sugaike had come down with the flu and been in bed for three days, but was now sounding better. How would he take it if I then confessed that, though he had telephoned me, I didn't know his number, and had something I wanted to discuss with him this evening? I had a momentary apprehension that Fujisato might take this to refer to some unpleasant news.

I could hear him say then, immediately aware of my apprehension, that in fact he had also been a little worried about him when he met Sugaike recently.

I was beginning to be drawn into an imaginary scene in which Fujisato and I proceeded to speak in hushed tones of how Sugaike was somehow deeply implicated with the man who had been wiping his sweating face at the airport station. But I finally dismissed the fantasy with the thought that if mistakes, including mistaken identifications and deluded ideas, generally could be said to be a kind of madness, then at least as far as that man in the airport was concerned, Sugaike would surely be the farthest from madness of the three of us. If Fujisato did in fact know Sugaike's number, and could tell me then and there, things would probably go quite smoothly. But if the answer to my question was left hanging, it would leave a puzzle in its train.

Then I concluded my thoughts with the decision that I shouldn't let it all worry me, but simply give up thoughts of recklessly making contact while Sugaike was still feeling weak. Recklessly, I murmured to myself again.

.   .   .   .   .

The cherry by the little pond was now half in bloom. From a gall on the big branch which, when snapped, proved to be mere rotten wood, a delicate circlet of twigs of white blossom had sprung forth with all the gay brilliance of a healthy young tree. It was now less than ten days until the date Fujisato and Sugaike and I had fixed to meet at Fujisato's house, but I couldn't believe the meeting would actually occur. Nevertheless, there was no word yet from either of them to cancel.

I had been able to discover that Sugaike was safe when I called his workplace the following day, and he himself came on the phone. He had settled down in the bed after our phone call, just to be careful, and gone immediately to sleep. When he awoke it was long past midnight. Startled that he could sleep so long at his age, he fell back to sleep again, and when he next awoke it was dawn. He added with a laugh that he had certainly slept, but then when he finally got up he had eaten an astonishing amount.

"I was a bit worried about you," I finally brought myself to say, "so perhaps, all things considered, I should just make a note of your telephone number."

"Oh, I never told you?" Sugaike's voice betrayed surprise. He quickly gave it to me. "Well, well," he muttered, and then he asked if I would be at home that evening.

125

"That was quite a surprise," he remarked when we spoke on the phone again that night, taking up our earlier conversation. "Imagine my never having told you my number. It makes sense that you never called me."

"The time before we met last autumn, it would be about six years ago now, just as we were parting ..."

"Yes, I was looking through my pockets for a business card to write my number on and hand to you when the taxi came, wasn't I? I remember I just raised a hand vaguely ..." His voice grew somber. "I wonder when I started to believe that I'd already given it to you?" he said to himself. Then suddenly his voice leapt again. "Wait, wait! I'm in danger of forgetting something else now! Right after you called during the lunch break today I had another call, from Fujisato. That's what reminded me. A double hit of senility, all this forgetting."

He went on to say that his phone call of the previous night had been to tell me Fujisato's proposal that we three meet up before long. This had launched him into talk of the weather, then my question had moved the conversation on to his illness, and talk of sweating had in turn shifted to the topic of the man at the airport station. "Perhaps I forgot to mention it because I have a feeling there may be something I don't know behind all your doubts about Fujisato. But no, I did intend to tell you at the end of the conversation. It's just that somehow it turned out that I hung up rather suddenly. And then I forgot about it completely."

"Is Fujisato really serious?" I asked. It was true; I could hear doubt about him in my voice as I said this.

"I thought it was probably just a polite gesture, too, but when he called today he pursued the subject, and asked if we'd agreed on the meeting yet. He said he would be looking forward to it."

"Looking forward, eh?" I said, and the air of suspicion I registered in the way I spoke made me suddenly fearful.

"Well, it will be fun, won't it?" said Sugaike after a moment.

"Yes, it'll be fun," I responded. My tone was still a little reserved, but I was at the same time amazed at how the word "fun" seemed to faintly tinge my heart like a word not heard for many years.

I wound up taking on the role of organizer for the occasion. This was quite appropriate, given the relationships among the three of us. Promptness is essential in such matters or the moment is lost, so we two compared schedules then and there. April first was a Friday, so we decided it should be the next Friday or early the following week, when the cherry blossoms had fallen and the crowds had dissipated.

Sugaike undertook to decide on the meeting place. Then, as we were about to end our conversation, he added, "I should have started with the question, in fact, but how is your family?"

"All well, thank you," I said, my tone matching his. Then, holding my breath a little, I asked, "And yours?"

"Yes, in the best of health as usual," he replied, then he added with a laugh, "'The best of health'—that's rich, isn't it!" and as he was about to hang up, he mentioned his address to me as well, just for the record.

It turned out that in fact Sugaike's house was not exactly along that road my mind traveled whenever we spoke on the phone, but a few kilometers to the west, at the southern edge of the neighboring suburb. As I stared at the address I had jotted into my memo book, I began to realize that I seemed to have seen these words before. It can occasionally happen that some chance will jog your memory so that you suddenly recall to the very house number the address of some friend deep in the past, or even someone now dead. When you pause in surprise at this, you turn out to have quite forgotten it again. There is only the sense of it having been there, clear in your mind, but you almost suspect that the thing itself was never actually present.

Maybe this feeling is of that sort, I decided, placing my hand on the receiver and looking at the clock on the wall. There was no possibility that I could remember Fujisato's number off the top of my head. I would have to take down the alumni book from the corner of the bookshelf. My eye traveled down the column of small print, pushing past all the names I knew, till I found his just above mine and copied his number onto the memo pad in large writing. In recent years, such searches had begun to take an inordinate length of time, while I endlessly ran my eyes vaguely up and down the list. I had even begun to conceive of a search as a major undertaking.

As I counted the rings, I was momentarily seized by a bizarre image of Fujisato asking "Who are you?" when I had given my name. If that happens, I'll take it in stride and politely explain the few details of what's occurred in the last year, I decided, pursuing the extraordinary idea while I waited calmly. Then my thoughts shifted to wondering how Yamagoe was doing these days, though in fact it wasn't so long since I'd heard from him. And then my thoughts began to burgeon and swell. Night after night the woman he lives with is no doubt leaving to him the decision of whether or not to have a child, and he, surely he is silently groping towards knowing with his own flesh the moment long ago when his father, crazed with angry jealousy against the world and women, first clung to his mother, almost ravishing her in the act of impregnation, and I saw the snaking line of the old canal road, and realized suddenly that Fujisato's house would be more or less midway between Yamagoe's and my own.

"Ah, thank you for calling like this. Have you worked out a date and time with Sugaike?" he quickly replied when I'd given my name, in a taut voice that suggested he'd leapt straight to the phone, belying the long wait before he'd answered. Even Sugaike, when his telephone call suddenly broke those long years of estrangement, had not commenced the conversation with such straightforward bluntness. I told him our conclusions about possible days, and he replied immediately that either Friday or Monday would suit him fine. Then he asked where Sugaike lived, and when I passed on to him the address I had just learned, he said, "Wait a moment, will you?" and there was a clunk as he put the receiver down. He didn't reappear for some time, then eventually there was the distant sound of a clear woman's laughing voice, and he was back on the phone apologizing.

"Would it be all right if you came to my house sometime Sunday afternoon so we could have some leisurely time together and then eat dinner here? I know it's Sugaike's precious day off, but he doesn't live far from here, so please see if this would suit him. I just talked to my daughter about it, and she was delighted with the rare opportunity. I lost my wife five years ago, so I'm afraid I can't offer you the spread I'd like to."

"Fujisato's house, eh?" said Sugaike when I telephoned to tell him, then he seemed to think for a moment, and continued, "That should work well. It seems right for us to meet at his place on Sunday, doesn't it?" Then when I told him belatedly that it would be his daughter who prepared the meal and that his wife had died five years ago, and asked him if he'd known, he said, "Is that so? Now I come to think of it, when we met the other day, I got the feeling that things weren't quite making sense from time to time. So it was different, was it?" His voice receding as if he was talking to himself, he continued, "Let's accept the invitation, since he's been kind enough to make it and his daughter agrees. Besides, we don't require as much trouble taken over us as we did when we were young. Fujisato and I were saying as much to each other with a laugh the other day."

I called Fujisato again, then Sugaike once more to confirm time and place, and so managed to complete the arrangements that evening. This was the day following Higan.

· · · · ·

Within the next three days the old cherry tree by the little pond burst into almost full bloom. Looking more closely, I saw that the little circlet of blossoming twigs was astonishingly rich with flowers. It was hardly what you'd call luxuriant growth, but somehow, perhaps because the blossoms spread themselves right up to the tips of the twigs, as they glowed there in the sunlight they almost appeared to be bending gracefully over the water. Even so, the tree seemed to half retain its old splendor. In the water beneath the bending cluster of blossoms stood a stout black pike that had once supported the large branch now broken and gone. The blossoms at their height only served to make the tree's remaining branches and trunk appear yet more like a dead skeleton.

The year when the heavy snowfall snapped the flowering branches, I visited the park a few days later. Beneath a sky that remained overcast and chilly, branches of various sizes lay everywhere beneath the trees, still covered in blossom almost completely open. Gardeners had sawn up the larger branches with a chain saw and loaded them onto the back of a small truck for removal, and small bits had tumbled off the back all along the paths, each still covered in fine blossoms and buds. Visitors to the park were sorrowfully gathering them up to carry home, and the scene looked like some mournful blossom festival. My own family brought some back as well, and put them in vases all over the house, in the hallway and living room and kitchen, and even in the study and the bathroom, so that the house was more ablaze with bright blossoms than our little garden with the cherry tree visible just outside. The faces of my wife and daughters shone pale in the daylight. One would have expected that everyone would be in festive mood, but in fact a strange state of mind settled over us, and we moved about in a subdued hush for several days. Finally the blossoms in the house all began to scatter, though not on any breeze.

I awoke early and heard outside the window the sound of a horse being led by. This was in fact a custom of many years. Yet the light slowly intensifying at the edge of the curtain was still faint, and it seemed too early for the students who these days took the horses to the park for their morning exercise. When I turned on the light of the alarm clock by my bed, I found it was only just past four. I lay back face up again, and waited for more horses to pass. I had also had the habit for some time now of spending time counting intently when I first awoke. I would, for instance, rapidly count up days, though I could no longer recall what the days were. It wasn't a bad idea to listen for the passing hooves, and count the horses. Sometimes I drifted off to sleep again while they went by. But today, there were no more horses. I heard only the one. Someone had led a single horse past in the dawn. The clop of its hooves continued on around the far corner where it would be lost to sight, then on still further, along the edge of the parkland, echoing back from the walls of nearby buildings so that this single horse sounded to my ears like the lively clatter of a large group. Then, at the point when the horse would have reached the park entrance and the sound of its hooves suddenly ceased, I counted that it was five days till the Sunday when we would gather at Fujisato's house. Having arrived at the answer, I was left with the sense that I had spent a long time over the calculation. Good heavens, I said to myself, the way I live means I can't even remember what day of the week it is.

A crime story in the newspaper haunted me. A man of fifty-seven had killed his son of twenty-four in despair. The man had been vice president first of a large company and then of its smaller subsidiary, and had gone on to spend eight years as head of its trading arm in the States before returning to Japan the previous year. His son had gone to high school and university in the U.S. When they came back, the son managed to find a job, but this hadn't lasted long, and since then he had hung around the house, sniffing glue.

129

At my age, I'd decided to adopt a suitably noncommittal approach to such news reports. I paid some attention to indicators that explained or hinted at the inner workings of those involved, but beyond that I resisted being drawn in by the story. I attempted to withhold judgment, and resisted being convinced by the story line. This attitude extended to the information given to help the reader fill in the general background to the case. Even if the story was written in a carefully objective style, it would rely on affective language that was common coin. Even when it was perfectly clear how the public would react to the news and make sense of it, though as a member of that public I accepted and noted this as one more piece of information, I nevertheless resisted being personally convinced by it. The result was that all I retained from the report was the basic chronology relating to circumstances and protagonists, and since the reports themselves were constrained in the detail they could give, my sum of information was a very rough and ready affair, dates of years separated by great gulfs of blankness, standing like mute stakes in the flow of time, with almost nothing attaching to them. Yet this only felt the heavier to me.

This story, however, was relatively detailed for its length. It was brief and to the point, written chronologically, giving ages and so on of those involved rather than focusing on the situation, and it didn't attempt to penetrate the incident further, for all its careful detail. Any emotional reaction was likewise repressed. At first reading I felt that the story had been written by someone who was in fact deeply intrigued by the incident, perhaps filled with painful empathy for the participants. I imagined that the reporter might actually be someone very close to those involved, and to find corroboration I opened another paper to compare the reports, but I found no mention of the incident there.

Once I'd read it, I didn't think much more about it. In some ways, I was forbidding myself further thought to avoid my imagination becoming drawn by the story. But some hours later, as I sat reading at my desk, I found myself repeating in my head the chronology of events that I had gleaned in my own fashion from the report; after a while I began to suspect that I had missed something in reading, or perhaps had added something that wasn't really there, or had begun to confuse my memory of the dates. This was also a habit I had fallen into recently. Suddenly the question began to trouble me, and I rose from my desk, went to the living room, and opened the paper.

The son's addiction to glue sniffing had begun ten years earlier. It's not that I had failed to notice this, it simply hadn't stuck in my head. Ten years earlier meant that it had begun before the two of them went to America. He would perhaps still have been in middle school. The father had joined his company the year before I left university. An old friend from that year had joined the same company the following year. I'd heard at the time that he had been quite depressed because he had hoped to be involved in the business side but had been placed in administration, until his enthusiasm returned when young company members were recruited to research the wholesale introduction of computers. This would have been around 1960.

Eleven years after he joined the company, the father had been sent to Southeast Asia, where he spent four years. A further eleven years were spent back in Japan before he went to the States. The report did not elaborate on either of these periods. This was only natural, since they were not relevant areas to touch on. In my mental chronology, these two stretches of time felt like blanks, gaps in the story, but of course this wouldn't in fact be the case. It was only now, in my own mind, that they were blank. Then I began tentatively to calculate the years again, and it occurred to me that the son might well have been born the year his father was posted overseas—and I found myself imagining the lonely father, lost in thought, the sound of an infant's tottering feet endlessly following now before him and now behind, and whenever the footsteps suddenly cease and he turns, he sees the child, each time grown older, crouched on the ground, deeply engrossed in playing with pebbles—and suddenly I was brushed with a quick shiver of pity. But the blanks remained blank.

I thought of them as blank, but it occurred to me that of course my own case was in fact no different. From Sugaike's point of view, for instance, despite our occasional meetings during the time, that same twenty-four years since the father had gone to Southeast Asia constituted a blank in my life too, as I simply sat at my desk at home. And with this thought, I pushed further speculation and imaginings aside.

However, past midnight the following evening, when I was already in bed, I was struck once more by the thought that I had made some important error in my reading of the chronology of the incident, and I used the excuse of needing another quick drink to send me to sleep, and slipped out of bed.

I searched out the newspaper from the pile of old papers on the shelf beside the bathroom, and opened it as I stood there. But the report was so clear and straightforward that even I could not have misread it. I went to the toilet, then in the kitchen I tossed back a quick shot of whiskey, and as its strange sweetness filled my mouth I castigated myself for being in rather low spirits for the last few days. Yet while this gloom had pervaded me, day by day the cherry blossoms by the little pond had been opening. Today I had seen the already-open blossoms strung from the weeping cherry like necklaces, their dense wings fluttering low over the pond. Tomorrow no doubt they would be flowering in a soft cloud, and beginning to scatter onto the water.

"Well, won't it be fun?" Sugaike had asked blankly. And I'd repeated the words in the same blank tone. I had spent the last half month exhausted and despairing at the image of us all sitting gathered there, three people who had lived our lives quite estranged from each other, with no possibility of anything we could talk about, all our efforts directed toward keeping at bay the bleak silence that would otherwise creep over the gathering; and yet at the same time, during these weeks I had begun to look forward to the event with increasing anticipation.

I went back to bed thinking to myself, half convinced, that at my age perhaps a heart filled with happy anticipation can easily shift to one filled with gloom.

. . . . .

Sunday was a beautiful spring day. I rose when the sun was high in the sky and stood looking out our glass living room door, and as I gazed at the cherry directly outside, now scattering its petals everywhere, I had to admit that I was sorry to be leaving the house that afternoon. Still, we weren't meeting until five, so until three or so at least I could spend my time as I wished, doing nothing, simply letting my heart fill with the blossoming branches shifting in the breeze. I was just deciding that, since the place was so close, I would be able to wait till after the race broadcast on television before I had to get ready, when there was a call from Fujisato suggesting we come a little early on account of the beautiful weather.

Apparently he'd just had a call from Sugaike, who said that as he was free that day he thought he would get himself ready after lunch and set off to stroll in Fujisato's direction, stopping in along the way at any parks where the cherries were still in bloom. He intended to walk as far as he could, but he only knew the directions from the nearest station to the house, and if he chose at some point along the way to take a cab for the rest of his journey, he wanted to know what he should tell the driver his destination was. As Fujisato was explaining, Sugaike had proposed that since he was likely to have time on his hands, perhaps we should instead all meet at about three at the nearby park with the hackberry tree.

"I'll be hanging around near the park at that hour, so just come along when you like," Fujisato said. "The park is easier to find than my house."

"That will be helpful for me too," I replied. "These days my instinct for finding my way to a new place has completely deserted me. Actually, though I believed I was quite clear on the directions I passed on to Sugaike, I was just thinking that I don't feel entirely confident about them."

When I replaced the receiver, I realized that I wouldn't be able to watch the race now. Though it was many years since the last time I went all the way down to the Kansai area just to watch this particular horse race, since that time I had never missed it on the television. Last year, just when I had turned off the TV after the race was finished, the phone in the living room rang, and my daughter's oddly bright voice had come down the line, laughingly telling me that she was in Tatebayashi and had broken her leg landing after a successful skydive, that a friend was now bringing her home after emergency treatment at the nearby hospital, and not to worry because everything else was fine. And indeed she did arrive home, smiling, that evening, but though she was quite well otherwise, the injury turned out to be a multiple fracture requiring surgery some days later. It was only early this spring that the simple operation of removing the bolt that had been placed in her leg was performed. And it was only now that I realized that it was exactly this Sunday one year ago that I had come across Fujisato in the hackberry park, after a gap of forty years. Of course I was aware that it had been around the same time. My memory of the scattering blossoms from that time was still vivid. But I had assumed that there was a week's difference, and the horse race hadn't served to connect the two for me.

"Well, then!" I muttered to myself, as if I should be setting about getting ready to leave that very moment, but in fact there was still some time to wait before lunch.

As I walked along the old canal road with my bottle of saké for the gathering, my eyes took in the sight of the cherries that lined it. This spring, I had been so impressed by the tree by the little pond that I hadn't walked down this road to see the blossoms, and now it seemed to me that the trees standing here gently scattering their petals in the breeze had grown taller. There was still a cold bite to the wind, but as I walked I felt the sun's rays on my neck and back. As I strolled on, struck by the sun's warmth, I pondered how even a trivial lapse of memory comes to your attention trailing a little cloud of guilt.

My plan had been to set off from home in good time and make my way slowly, but I found myself approaching the corner on this side of the park well before three o'clock. I looked on down the road, and saw the hackberry tree against the pale green mist of the spring trees beyond, looking as if it too was in full bud. I narrowed my eyes and walked slowly towards it, wondering how long the big tree would be able to maintain this illusion. For a while it remained in healthy leaf before my eyes, then the broad daylight began to lend this effect an air of uncanny illusoriness, and the next moment it was suddenly revealed in its true form, as a broken and rotting tree. There was something both humorous and at the same time heartrendingly humble and vulnerable in its appearance. I hurried over sympathetically to look up at its trunk, and was frowning at the sight of what seemed a thick matted net of purplish capillaries smothering the dry bark when I heard the faint sound of music somewhere nearby. Sensing a dark trembling of human breath within the bright sunlight, I turned, and there, sitting on the bench where on a previous occasion the vagrant had been stretched reading a comic magazine, his padded form buried in a colorful sleeping bag, now sat Fujisato and Sugaike, looking rather bashful.

"In the end I made it all the way here on foot," said Sugaike in greeting. "It's what they say, isn't it—old men have strong legs."

"I got here half an hour ago and he was already sitting here," Fujisato chipped in. "He looked just as if he was someone who lived around here."

"I'll join you in the sun, if you don't mind," I said, and seated myself beside them. The three of us sat there quite simply together.

Nevertheless, my ears continued to be haunted by the sense of music in the air. It could have been the hum of bees flying past, but sometimes it sounded like a snatched phrase from an organ chorale, and it never settled into silence. On the other side of Fujisato, Sugaike apparently noticed my confusion, for he took out a little radio cassette and showed it to me.

"I'd turned down the volume and forgotten it. As I was heading out the door, I picked it up, thinking I could sit down in some park on the way and listen to it. But then when I telephoned just to check, we pushed the time forward, you see. If that's the case I won't need it, I thought, and put it down again, but then I remembered that he said he'd ask you if you wanted to come early too, so I went back and picked it up again. Funny, you coming out after lunch like this, with such an important race on today."

"I didn't realize," Fujisato put in apologetically.

"It's a fine thing to listen to the races on the radio while you look at the blossoms," I answered. The soft music did indeed seem to be a chorale. I remembered having several times seen in a little European town an elderly-looking Japanese businessman at midday when the church organ played, drawn by the music to slip out from work during a break and casually approach the bench in front of the church, where he would then sit huddled right at the edge, eyes closed in concentration or perhaps in drowsiness.

We began to talk about the resignation of the prime minister two days earlier, and then suddenly it was time for the race to begin. Sugaike was the first to realize, and he switched the radio back on.

We three sat there listening, with faint smiles hovering on our faces. A bystander would no doubt have seen us as a picture of three old men sitting in a row basking in the sunlight and grinning vaguely from sheer enjoyment.

"Okay, that's enough. That's what I thought would happen."

"Did you win?"

"No, I didn't place any bets."

"You were listening so intently I thought you must have."

Fujisato was contrite again. "I kept you from watching it this year, didn't I?" he said regretfully. I was about to reassure him when he suddenly turned to look to the right and continued to sit gazing in that direction. Our eyes followed his, and we saw a slim young woman standing at the edge of the park, staring intensely at us with a puzzled air. Fujisato nodded to her, and her face broke into a smile, but then puzzlement overcame her again; her gaze seemed on the point of being forced downward when Fujisato's smile gave her fresh courage and a smile at last spread across her own face again, a smile suggesting she had reached us from along some far, faint road. She welcomed us, quite forgetting to bow in greeting.

"There's no need to worry. I'll bring them along shortly," her father responded, an air of intimacy in his look.

11
Garden Guests

He had learned from his late father that the place was built in 1939 or 1940, and until the war it had been the home of a military man—so Fujisato informed us when we three had settled into the guest room. His family had consisted of the two parents, his older sister, and himself. They had moved here nine years after the war, so the house would not have been old by our present standards, but for Fujisato, then in high school, it had seemed a thoroughly gloomy and unpleasant place, and he had wondered why his father had to buy this stuffy old house at a time when nice new houses were at last springing up everywhere. Meeting my eye, he told me with a laugh about the strange smell that seeped from the corners at night in the rainy season, permeating the place as everyone slept, about the rumors of the wild life led by the previous inhabitants, and about how the military man had supposedly ended by being executed in some foreign country. I realized that he would be referring to the period in his life when I used to come upon him in the early morning classroom, sitting alone by the window, gazing out.

However, Fujisato went on, his mother had died, then his father, he himself had passed fifty, and his son had married and moved overseas, and now, with the time to gaze around him and observe the place, he was impressed at how simply and durably it had been built. He decided that the relative lack of comfort in the design could be attributed to the somewhat strained lifestyle and tastes of the youthful military man; in fact, what amazed him now was how he could have spent all these years considering the house to be nothing more than a hopelessly lumpen old veteran of a dwelling that had withstood the best efforts of his mother's years of polish and later his wife's similar attempts to get it into decent shape.

"It's true," said Sugaike, cocking a knowing eye towards the lintel beam, "it's very well built." I recalled the unusually plain and modest entry hall. The wooden floor was raised quite high, and the slender wall pillars did not bespeak an old house, but glancing up as we entered the verandah passageway just now, I had noticed the thickness of the round beams. The rafters that extended out to the veranda awning were likewise sturdy.

"It's a typical bungalow," remarked Fujisato.

"Does it have an inner corridor?" Sugaike asked.

"Just a little one. What about yours?"

"Yes, and talk about gloomy! The air raids made a fine clean sweep of everything, but that was just the other day."

"What's it feel like to live in the same place for forty years?" I inquired.

"Well, I spent a total of eight years living abroad, of course."

All three of us gazed around the room, as if counting up the years.

"You've turned it into something very nice," observed Sugaike. It sounded a little like a subtle apology for his impertinence. I was impressed at how he had managed with his remark effectively to ask after both the mother and the wife who had run the household, but then I set about calculating the passage of time again, with the thought that by the time Fujisato had come to view the house in a new light, his wife would be dead in only a few more years. My thoughts were interrupted by the words, "Ah, here's my daughter." I swiveled around to see her suddenly waiting there, kneeling in the corridor at the opened sliding door, the tea tray balanced on both hands. She made a formal greeting when I turned.

· · · · ·

"Well, well, some young people are so quiet these days," Sugaike murmured, his eyes turned toward where the girl was kneeling almost invisibly in the recesses of the corridor.

"It's not that," responded Fujisato with a deprecatory smile. "I spoke to her on the matter recently, in fact." I assumed he was referring to the need to behave in a modest and maidenly fashion, but he went on, "'Don't walk about in the house so silently,' I said to her, 'and don't just come to a sudden standstill nowhere in particular like that.' And she came back at me with, 'Well, you do exactly the same thing yourself these days.' And it's true, I do. We've both become very quiet around the house."

Sugaike stepped in at this point with the light remark, "I've heard that people can start to talk to themselves constantly." He cocked his head thoughtfully as he spoke.

"I apparently do that," Fujisato said.

"That must be why you don't hear her moving about the place," I chipped in, to help keep the tone light, but Fujisato responded, "When I see her there sometimes, it can take a few moments before I speak." Sugaike and I both fell silent at this, and sat gazing out past the corridor where the girl had been sitting, onto the darkening garden beyond.

The grass beyond the veranda still retained a wintry dryness, perhaps because of the lack of sunlight. The lawn extended back and was lost among the distant garden plants and flowers, increasingly unkempt in its farther reaches, and the spring flowers were past their peak, beginning to be replaced by flourishing grasses. This view in turn merged back into a further grassy field—at first sight quite untended though with evidence of a tending hand here and there—which came to a halt at the stone wall in front of the next-door house.

"It used to be a Western-style garden," Fujisato told us. "There was a garden bed over there, with roses and so on in it. My mother began to prefer grasses to flowers in her final years. Maybe she didn't have the perseverance for gardening that she used to. So this is what it turned into. When my wife came back from our time living abroad, she preferred it like this, and she started bringing in all kinds of wild grasses. It makes for a lovely, peaceful garden in spring, but it can get quite oppressive during the rainy season. They grow so thick that they half bury the stone wall there. But even so, there'll always be the odd flower showing through here and there. And it's impressive in autumn too."

"It must be a subtle business to keep it looking nice like this. I suppose your daughter looks after it now."

"I do some gardening too."

"I'd guess that's the area where a man's hand has been at work," remarked Sugaike, and when I looked in the direction he was pointing, I saw what he meant. The plantings in the area of the small, mounded hill had a somehow stiffer, more labored air that was at odds with the gentle atmosphere of the garden as a whole.

"You guessed it. That's where Dad has been having his battles," Fujisato said rather shamefacedly.

"It's a woman's garden," Sugaike said, gazing calmly out over it.

I now began to puzzle over Fujisato's remark about the gap in time between seeing his daughter and speaking to her. If he received the impression that she was suddenly standing there unexpectedly before him, surely she would feel likewise about him. She was apparently twenty-seven. When she had stood there in the park, my first impression had been of a girl who was terribly shy, but now that she was here in the company of guests, she was in fact quite composed. I gathered that she wasn't housebound, but went out to work four days a week, and would happily go off on overseas trips. When Sugaike remarked that it must be a bit depressing having to spend time with her father's guests, she replied that her father was quite delighted that we had come to the house. When she took our orders for drinks and retired, Sugaike called after her, "Be sure you come back and join us again soon." I was alert to her rather humble "Me?" But when he went on to say, "I found some Toscana wine and brought it along," she responded with a straightforward delight. She seemed to be adept at answering questions, but before the answer emerged there was a moment when she first drew breath and grew unfocused, as if reaching for the words. Her voice was clear, though soft. Its slightly rough edge of hoarseness and her habit of drawing little breaths

138

between phrases gave the unsettling impression that she might suddenly come to a halt at any moment, though in fact this never happened and the voice flowed easily on. Although she continued to smile when she had finished her reply, she seemed once again to be tuned in to some distant place; once she had left the room, this presence bequeathed to the listener a lingering sense of quiet in the air.

"Ever since I was a child," Sugaike said, "I always had a bad impression of my father's guests, you know. That's why I was a little worried for her."

"Do you have any children?" Fujisato inquired, and for the first time I heard that he had an older boy and a girl. They both had long since found jobs, but neither showed any intention of marrying.

"The boy moved into his own apartment on the grounds that he always gets home from work so late. He had the nerve to babble something the other day about how I must come and stay occasionally."

It was then my turn to be asked, and when I replied that I had two girls, but that there was no sign of either of them marrying, Fujisato sighed and said, "Well then, we're all in the same boat."

"It's that old story about the man who can't follow his dream of shaking off the world because there's a daughter hanging around his neck, huh?" said Sugaike drolly, and we all sat gazing at the garden once more. Our gazes softened with contentment at the sight of the changelessly gentle garden, and flowed naturally together through the grass to our left, tracing the shadow of a faint path that made its way out to the neighboring wall.

. . . . .

The saké had been served and the light in the garden was fading fast when Sugaike brought up the question of the path, inclining his head toward it and sketching its route with his hand as he asked, "Would that little track be a cat path? Though actually it looks as if it goes in the direction of the gate in the neighbor's fence ..." Apparently this gate was visible from where he sat. As the sun sank, the shadow of the line of the path grew more distinct.

"Ah yes, that. It still hasn't disappeared, eh? Someone used to come in every night along there in the summer two years ago," replied Fujisato. "It gets so covered in dew during the night that I cut the grass there for him. There used to be a path there once."

We laughingly objected that it wasn't the season for ghost stories, then settled down to hear the tale.

It was the eighty-four-year-old who lived next door. It began one stiflingly hot night past eleven o'clock, when Fujisato was sitting out in the corridor facing the garden with the glass doors open and a mosquito coil beside him. There the figure was, standing out on the lawn in his dressing gown. Fujisato had been deep in thought, and hadn't noticed him approach. Even now, when the figure stood in front of him, he was oddly unsurprised.

"Good evening," Fujisato said, offering him the flat straw cushion he'd been sitting on, and the old man came over, stepped onto the stone below the veranda edge, settled himself onto the veranda, and launched into a complaint about how the summer night air was bad recently, everyone was using air conditioners these days, it made the nights terribly steamy and hot, and he could scarcely breathe. There was indeed a white fog lying over the garden as he spoke.

A white fog lay over the old man's eyes as well, and the color of his pupils was faded around the edges. Until about a year ago, he had looked in vigorous health when out on his walks. Now his eyes met Fujisato's, and he seemed to take him for the young lad next door that Fujisato had once been, for his voice took on a hectoring tone. Listening to him, Fujisato felt the image of his own father in life hovering now near now far. The man may have been in his eighties, but his eyes still gleamed astutely. Then, from around autumn of the following year, those eyes grew large and vacant, the face took on the air of a kind of monkey mask, and he stopped acknowledging Fujisato even when they passed one another. And since spring his decline had been rapid. Though he was still reasonably mobile, every time he went for a walk he would apparently get lost and have to be brought home by the local police.

He had lived in the house next door since before the war. When the Fujisato family moved here, there was a little door in the stone wall between the two houses, painted blue, more in the Western style than the usual wooden door, and a path connecting it to this house was clearly visible. The neighbor worked in one of the big munitions companies, and Fujisato's father used to joke about how he and the military man in our house were probably secretly in cahoots; and indeed, to judge from this path, there was clearly some backyard communication between the two houses. Fujisato's mother too was very friendly with the neighboring wife, a woman now long since dead. His father said he often came across the neighbor on his Sunday walks. Fujisato had no memory of how the rotting door came to be replaced, but he said the door had never been locked from either side. Once or twice it had provided a route for thieves, but neither house had suffered any loss, and they were content to leave the back way unlocked, as long as the fronts of the houses were carefully secured.

The old man told a story of one summer night during the days when the area had still been given over to fields and orchards. In those days there were no dwellings other than farmhouses, so it must have been before the Fujisato family moved there. For an old man's reminiscence it was remarkably coherent, neither rambling nor repetitive, and in comparison with the times when he would accost Fujisato out in the street and talk to him, he now spoke easily and straightforwardly, without forcing the conversation on him, and with a gentle calmness that made the old man seem suddenly

140

much younger.

He said that late at night the breeze had carried in the scent of water, and in those days it had been much easier to sleep. As he spoke, he would prompt his listener from time to time with "you'll remember" or "wasn't it," as if the past he spoke of was not fifty years ago but a mere decade or two back, and when the old man proceeded to sympathize with him over the problems of having lost his wife, Fujisato began to suspect that the old man was in fact addressing his father, rather than himself. Then the old fellow lowered his voice and continued, "Apparently this entire area, including your place and mine, was originally a field. It seems the men have generally survived the women in these parts. My son's quite resigned to the same fate," and he looked Fujisato in the eye. This was surprising enough, but just then a voice was heard behind them, and when Fujisato turned he was more astonished to see that his daughter, who ought to have been asleep, was standing there with a tray of tea and cakes for them, as unperturbed as if a normal neighborhood guest had called in. The old man looked abashed.

A little later, a light came on in the back of the house next door, and Fujisato sent his daughter a look that asked her to telephone them. The woman was shocked and deeply embarrassed to learn what had happened, and in no time a young lad, no doubt a grandson, had arrived at the front door to fetch the old man. His untroubled expression suggested that they probably had to cope with much the same sort of thing day and night. When it happened a second time and his daughter rang next door, the woman confessed tearfully, "It's wearing me out," and followed this up with bumbling apologies. From then on, though not exactly every night, it regularly happened that when Fujisato was out taking the cool on the veranda late at night, unable to sleep for the heat, the old man apparently caught sight of him from somewhere inside, and in a little while the gate in the wall would creak open.

"It's a funny thing," Fujisato went on, fixing his gaze on the gate now rapidly disappearing in the fading light, "but when someone's standing on the other side, it looks distinctly white."

It would take some time for the old man to make his way through the grass to where Fujisato sat, but he waited silently, feeling that if he addressed the old man it might make him come to a halt. At last, relying tentatively on Fujisato's welcoming expression, he approached the veranda and settled himself down on the edge with his feet on the stone below. Apart from the fact that he obviously considered such a visit at such an hour to require no explanation, there was no particular sign of senility in his behavior or speech. He made himself comfortable and launched into general chat. The tone was plaintive, but hardly indignant or incensed. In the course of these conversations it became clear to Fujisato that the old man was living in a present that was roughly a year earlier, and having realized this, he could follow the talk more easily. It seemed that for the old man time had come to a halt with the previous summer. Nevertheless, the things that caused him anxiety were still more or less applicable to the present world situation. Indeed, his words could sometimes almost be taken as prophetic. Fujisato was privately amazed and impressed by this, and half-doubtingly he pressed the old man with further questions, but he reached the conclusion that for the old man the previous year simply did not exist.

One night there had been a rain shower earlier in the evening, before the muggy heat had returned, and when the old man arrived at the veranda his dressing gown was soaked from the passage through the grass. Fujisato asked his daughter to bring a towel, and as the old man carefully wiped his feet he remarked, "I seem to have come a long way." Looking on, Fujisato decided that he would spend half a day the next Saturday cutting back the grass as far as the gate, but when he came home the next evening he saw that the path was already cleared. When he asked his daughter about it, she said that the old man had truly looked as though he'd arrived from some distant place as he sat there wiping his feet, and she felt later that she should have stepped down into the garden and wiped them for him. Because it had been a path for a long time, she said, the grass wasn't deeply rooted and it was quite easy to pull it out, though in fact her hands had been rather cut about by it. The old man didn't seem to notice that the path had become easier.

However, the old man had died at the end of the year. As Fujisato made his way around to the house for the wake, he reflected that this was the way the young lad had always taken when he came each night that summer to take his grandfather home, for some reason avoiding the side gate. After the incense for the dead had been offered, the woman of the house had come over to apologize and thank him specially for putting up with all the disturbance that past summer. She began to cry, and went on to say that the old man had expressed his gratitude until the end that Fujisato's daughter had cut the grass on the path for him. He must have watched her do it from somewhere inside the house.

"No, that's not right," Sugaike broke in. "That's where your observations slip up. It's midsummer, near midnight, when people are in bed and scents grow vivid. The old man would know from the air of that path that a young girl had cut it."

The alcohol was beginning to have its effects. I looked at Sugaike, surprised that he would display this degree of sensibility. "Weren't you in fact waiting there for your nightly guest, staring at the gate?" I asked Fujisato.

"My daughter accused me of the same thing at the time," he replied. He said she had told him he was attracting the old man to come over by waiting out there like that looking at the garden at that time of night. As a result, he did his best to keep away from the veranda late at night, but there were times when he just couldn't sleep. The old man didn't always come along

142

on these nights. Yet there were times when he hesitated on the verge of going back inside—he had recently stopped closing the shutters on summer nights, but if the glass doors were closed and the curtains drawn, the old man would find himself standing out in the garden in the dark, and Fujisato said when he pictured this, he couldn't bear the thought. Then, sure enough, the gate would creak open. "Anyway, I certainly didn't find his visits any problem," he said a little defensively. Though the old man didn't show any signs of true senility, if his flow of thought was interrupted it became impossible for him to answer the least question. If you continued to press him, he would gaze apprehensively around the garden, with an expression like that of a child preparing to burst into tears. Fujisato therefore felt he had to accept the offer of the old man's ramblings as one would a frail object, and then found to his surprise that it was actually quite enjoyable simply to sit there with him, calmly nodding and interjecting an occasional response that supported the direction of his talk. The old man never grew vehement when his opinions were echoed. Though his tone was complaining, he wasn't resentful of anyone. Perhaps this simple, sorrowing tone, which seemed to have long ago dealt with its original emotional content, made it easier to hear him out.

While complaining about how hard it was to sleep, the old man would proceed to report subtle shifts in the night air from moment to moment that affected his ease of breathing. As he listened, Fujisato found himself easily persuaded of the truth of the old man's observations that summer, though now, looking back, he said he couldn't recall why, or just what subtle shifts they had been. He even accepted quite naturally the sudden turn of conversation when the subject of the night air was replaced by some more mundane topic.

One night towards the end of August, when the young lad's oddly bright voice called him from the front door as usual, the old man stood up from the veranda remarking, "This may be the last time I can come." Three nights later, however, he appeared again quite early. Still inside the house, Fujisato found his eyes meeting those of the old man, who was standing in the garden. That night, the old man drew in a deep breath and remarked that the air was suddenly much easier, from which Fujisato concluded that he was feeling relieved that summer was almost at an end. He responded in pleasant agreement, but the old man's reply was, "Finally breathing easy like this is a sign that I haven't long to go now," and while Fujisato was struggling to answer the old man rose to his feet, though he hadn't been there long at all, and made his way back through the garden toward the gate in the wall. He walked steadily off along the path into the distance, bowed slowly when he reached the gate, and disappeared. Fujisato heard the latch close firmly on the other side of the now very warped gate. And he never came again. Once September arrived, he got his daughter to ring next door and inquire after the old man, and he was reported to be as usual.

"What can he have meant by saying his breathing became easy?" Fujisato asked.

"Maybe he was talking about the loosening up of the boundary," I said, searching my own experience of illness.

"Hey, here he comes," said Sugaike suddenly, peering into the darkness of the garden. "It really is a cat path. But he's turned and gone straight past us without so much as a glance."

The three of us craned forward and down, following the shape that moved across the far edge of the lawn as if parting the dusk.

"He's absolutely intent," muttered Sugaike. "I wonder what he can see ahead of him."

·   ·   ·   ·   ·

Beneath the latticed window was a long, tin-plated sink, with a faucet at one end, though the fittings were long since out of date. Here hung a hand-basin, or rather one of those pot-bellied vessels for holding water.

As I quietly washed my hands, I seemed to be looking at myself from outside. I recognized, too, the sensation of raising my eyes to the ceiling above the window as I washed. There was a solidity to the house, even in the bathroom area, and I recalled the house our family had rented forty-five years ago, an old place that had survived the Great Earthquake of 1923, in which the rafters over the little window at the hand basin down at the end of the inner corridor were visibly tilted. Whenever I came out of the toilet and ran the water there, my eyes would go to them. This repetition used to irritate me as a child. The floorboards along the corridor likewise conveyed the feel of the building's warp, and you chose where you stepped with care.

There are few situations when you become so disoriented as those times when you have a lot to drink in someone's home, and leave the party to visit the toilet. It was just past eight in the evening. I had been here for four hours already. The toilet was situated at the right-angle bend in the corridor, just beyond the guest room, and from the corridor I could hear the low murmur of the other two, deep in conversation.

At some point, these two had grown interested in my daily life for the last twenty-five years. It began when I was asked whether I was more of a morning person or night owl, and I replied that I was a morning person, but added that I wasn't a typical one, since I got up and went to bed late, though my working hours were confined to the time between noon and nightfall. I had always thought of my daily routine as hardly worth mentioning to others, nor indeed something that should be talked about, so I was prepared to leave my explanation at that, but their faces expectantly waited for me to go on. So I found myself proceeding to confess that in the depressing hour before I began work around noon, when others had long since begun their working day, I would wander around the neighborhood, and I had never been able to shake myself free of the odd feeling, as I did so, that I spent my days doing nothing. Did I feel that way every day, they asked, and I replied that there were times when I didn't, but on the average it could be said to be every day, yes. For twenty or more years? they asked. Yes, I replied, all through that time, though this and that had happened, I had lived this life of strict routine—adding defensively that I wouldn't have made it to this point if I hadn't. At this, the other two wrinkled their brows and fell silent.

"It must be a quiet life," Fujisato finally said. "See, even when the people you're with go silent, you're quite unbothered."

"No, I'm actually quite busy. It's a bad thing," I replied spontaneously. "I spend my time frantically attending to this and that and never do anything properly. The end result is the same as if I just kept quiet and said nothing for half a day."

"Don't you find yourself going a bit crazy, spending every day in the house like that?" Sugaike asked. "Or are you just so used to it now?"

"Well, to begin with, I never get used to it. I'm just levelly measuring out my days, a little at a time."

"Damn," said Sugaike with a laugh, glancing at Fujisato for confirmation, "and here I was, thinking you were a master of leisured seclusion. I was planning to come to you for a bit of advice."

"It's as though someone in the know has turned around and warned you that the insurance you had quietly taken out against your old age is actually useless," joked Fujisato, rather surprisingly.

"I'm here to guarantee you that you don't achieve serenity by holing up at home," I replied, picking up on the joke a little. "And this 'serenity' is actually quite a turbulent sort of thing, you know."

This is when Fujisato confessed that he was intending to retire from his company before summer. His tone was so light that Sugaike didn't pursue the remark with a question, and the conversation felt poised to move on to other subjects. I imagined that people must maintain a certain reticence on the topic of their plans following retirement. And after all, Fujisato's situation was very different from Sugaike's.

Fujisato took up the conversation again, saying, "Remember that really hot summer we had four years ago? I spent maybe one night in three sitting out there on the veranda looking at the garden. I watched it till it began to grow pale in the dawn. I was always late home, too."

"Yes, it was hot that summer, wasn't it?" responded Sugaike. I felt that with these simple words something had been communicated between them.

"I used to wonder at how different the garden looked, now that my wife had died. Still, it's an odd thing. I'd looked at that garden for decades before I knew my wife, but now when I looked at it, I kept feeling that it had lost its familiarity. It's certainly not a big garden. You can't see much beyond the edge of the lawn at the moment because it's night, of course. And once this little patch had begun to look strange to me, it was impossible to pull things together again and retrieve the feel of knowing it. The first thing I thought was that this was my just reward for having never paid the house any attention all these years, and I do think that's partly true. But then I became aware that it was a sign that my physical and mental powers were gradually ebbing. It's as if when your strength begins to fail, your spatial grasp becomes weaker. Also, the garden had gone through various changes over the years. I'd unconsciously been seeing in it a kind of quiet historical transformation. I mean, if that hadn't been the case, I wouldn't have been able to feel so familiar with it. But now, when I tried to put the changes into some sort of clear order in my mind, my strength wasn't up to it. In the end, my eyes would grow tired, and I'd be so sick of looking that I'd sit there simply listening to it. When even a light breeze passes through, you can hear the leaves and grasses whisper over the garden, you know. I began to feel that I was more familiar with this sound than with the look of the place. Then the blades of grass would slowly grow visible, and the garden would begin to float up, like a soft white hollow. When I saw this process begin, I'd go back to bed before the light grew any stronger. On days when this happened, I would always wake three or four hours later after a deep sleep and find that everything looked astonishingly clear."

"Yes, I know what you mean by 'clear,'" Sugaike broke in, smoothly taking up the topic with a bright smile. "Everything stands out vividly, doesn't it? And wherever you can read the meaning of things, you do it quite effortlessly, and your judgments are quick and true. But it's a sign that your tank's close to empty, in fact. Later you scratch your head and wonder if that's really the way it was, but when you go gingerly back over everything you rarely come upon any big mistakes. All the same, you know that it's a clarity that comes from being near the end of your rope, mentally and physically."

"Yes, and if you take it a step further, you're in trouble."

"You're already in trouble, actually. I've had it repeatedly, and never come to much grief, but I feel as if I've come through a difficult pinch. People think you handle things by working up a great head of steam and powering through, and in general I agree. But in fact it's not true. There's just that glimmer of clarity, and you stagger along making your way through a narrow pass, that's how it goes."

"I've seen a lot of men who never manage to shake the madness that this repetition brings on, you know."

"You're caught off guard, aren't you, particularly when you're young. There's a stage before it all becomes deadly earnest, isn't there? It's not that you could see things all that clearly in the first place, and you don't actually progress far with one temporary experience of it, so things begin to get difficult, till you find you have to as it were stand a few inches back from yourself and signal to yourself in order to control the slide into excitement that takes over after a while. And don't you find that when your eyes meet your own eyes, and both see the others looking so astonishingly driven, you burst out laughing?"

"Yes, I guess I've ventured a toe into that sort of thing, now that you mention it. No, to tell the truth I've actually stood before it with both feet firmly on the ground together. The tension of it went on for three years, and I had to endure it for two more years after that, with my position getting worse and worse. But oddly, during that time I grew more and more able to stand it. I guess it was a good thing I realized I'd reached my limits."

"How many years in a lifetime can one stand the tension, I wonder?" said Sugaike, looking thoughtful. "Not many, I should think."

"But it's a bit ridiculous to talk about staring at your own garden and realizing you were at your limit, isn't it? I felt it clearly before the thought was formulated, you know."

"Happy is the man who's had his own garden for years."

"Yes, but that familiar garden turns into something unknown, don't forget."

"Even so."

"I was given leave from my responsibilities for two years, and allowed to spend ten days hiding away in the house, and yes, it was a turbulent experience, you're right. Late at night when things had at last grown calm I'd come and sit on the veranda, and instead of pondering my past and future, my thoughts were entirely taken up with wondering what to do about the garden. We had to do something, you see, or it would turn completely wild and unrecognizable. I thought perhaps it would actually be better if it did, but on the other hand I had a feeling that if the garden went to ruin, the house would start to rot too. In fact, all I did was stare at it. I didn't have the physical or mental energy to lift a finger. My son and his wife were due to have a child soon, and I wondered whether they might come back here and either knock the place down or sell it. Towards the end I even felt that if that was how things went, well, that would be okay. I was even imagining the scene of the bulldozers coming in. We've had a hard time of it, haven't we, and then there's that tendency to shrug things off with the thought that it's only one's just desserts in life. You even find yourself getting excited at the thought of what will happen to you, and feeling inclined to lend a hand in the destruction. This is the point when the old man from next door made his entrance."

The two of them chuckled. I had been caught up with the trivial question of what people do once they retire, and had listened with bated breath as the conversation swerved off in this extraordinary and unanticipated direction. Their laughter took me by surprise, but I nevertheless heaved a sigh

147

of relief.

Sugaike took the lead once more by closing the discussion with the remark, "Well, that's the way of it." He went on, "We're all fifty-seven, aren't we? Okay, let's each talk as optimistically as we can about our future. I mean just amazingly optimistically."

Fujisato was the first one to be asked. He said he planned somehow to spend the next two years doing nothing. He couldn't really see beyond that, but he felt he would change during that time, and that was what he pinned his hopes on, that was the most optimistic thing for him this year. But first, he said with a painful grin, he had to see to his daughter, and he went on to make the strange remark that perhaps there were occasions where the father retired from work in order to get his daughter married. If not, he said, the father couldn't gain his independence.

Sugaike was next. He said that he planned to draw things out. He'd been preparing a bit at a time over the last ten years, so he was already in quite a good position, and though he'd no doubt have to change companies a few more times, he may well go on working into his seventies, this was his most optimistic scenario.

Then their eyes turned on me. "Well," I said, "I'll just go on optimistically from day to day, as I always do." They fell about laughing with pleasure at this, and I laughed with them. Seizing the moment, I made my way to the bathroom again.

It is not only tedious but downright unpleasant to find yourself alone in someone else's house listening to the voices inside. When I turned off the faucet and the water had run down the pipe, I suddenly found the hushed voices in the other room had become clearly audible.

"Ah yes, well, they effectively went bankrupt about three years ago, and things took a sudden weird turn. That's precisely when all the wild behavior started." It was Fujisato's voice, speaking in a tone utterly different from his previous one.

"So that's the way it was, eh?" Sugaike sounded as if he'd be nodding as he spoke. "Talk about high-handed! I thought at the time it was a bit too much to be explained simply as panic at things getting precarious."

"People just stop being normal when they're pushed to the edge over money and violence and threats like that. Right to the very end. Of course they don't have a moment to think. They seem to stop being conscious of the fact that they're at someone else's mercy in all this. You see the same expression on all their faces. You just have to see that look, and you can pretty much guess what's going on."

"And your daughter?"

"Yes, she saw right through it. One evening she cornered me with questions. I couldn't deny it. I felt bad at how I'd left her wounded. I was just too insensitive to notice. My wife had died, see. I'd never dreamed that as a father I'd … and she as a daughter … but when you come to think about it …"

At this point I ceased to be able to hear the words, perhaps because the voices had grown hushed again, or because shame at seeming to eavesdrop had caused me to hastily muffle the sound by wiping my hands. When I had put away my handkerchief and was walking back towards the bend in the corridor, Sugaike was saying serenely, "When I glanced out the window, the propeller had stopped turning. It was a twin-engine airplane. 'Such an old-fashioned plane must actually be pretty safe, mustn't it?' I felt like asking. I looked round the plane and there sat the passengers, less than twenty of them, and when our eyes met, they had this expression that seemed to say 'Now what?' I looked down, and there we were, right over the Andes, like some eagle. Still half an hour to landing. So how do you think I spent the time? I dozed off. And can you guess what I thought before I went to sleep? All I did was murmur in my bad English, 'Jis izu a pen.' That's the level of my reaction, you see."

"I'm much the same myself."

Taking Fujisato's voice as a cue, I turned the corner and came face-to-face with Sugaike's daughter, as with a flower in bloom. She was flowing smoothly towards me down the corridor, bearing in her hands a tray holding wine, corkscrew, and wine glasses, and when she saw me she gave a little lift to the breasts beneath her blouse, tilted her head slightly, and sent me a smile.

Then, before she knelt at the edge of the guest room, her gaze went into the room and she paused there, calmly looking ahead, her profile suddenly that of a person solitary and intent.

It was her father's face that she seemed to be gazing at.

12

THE BANQUET AFTERWARD

In my morning dream, I was looking up at the narrow line of stone steps that climbed to the top of a mountain. I could see in the pale evening light how the soft shadows that lay in the foot-worn hollow of each stone step, half-buried in the earth, were layered one upon another up the staircase, creating a gentle wavering pattern. I woke with a sigh, knowing that although the place was unknown, this path was one I was long used to walking, indeed was deeply intimate with. I had been suffering, as I slept, from a sensation of deep exhaustion in my knees.

> —My soul is young, young as if newly made. No, younger
> even than that. I wouldn't even be surprised if it had grown even
> younger tomorrow than it is today.

My eyes paused as I read these words in an old book, and I was struck with the thought that Fujisato had said something very similar. There had been no communication from either or Sugaike since our meeting. I had intended to send a simple thank-you note to Fujisato, but something held me back, and I hadn't yet got around to it. The impulse to telephone Sugaike had also felt like superficial curiosity, and while I was hesitating the chance had passed. It seemed to me that in fact it was probably appropriate for us all to relax again for a while into our former estrangement.

That evening we had all, including Fujisato's daughter, ended the meal in high spirits after Sugaike's wine plus two more bottles from Fujisato's cellar had been opened. Fujisato and I then saw Sugaike, who was loud in his praises of the daughter, off to his waiting taxi, and returned together to the road beside the hackberry park. We were on the point of going our separate ways when Fujisato suddenly made his way into the park and towards the bench, as if something had caught his eye, so I followed, thinking he may have something he wanted to say. Then I saw that a large shadowy form lay on the bench. It called out, a word that sounded like "bodhisattva." Fujisato stopped. "So you're back, are you? It's been a long time," he said. The tip of a white hand emerged from the neck of the sleeping bag and casually beck-oned three times in our direction. The bearded features, lying there face up, smiled shyly. "Goooood night," came the drawn-out response, immediately followed by the sound of snoring.

"He's a friend of mine. Let me see you off," Fujisato said, and began to walk.

Late one cold night at the end of winter three years earlier, Fujisato told me, when he had been about to cross the park on his way home, the man had been ensconced there cross-legged under the hackberry tree, and had asked Fujisato to help him. He'd been drinking something rough, he said, and he couldn't stand, so he asked for a shoulder to support him as far as the bench. Bracing himself against the dreadful smell, Fujisato had helped him to the bench, where the man had again asked for his aid. He wanted Fujisato to fetch his bag, take out the sleeping bag and spread it on the bench, and when he had helped ease the corpulent body unsteadily into it, bottom first, and done up the zipper, the man requested with great solemnity that he strike him gently three times on each shoulder. When Fujisato did so, the man fell asleep.

"He seemed to be calling you a bodhisattva."

"He first addressed me with the words 'Hail bodhisattva! Excuse me, bodhisattva,' and ever since then he's made a point of impudently address-ing me this way."

Since that time, whenever Fujisato was on his way through the park late at night, the man would call him from his sleeping bag. In the beginning, Fujisato would simply greet him and pass by, but after a while he took to pausing there perhaps once in three times. The man would tell him tales of how he had eaten something sweet that day that hadn't agreed with him, or had chosen not to have anything for the day, or had been bothered by some woman who was hanging around him. Whatever it was, he spoke quite sternly about it, but there was a certain natural charm in his manner of speech. Fujisato discovered he seemed to be growing fond of him. It was a season when the days were beginning to brighten, and whenever he real-ized he was likely to be crossing the park on the way home late that night, he would go out of his way that evening to buy some sake and snacks as a gift. There were times when a bottle of cheap spirits lay secretly in his brief case during an important meeting or interview. For a while, he seemed close to being an alcoholic.

When asked, the man told him he was forty. But he added casually that if you asked him ten years from now he'd still be forty if he was alive, and if you'd asked him ten years ago, and he was certainly alive back then, he'd have been forty as well. One night, when the season had grown hot and he was lying stretched out on top of the sleeping bag, clad in T-shirt, shorts and an old-fashioned stomach band, he looked up and gazed intently into

151

Fujisato's face and pronounced, "You've lost the look of one who'll die by the sword, bodhisattva." "Can a bodhisattva die by the sword?" Fujisato asked him, whereupon he coolly replied, "Being cut down can be a form of religious austerity for a bodhisattva, you know." Then he went rambling on, thoroughly pleased with himself. "Your face has got softer. It has the look of a woman now. Yes, not a bad thing. Must be your mother's face I think. But it's just my personal opinion that it's not a bad thing."

"So there you were, being called a bodhisattva by someone who reads fortunes in faces, and being visited every night by the old man next door—a merry life."

"Merry—yes, now you mention it, I suppose it was quite merry. It was indeed merry."

We had arrived back at the corner of our earlier meeting. Some flowers still hung on the young tree there.

We must have been talking and laughing together; yet a change of register in a memory can occur in a short space of time, and day by day, as I recalled our conversation, it seemed to me that in Fujisto's voice, and in mine in response, there was a dying fall. It was just the opposite of that time almost a year earlier, when we had walked together along the old canal road, and Fuisato's voice had grown brighter the gloomier his talk became. His talk then had been of a boy who committed suicide forty years earlier. Could it be that the space of three or four years was enough to act like the hollow of a resonating chamber, adding a brightness to the voice?

It did seem that there had been a time when Fujisato's life was in danger. Ignorant as I was of the ways of the world, I could not guess the circumstances, nor what sort of danger he had been in, nor to what degree. Sugaike had stepped in to mediate things with his tale of the half hour he had spent airborne in the lame old twin-engine airplane, but from this it was still difficult to guess the severity of Fujisato's difficulties. But it must be the case that when a man feels himself in danger, no matter how calm he feels or how inclined he is to forget it for much of the time, both face and body would reveal his difference from ordinary people. A vagrant who had left human relations behind would no doubt be able to sniff this out in someone, or at least to discover it at the moment when it suddenly ceased. The truth can often dwell in words that tumble haphazardly from the mouth.

As for the woman's visage that he claimed had begun to show through, perhaps it's true that a man's face takes on this look once the physical danger has somehow been transcended. Or it may be that this was the man's own way of smoothing things over. From what I could judge both from Fujisato's words and my own brief glimpse, he was a man in whom the sentiments of an infant for its mother remained, frozen and intact. "Your mother's face" might well be his own projection. Or perhaps it was a gift in gratitude to this temporary bodhisattva. One does hear tales of the beggar who gives some unexpected gift, after all. But what if Fujisato had suddenly felt from this man's words the sensation that his daughter's face was showing through his own, and by way of her face, the face of his dead wife? And what if this had occurred during the time when his state of danger was continuing, and when his thoughts and fears were directing themselves more to his daughter than to himself? What then?

"It was indeed merry," Fujisato had murmured to himself, as if discovering the word first from me. His voice was dark.

I waited for these words to be followed by a fresh burst of laughter, but his mouth stayed clamped shut as he surveyed the scene around us. It was a cramped little three-ways corner, but his eyes took it in as if gazing over some wider space. There was no glitter of suspicion at the presence of anyone strange in the area. Rather, drawn as I was by those eyes of his that seemed withdrawn into his inner being, I felt for an instant that a great throng of shadows had suddenly gathered about us in the darkness.

When Fujisato's daughter joined our party, Sugaike took the conversational lead.

"I have a habit of talking in my sleep," he began. "I gather your father talks to himself around the house, is that right?"

"Yes, well," replied the daughter, looking as if she were searching again in some distant place for the words. "He talks quietly and happily to himself. When I go to check, he's there calmly reading a book. He looks at me quite oddly."

"I'm not aware of doing it," her father said with a laugh. "When she tells me, I start to get the feeling I've been talking. I've always had a habit of believing it when a woman tells me such things."

"And when you leave the room, you hear him talking again," Sugaike interrupted, whereupon the girl replied, "Hardly," and seemed to turn away from him a little. However, she went on to ask, "Do you talk loudly in your sleep?"

"It's not loud, but it's distinct. I'm told I speak quite clearly, voice and tone both, more so than when I'm awake, in fact. But no one can understand a thing I'm saying. My daughter tells me she always has to listen when I talk in my sleep, and it feels weird when she can't understand it. Mind you, she couldn't hear it from her own room."

"So it's not the kind of sleep-talking that worries the family," the girl said.

Sugaike opened his eyes wide in reaction, as if to say Ouch!, and turned to me. "What about you?" he inquired.

"There are times when I feel as if I've been endlessly yelling even when I haven't spoken for half a day," I said.

Both father and daughter laughed happily, and as they did so, there was a long moment when their faces looked identical.

153

Sugaike indicated with his head in the direction of the veranda, and began to ask about the garden. He seemed to have complete recall of all the flowers and shrubs in the garden, though they were now invisible in the darkness, pointing to each in turn as he asked, and the girl, apparently impressed by the quality of his questions, was drawn to respond with details, even down to when each was planted. At length, the two sat facing the garden, separate from us, in a conversation of their own. Their voices as they sat there sunk in passionately detailed talk grew hushed, occasionally swelling with a gentle warmth, while distant, entranced smiles hovered on their faces. Listening, I was impressed at how well she fitted herself around the man's flow of interest.

"Your father seems to have viewed it as some wild, unkempt place, but you've been doing things to it all along, haven't you?" Sugaike asked, straightening his back.

"Yes," she replied, and her face reddened. "When my mother was in hospital, people told me that it was bad for an invalid if her garden was left to go to ruin, you see. That's how it started, and then later it was just a habit I'd gotten into. But the limited amount I can do with it still kept it a wild garden."

"Still, I'd say there's something of your spirit in the way this garden looks," Sugaike remarked, and then he let his eyes wander over the garden without seeking a reply.

"Grass is a powerful grower. It's always getting the better of me," said the girl, lowering her eyes, almost as if her words were an unanswerable question. Then she pushed the hair back from her forehead with her fingertips, and proceeded to say something very similar to her father's earlier words that evening.

"I was born in this house, and though there was a while when I lived abroad, this is where I was brought up, so I never actually spent time really gazing at the garden and taking it in. When the time came to actually go into it and stand there in the grass, I had no idea what should be done with it all. All I could do was search out the places where my mother had done things, and follow those as best I could, but of course while she was ill at home, spending much of her time in bed, the garden inevitably suffered here and there. That was all very recent. When I find I can't recall this recent time, I realize it's visible here in this unknown garden. I'd often just stand there in the grass, staring blankly at the veranda. It was during the day, so no one was about. I realized that my mother had sometimes done the same thing, looking back at the empty veranda from the garden as if something puzzled her. But she hadn't been brought up here, of course."

There was a shrillness to these last words that struck her guests. Her father chimed in at this point.

"My wife used to be there in the garden asking my dad on the veranda about some detail of how the garden used to be, I remember. If she asked me, I'd only give her some vague response, and wouldn't be drawn on the subject, but dad would throw himself into trying to recall things for her. The garden got pretty overgrown after my mother died, too, you know."

"I gather your father spent many a late night sitting out on the veranda staring at the garden?" Sugaike asked the girl.

She gave a laugh, and replied with another question. "So you knew that?" Then she nodded silently.

Sugaike pursued the subject. "I imagine his expression got calmer as you gradually took the garden into your control?" At this, she gazed at him, though with a solitary look, and when she seemed to have lost consciousness of herself altogether, suddenly she burst forth with a cheerful laugh, "I suspect he had no idea, till the guest from next door appeared."

"Actually, I'd begun to notice before then," her father said defensively.

"You were setting your mind to how you could restore a sleepless man, as you worked in the garden," Sugaike declared, and he struck the table gently with his fist. "Well then, let's have a bottle of wine from your father's precious store."

The girl rose lightly to her feet.

. . . . .

Sugaike had understood the situation thoroughly. He had very quickly comprehended the reason behind the rather incomprehensible invitation we'd received, and had played his guest's role well for the father and daughter, though what he was thereby helping to achieve was unclear. As for me, although I didn't understand the situation I followed his lead, and together we played our role in helping to guarantee the present peace of mind of the household. There are after all circumstances in which the presence of magnanimous guests is needed to ensure the home's sense of security.

"Thank you for this evening," said Fujisato, raising his glass. "Yes, thank you very much," his daughter added, bowing her head to us. Their words resonated with a real gratitude not normally present in the host's expressions of thanks. Both Sugaike and I had an appetite for alcohol, and when the bottle was empty Fujisato and his daughter happily conferred about which wine to regale us with next.

When Fujisato cast his eyes over the deserted crossroads and murmured, "It was indeed merry," had he perhaps also had in mind the scene of the evening we had just enjoyed? He said no more, and we parted with the laughing words "Let's get together again," but as I went off along the dark road, I was struck with a sense of guilt. I realized on reflection that as guests both Sugaike and myself were strangers for Fujisato quite as much as or perhaps more than the vagrant in the park or the old man from next door. We had been invited as guests for that very reason. He had wanted us to come as strangers and relax in his house. Sugaike had grasped this better than I, and although he was potentially in a slightly awkward position with Fujisato, he behaved like a long-lost friend. I had been far less aware of things, and had maintained a certain half-hearted reserve, but insofar as I had relaxed there, I had been afforded a thoroughly warm welcome. The gathering had been a merry one.

Next morning, there hovered in my mind an image of Fujisato returning home and thanking his daughter for her labors, then gazing around the guest room with a puzzled air, wondering just who had been there. His daughter had come to clean up the dishes from the table, and was again watching her father from the threshold of the room.

Still, with increasing age, the day before ceases to feel so close. Two weeks after the Sunday visit to Fujisato's, on the other hand, I could recall the words he had spoken a year earlier as if it were yesterday I had heard them. It's over …, he said … The sense of it spread over everything in the world, like something heaven-sent. He was speaking of a morning classroom forty years in the past. Fujisato was staring at the ledge beneath the parapet on the roof, where someone had leapt early one morning in the rainy season. Staring, as he sat there each morning in the front seat by the window of the empty classroom before the first math class, staring until his hair stood on end with the force of the plunge down from his own feet. As I had listened to him tell the story, I pictured the scene as if I were peering diagonally down at the ledge where the boy who was about to die had stood. It seems a visual image of a forty-year-old memory naturally takes on a bird's eye perspective. The view from the third floor window would of course have had the roof ledge above eye level, indeed Fujisato's gaze would have been on the wall beside where the boy's feet had already stepped into air.

Immersed in the urgent moment of that fall, he was seeing the figure of the boy as he was three days before it, staring up into the great ginkgo tree in the schoolyard. This was how I had come upon Fujisato, and sat down in the far back seat, near the rear door of the classroom. Fujisato remembered that we sat diagonally opposite each other, and I too had been aware of it at the time, indeed it was the kind of nervous awareness natural to a youth. Fujisato said it was a cold morning in the rainy season, but all I remember is coldness and darkness. As soon as I sat diagonally beside him, Fujisato felt our two gazes travel along a single line of sight, changing the feeling of the wall they were directed at, drawing him in with a sudden strong sense of the absence of a person there. This sense of absence perhaps meant that Fujisato was gazing at what he could not in fact have seen from that third floor window, the place where the boy had stood. From behind him, my own gaze pushed his forward.

Then, Fujisato said, he realized that I had moved from another school, and therefore would not have been here when the suicide occurred, and as he continued with relief to stare at the wall, the feel of it underwent a further change. It wasn't exactly that it softened. Now he felt a shiver of fear. The boy's figure continued to plunge, as it gazed up at the treetop. The landscape outside the window was fraught with the danger of imminent destruction. A desolate vastness slowly began to swirl inside his head, a huge emptiness in which even he himself was not present, and within that languorous swirl lurked an intense urgency. And yet over all this there descended the feeling that it was over.

It descended, he said, also over the sense of strangeness in the fact that for me, diagonally behind him, the event had not even occurred.

It was understandable, I could see, that for Fujisato it should seem strange that someone with no knowledge of the event could be sitting there. I could imagine such an ignorant person might in fact exert, over one who was suffering from the knowledge of the event, a powerful sense of contradictory familiarity with it, one that might lean either toward malice or propitiation. The astonishment that for this person it had simply not occurred would finally return in himself, bringing with it the chance for a feeling of relief that it "was over" to spread through him at last. Would I too, as I sat there puzzling over my math problems, have been included in this sense of all being over?

Fujisato said that after this, each time we were alone in the classroom together early in the morning and he sat staring at the wall, the sense of completion grew deeper, indeed during the next twenty or thirty years he continued to call up this feeling and hold it close whenever he was driven into a tight spot in life. The deep peace of this conviction allowed him to stubbornly hold his own against competing reality. He seemed to have managed remarkably well. The end of the story was that he earned the reputation of being mad, and what was worse, rumor had it that it was feigned madness. For all the changes that this peace would have undergone with the years, it would no doubt have retained as its essence that fervent peacefulness that descended after the boy's plunge. My own absence from that event would also to some degree be included in this. Perhaps this absence was the same intense absence as that other one.

I also heard from Fujisato as he talked a year earlier that although he had clung to this feeling until his forties, once he passed fifty this clinging had gradually grown gentler and he had come to feel at one with it, so that recently he felt that he was not far short of being able to view everything as being over. At that time, I hadn't heard of the rumor that he was mad. There was no way I could have known of it. When I first heard of it from Sugaike on that street of a foreign city where we had met, we were just leaving the restaurant after our lunch together, and I did not immediately pursue the topic. Walking beside him a little later, my voice as I came back to the subject with "So he's mad, you say?" was somehow imploring. Sugaike then spoke of the rumor that it was feigned, adding that he was the butt of resentments over his position at work, and it was hard to credit that the rumor was true, though he casually suspended judgment by saying that such things do have a life of their own. This sat comfortably with my imaginative inclinations, which suggested that the person constructed by rumor could be conceived to exist independently of the actual man himself, and for this reason I accepted Sugaike's words. But after I returned from my trip, whenever I recalled Fujisato's face something in me frowningly resisted the thought that this man was mad, and I found myself puzzled that I should be feeling these aspersions almost as personal insult, for all the weakness of my connection with him. At the same time, however, I felt the shadow of a memory of nodding in deeply reassured acceptance as Fujisato had coolly related to me how he had gone crazy some years earlier. I was aware that this memory was false, yet I also thought that if indeed that man were to be mad, it would in fact be a madness akin to a gradual, almost ecstatic return to sanity.

I had no idea that Fujisato's life had been under threat.

. . . . .

Who had said that it was under threat? I wondered some days later. Neither Fujisato nor Sugaike had used these words in what I had heard from beyond the bend in the corridor. I had the feeling that even when I overheard them speaking together in rather problematic fashion on the subject of Fujisato's daughter, I had felt no particular dismay other than that of finding I had listened to something I should not have heard. At this point their voices had receded, and when I heard Sugaike telling his tale of being in the airplane with the broken propeller, I heard it simply as a new topic of conversation between them. "That's the level of my reaction, you see," Sugaike had concluded, and Fujisato responded with, "I'm much the same myself." It seems that this was the moment when the words "physical danger" had first come to life in me, and I proceeded to go back over the conversation with this new idea. When I rounded the corner of the corridor, Sugaike's daughter, approaching with the assembled wine glasses, appeared to me like the blooming of a white flower.

I was impressed that day at how Sugaike and Fujisato fell into a kind of familiarity of tone with each other that suggested the friendship of eighteen- or nineteen-year-old youths. In fact, they met through work in their mid forties, and it seems that there had been no further contact between them to speak of. I wondered as I listened whether Sugaike was fitting his manner to that of the old schoolboy relationship he knew Fujisato and I to have, but from the moment I came back from the washroom, I heard his tone with new ears. With both these men, it was the ease of relief that set their tone. The guest was soothingly assuaging the dangerous experience his host had gone through, and the host was accepting this gesture of pacification.

Things would grow more cheerful only to revert again to chill, and the chill would in turn bring a return of the good cheer. In time, I too became part of things, and the three of us created a peculiar state that was both playful and tending to sink into something darker. But the daughter's smiling face increasingly bloomed with high spirits as this situation progressed. Observing this gave Sugaike a look of satisfaction, though his face betrayed a hint of exhaustion.

Now at last I was free to contemplate the idea that Fujisato had been mad during these recent years. It seemed to me that in his own stories, his daughter revealed herself as saying as much. But this madness had not been a question of when, for how long or in what way. He would have been minutely mad over a number of years, and during that time it would not have been visible to others. From what I could make out of the business world's rumors conveyed to me by Sugaike, Fujisato had gone mad, or pretended to do so, and resigned his position roughly a year after the economic collapse of that period had first become obvious. Rumor also had it that he had taken six months off work at the time, but I judged that the atmosphere that evening was such that he would have spoken of this if it had been true. He himself had said that the time he was released from his position at work was the year before last, the year the old man had appeared in his garden in mid summer. He said he had taken ten days off work then. This must have been the origin of the rumor that he was mad. In fact, Fujisato seemed to have grown more at ease with things by that time. Then, the following spring, he had come across me after forty years in the hackberry park. Recalling his face, I realized that he looked calm and at ease then too.

It was three years ago that the vagrant in the park had remarked that his face had lost the look of one destined to die by the sword, which would make this the year before the appearance of the old man. The very hot year was the year before that. He had noticed that the deeply familiar garden appeared strange to him and realized than that he had reached his limit; his situation worsened during the following two years, but he had gradually found that he was more and more able to bear it. He said that the strain had continued for three years up to then.

At this point in the story I recalled that he had said his wife died five years ago, which meant, I realized with astonishment, that it must have happened the year before that hot summer. An incomprehensible miscalculation had somehow crept in to my understanding of events. When Fujisato began to talk about that summer, I had certainly understood him to be describing the state of mind he was in after his wife's death. Yes, I thought as he spoke, I can understand how the garden would take on a different look. And then in the space of a moment, when Fujisato confessed that it was at the end of three year's of strain in his life, his wife's death had been pushed back in my mind to the beginning of that three-year period. Otherwise, I would have taken his passing references to the perilous situation he found himself in at work as the result of the yearlong state of extreme psychological fragility that followed on his wife's death. Yet even Sugaike, who should have been alert to these things, had taken the references to his perilous state to refer to something that derived from physical and mental exhaustion. And even Fujisato's own description of seeing the garden as strange and unknown seemed to be about something other than what would be a quite natural response to a well-known garden that was seen now from the defamiliarizing perspective of one newly-bereaved.

He had said the stress continued for three years, and that it was about a year after his wife died that he had found himself against the wall in his work, so his vision of the estranged garden must in fact have been a result of his dangerous situation. He had stated that his strength was exhausted to the point where he couldn't mange to adjust his vision of the garden back to that of something already known. This suggested that the sense of danger of his position could no longer be willfully suppressed, and manifested itself in the view of the garden. Yet from his tone as he looked back on this time, somewhere within the astonishment with which he gazed there hung already a sense of relief. Perhaps, then, the danger was already beginning to pass, and came to him now as a visual atmosphere. Being who he was, he would have dealt with this danger without agitation or tension, but rather with patience if not calm. Perhaps even fear can take on an aspect of moderation. But over all this, over the caution and the fear, perhaps over whatever resolve he had made, the quiet of that sense of completion had descended ever more deeply with his wife's death. His so-called madness was surely nothing other than this inner quiet.

The physical danger revealed itself in the sight of the unfamiliar garden. The quietness of the sense of completion, with its overtones of extreme tension, passed. Mind and body made no effort to resist it. He seemed paralyzed to save himself from it. Imagining how it would be if a human form emerged from those grasses, whether he would be capable of registering it as real, he felt the sense of fear itself crouching there within the awareness that things had reached their limits. Staring within and without himself, wondering if what he saw was the premonition of his own extinction, he was astonished to find instead that it was a sense of normalcy making its way up through him from the depths.

And then, later in the house, happening to register the sight of his daughter, he was suddenly surprised to recognize the tension that came over her features when she felt his gaze. He realized now that she had been quietly watching over him all this time, so calm and unshaken, and felt instead a fear rise in himself at the thought of how he must have become. Perhaps in that fear too there was a sense of relief.

"I did hear in a very roundabout way the rumor that you weren't too well for a while. When would that have been?" Perhaps there would be an occasion for me to slip this question to Fujisato himself. But equally possibly the matter would never be brought up between us. My imagination began to go around in circles over the question, and as I was on the point of bringing it to a halt, I felt a sense of suffocation, as if a silence that had begun to open had closed over again, something that would last a lifetime.

"It was the year before that hot summer. No one was aware of it, and I myself wasn't aware that my daughter was." Fujisato seemed to nod. But then he went on, "No, that's not right. If we're speaking of being mad, I think it began after that. I might still have been mad when I ran into you last spring. If I hadn't been, I don't know that I would have recognized you. Even if I had, I don't think I would have approached you like that without being able to remember your name."

And I believe he laughed merrily as he said these words.

13

MIMICKING THE CUCKOO'S CRY

"It must be three months since we last met," I said, my eyes moving to the wall in front of my desk. No calendar hung there. It was two years since the calendar had suddenly become irksome, and I had banished it to the bookshelf behind me. Sometimes you can suddenly relinquish a habit of many years, and never look back.

"Are you back home already this evening" I asked, then suddenly remembered and added, "Oh of course, today's the Emperor's Birthday holiday, isn't it?" Yamagoe laughed. "It's called Green Day now," he replied.

"Back when the blossoms were in bloom I found a garden with fine cherry trees, and I was intending to invite you to come and see it the next day, but life suddenly got complicated and I was overwhelmed by things to attend to ..." he went on apologetically, his tone as always remarkably old-fashioned and formal for his years.

"A garden with good blossoms, eh? I'm sorry I missed it," I responded, and for a moment I couldn't quite recall whom I was talking to. Then Yamagoe began to speak about a certain woman from the hospital. He gave both her family and her first name, said that she was sixty-six, and asked if I'd known she was in hospital after breaking a bone. I hesitated over the name, which meant nothing to me but which I had a sudden feeling I recognized because the surname was an unusual one. However, Yamagoe went on without waiting for an answer, to inform me that she had died. It seemed that the same family and first name had appeared in the list of fatalities from the airbus that had crash-landed at Nagoya airport a few days earlier. She was listed as sixty-nine, so the age also fitted. She was said to be from Gifu Prefecture. She'd been visiting her son in Tokyo when she fell and broke her leg and was brought to the hospital, but it wasn't a bad break and things were looking good for her, so she'd told Yamagoe that once her leg was better she intended to join a tour and see a bit more of the world. She added that she had never been to Taiwan. Yamagoe concluded that this must be her.

The plane had come from Taipei, and apparently many of the passengers had been elderly members of a tour group.

"It was last week, wasn't it?"

"No, three days ago." His voice sounded youthful and indignant. Days pass before you notice it, I thought crossly. Why this haste?

"Did you get to know her well in hospital?"

"I lent her a hand on quite a few occasions," Yamagoe replied in the same tone of voice. "In a manner of speaking, since we were both in wheelchairs. I was more under the weather than she was, and she told me off for it. When I complained that I had no appetite at lunch time, she told me I should raise my eyes to heaven and thank providence that I'd been able to work hard all morning, since we invalids were working in our own way just as well as the next man. It was a day when the rain was bucketing down outside, I remember."

"Yes, invalids suffer all day when it's rainy, don't they?" I said with a laugh.

I recalled a scene from ten years ago, when I was traveling somewhere on a train. A large family group of tourists from Hong Kong were gathered in a noisy crowd, sitting together and exchanging rapid chatter hither and yon in all directions among themselves. I was particularly interested by a beautiful youth of about twenty and a fat and florid-faced woman in her fifties who were talking animatedly together, gazing into each other's eyes, and my companion, who could understand Chinese, leaned over and whispered in my ear, "They're talking about food, about what they'll have for dinner tonight."

"I once changed her bedpan for her in the night," Yamagoe went on, his tone unaffected by my attempt at a laugh. "Just washed it and brought it back, since I was going myself."

Instantly, the unknown dead woman assumed a more vivid existence for me, and I saw before my eyes the long hospital corridor at night. Lying awake on nights when it was hard to sleep, it was never long before you heard someone going down that corridor. There was the sound of running water. Sometimes, no matter how hard you listened, it seemed that the person never returned. I don't know how much of these sounds were real.

"You weren't in the same room, surely?"

"She'd call me in as I was going past in my wheel chair down the corridor. She'd say my name behind me, in a small voice. I'd go on quite a way before I realized what I'd heard, and turn back. Those hospital rooms had the door open even at night, you remember. She'd laugh and say she found herself calling to me from the bed when she saw me passing."

The bathroom and toilets were on the right half way along the corridor, the laundry was this side of them, and the disabled access toilets were right down the far end. Waking from nightmare-haunted sleep, that long stretch of space seemed to extend tranquilly out from the mind like a natural continuation of the body's pain. It tilted quietly forward, and there was an oppressive sense to it.

"I can see why she stays with you," I murmured.

"Yes, and there's something else too," said Yamagoe, his voice dropping to a hushed tone. "I remembered how we'd talked once in the common room after lights out about that jumbo jet accident, it would have been six years earlier, where it lost the tail section, and that careful list of reasons for the suspicions about the cause of the accident."

"Who said that? I did?" I had no memory of it. It was certainly true that I had long had reservations about the explanations for that accident, and there was a time when it had weighed on my mind quite a lot, but I'd surely forgotten all about it while I was ill. I found it hard to believe that I had talked about such a thing when I was in my difficult postoperative state, and to a young man in even more precarious health than I was.

"I must have let my tongue run away with me, pretending I knew more than I did."

"No, on the contrary I remember being most impressed with the way you carried out your fine analysis from the starting point of the overall common sense understanding of it, going into the minutiae of the seconds either side of the supposed cause, that explosion of the isolating barrier, almost as if you were stroking each detail."

"How terrible of me."

It must have been a continuation from Yamagoe's confession of what an unfortunate year that year of the accident had been for him, with his sister's death and other problems, so I had been doubly insensitive.

"Someone who's managed to get through an illness tends to enjoy that sort of talk, don't they, because they're still scared. But I remember you hadn't yet had your second surgery."

"I remember you frowned over the fact that you felt a bit squeamish to be sitting there safely as you discussed the ins and outs of other people's predicaments, talking about the airplane's flight recorder and voice recorder and other such details. You also said that the dead are quiet, and if we living feel that quiet as a fixed point, we quickly find ourselves falling towards it."

"What appalling things I say."

"You know, with this recent accident I had my doubts about the course of events between when the plane was calmly preparing to land and that moment when no more information became available. I went over the reports every day, and in the process I found myself drawn right into it, till I was inside each second. I was strangely elated. It was a feeling quite close to rage. I remembered how you laughed when you told me in that common room about how perturbed you were by your own rage when you saw the thickness of the line used in the flight recorder's line graph recording the changes as they happened, and the way you'd been incensed that they'd set it up like this to blot out the individual seconds. That's why I took it into my head to telephone you now."

"That brings us to the point by a very strange route, I must say," I replied, bewildered. I proceeded to ask about his recent circumstances, so that at length the topic moved on from the plane crash, and Yamagoe reported all going as usual. "I'm living easy," he added. We chatted a while longer about this and that, but it seemed he had no other purpose for calling. He mentioned that he was thinking of going off to take a look at somewhere distant during the summer vacation.

After we hung up, I thought about my relative lack of interest in this recent accident, and reflected that an extra decade of life meant that these days, though at the time it's all very exciting, before long a reaction of evasion or rejection seems to creep over one.

Some days later the papers carried a photograph of the passengers in the plane, taken at some stage before the accident occurred. Apparently some film from a camera had been safely retrieved from the wreckage. It did look as though there were a lot of elderly women. No doubt they were accustomed to trips abroad, but the look of relief on every face was typical of those their age who have arrived back inside home territory again, suggesting that the photograph was taken not long before the journey ended. I peered at the faces, wondering if I might recognize one of them. An image came to me of the long hospital corridor, thick with the gathered insomnia of the patients, but only row upon row of smiling faces greeted me from the photograph, sending my gaze skittering off them.

My mind slipped into its dull-witted calculations. If she were seventy, that meant she would have been twenty-one when the war ended.

. . . . .

One fine Sunday morning before the rainy season set in in early June, I dropped into a second hand book stall in the market that was held beneath the row of now leafy zelkova trees in front of the equestrian park. I picked up one of the volumes of a World Literature series that had been a big seller almost thirty years earlier, when I too had owned several volumes, and just then someone tapped me on the shoulder from behind. I turned, with a sense that whoever was there was quite a large man, and there was Yamagoe, smiling at me.

"You're a big man, aren't you!"

"I'm only one meter seventy-seven centimeters, you know."

"You're still big."

"You probably feel that because you were bending over."

It seemed that he had likewise seen me as small, though I'm one meter seventy-one centimeters tall. I recalled an article from when I was a child, about some important person who had been found dead on the railway bank on a day of heavy rain during the rainy season, whether from suicide or from a train accident was never determined. The piece had traced his movements up to the time of the accident, and reported his height as being five foot eight in the old way of counting. He would probably have been in his fifties too.

It was a fine early summer day with a breeze, but the faint smell of old things that wafted from the various tent stalls set up along the tree-lined street, reminiscent of the smell from an old house when a family moves out, hung motionless in the air. These were not antiques, or of any great age. They were household furniture that had been repaired rather than thrown out, things like electrical goods, audio sets, electric guitars and so forth, yet it seemed even such things on the whole could not evade a subtle decay. This was the sort of summer flea market that was set up in imitation of those earlier markets that used to be held at the end and beginning of every year in these parts, where in the early days the local farming folk used to gather and which in more recent years had flourished, drawing people from far and wide. It was run by students from the nearby university, who provided a now rare sight as they rushed busily about dressed in pink traditional workmen's coats, throwing themselves into the work. To judge from the prices that hung from the items lined up in the front row, there would be quite a run on the household wares they were selling.

I must have been quite engrossed in the book, for one of the pink-coated young men came over and cheerfully informed me it cost two hundred yen, a very cheap price, and I decided to hand him the couple of coins for it. It was a collection of the works of two authors, one of whom was a nineteenth-century Austrian writer whose work I have always loved. The prose was calm and strong, but in his last years he had been unable to bear the physical suffering of his illness, and committed suicide. Original aside, the new, simple translation that had appeared to great accolades in the mid-sixties had failed to impress my youthful taste.

"This book could be the one I sold at some stage, you know," I remarked.

"How have you been since we last met?"

"Fine, thanks."

We made our way side by side through the crowds, making automatically for the park. Truth to tell, my wife's father had been in hospital since mid-May. He was eighty-five, and had had a bad heart for many years, and now on top of that had developed a touch of pneumonia. He seemed to have grown very frail. Occasionally he forgot where he was, and asked if he was in a storeroom or in a government office. My wife's home town was up in Fukushima, and her mother was now living there alone, so her daughter-in-law and daughters took turns going to stay with her from distant Tokyo, and

166

my daughters went to help out too. A week after he was hospitalized, I took a day and went up to see him in the hospital in Fukushima. He hadn't seen me for three years, but he immediately recognized me and called my name, rather in the manner of calling a roll. When he relaxed, however, he seemed to hover on the edge of delirium. He was having trouble with the pipe that was inserted into his nostril. Even without this problem, his weakened heart and lungs meant that he couldn't speak easily. He said he saw all sorts of things. That morning, he had apparently asserted that he was in the cabin of a boat. The hospital looked about thirty years old, but despite its modern architecture it was aging rapidly, and the place was indeed a little reminiscent of a salt-corroded ship. Looking around at the exposed plumbing that ran along the walls, I recalled the hoary old government office I had once worked in myself, and could quite see why he mistook the place for an office. My mother-in-law said that he was stable now, but had been in a critical condition when he was first hospitalized.

I left the wardroom and went to the smoking room for a cigarette. From its window I noticed a large terrace one floor down, that doubled as a clothes-drying area, so I went down and there discovered an empty racecourse directly before my eyes. It looked so clear and vivid, almost within hand's reach, that I was somewhat stunned. It almost felt as if I had crossed to the realm of the dead, and was staring back across into the living world.

"Things look different now from the way they looked in hospital, don't they," Yamagoe remarked at this point, and I was startled at how he seemed to have read my mind. He was looking in the direction of the leafy, early-summer wood that stood beyond the equestrian exercise ground with its bright green grass. We arrived before the exercise ground and both lit cigarettes, then climbed the bleachers beside us, and Yamagoe went to sit on a sunny bench away from the shade of the roof. Mentally noting that this choice was typical choice of a young man, I joined him there. Then he began,

"Remember how one had a one-hundred-eighty-degree view from the common room in our wing? It was on the seventh floor, and the hospital was in an elevated place too, wasn't it? I used to go to that window many times a day, but no matter how I gazed out at the scenery, telling myself how impressive it was, I never could feel I was really gazing at a fine view. I put it down to the fact that I was looking through a pane of glass, but even when I started using crutches and could go about outside, it took a while for that landscape to stop feeling to me as though it was seen through something like glass. When you're suffering, you're locked on the inside of the suffering, aren't you?"

"I remember looking out at that view of Mt Fuji straight ahead of me in the evening sun, with a hopeless feeling," I said, tasting again that stifling sensation. "And you were in there three times as long as I was, weren't you?"

I did indeed notice Yamagoe there in the common room, at a stage before we had begun to talk, sitting in his low wheel chair by the window peering out at the landscape. Though it seemed likely many of the patients, their family and other visitors would look out through the window like this, in fact it seldom happened. One other patient, a woman who must have been in her eighties, would also draw up her wheel chair to the window. She was someone who at first had seemed permanently bed-ridden with a severe illness, but then had suddenly begun to appear in the corridor, busily plying her wheel chair. At one point a middle-aged couple, whom I judged from their tone of voice not to be her son and daughter-in-law, came with her to the common room, and I heard them trying to cajole her into coming to live with them, assuring her she was more than welcome any time. She didn't reject the offer outright, but simply let them talk without deigning to acknowledge it when the crucial words were said. I gathered that she was determined to go on living by herself, though it seemed she would have to do so in a wheel chair. But then, some days later, there she was on crutches, her back severely bent but nevertheless standing. With intense effort, she managed day by day to walk greater distances, and even after she had begun to walk quite well, one would often see her go to the window and gaze out at the scenery with the thoughtful expression of a young girl.

"Just the other day," said Yamagoe, changing the subject, "I went to Akasaka just on evening. I went round past Sanno and was just going to go on to the Nagatacho valley area when there it was, still standing there unchanged, that burnt out ruin."

I realized he was talking about the hotel that had burned down, with the loss of more than thirty lives. I too had gone past it the previous autumn, and sighed as I recalled that it would have been back in 1982 that it happened. This was also the year that Yamagoe's father had died in his late forties from cancer. He had told me this himself in hospital. Here was the same subject of hospitals coming up yet again.

"That happened the year I entered university, you know, and there it still stands, just as if it had burned down only last month. I could almost smell the stench of smoke still hanging over it. Why would they leave it looking like that for twelve whole years? I gather it hasn't even been auctioned off yet. I suppose the court case dragged on, and the boom economy sent the land prices up too high, and then the bust brought them down too low, and no doubt the cost of razing it would be enormous, but who's going to put up that sort of money to take on an ill-fated place like that unless they clear the land and leave it there for a while? They have to decide to demolish the thing before anything else can happen. It's sheer pig-headed obstinacy on somebody's part to leave it like that, I thought when I saw it. I stood there looking up at the blackened window frames, and it began to feel a bit creepy as I speculated that people were generally more than happy to compromise the point as soon as profit became the issue, and here was an example of how a set of circumstances can reveal some quite abstract level of obstinacy. Mind you, there I was myself, standing stubbornly in the road in the dark ..."

"A piece of land that's undergone a huge drop in price is like a ghost in itself," I remarked. "The old idea of a place's ghost may well have transformed into its price tag, in the present age."

I was ducking the issue with my attempt at a joke. I had a guilty feeling that Yamagoe's thoughts on obstinacy were obscurely directed at people of my own generation. It was not on the whole a generation inclined to stubbornness, but it may well be that we did have some attachment to such scenes of desolation. In fact, the high school I had gone to backed onto the site of this hotel. The school was above the cliff, and the hotel below. The suicide who had caused Fujisato such suffering had leapt from the roof of the building beside that cliff, though it was into the garden and not on the cliff side that he fell. There was no hotel there at that time, and the school buildings had long since been replaced. I had had my wedding reception at that hotel.

"There were some ghosts there for a while that had a huge price hike and were very full of themselves, weren't there?" I went on.

But Yamagoe was not to be distracted. "I had a chilling sensation that there were people looking at me from those high windows," he said. "It felt as if they'd been staring down for the last twelve years."

It had happened at the beginning of February, I recalled, making a weary calculation, and was followed the next day by the accident in which the pilot suddenly went mad and put the plane into reverse just short of Haneda airport, plunging it into the sea with a loss of more than twenty lives. Two days before the hotel fire, I had gone with friends to the resort area of Izu, and we were staying that night in a Japanese inn at the bottom of a cliff when a quite strong earthquake hit. Around that time, Yamagoe's father had still been up and down from his bed at home undergoing treatment, and I recalled Yamagoe telling me in the hospital how he watched all the television reports of both accidents in grim silence. He hadn't spoken his thoughts. He had died just before summer that year. I thought of how he was several years older than I, but since his young days had ill-willed the human world and prayed for its devastation. For all their love and compassion, he saw in both his submissive wife and the children that she bore him this same cursed human world. The eldest son who had died in infancy while he was still alive, and the daughter who had died, fresh out of college, soon after her father, were both taken by traffic accidents. The son's death coincided with the time when the nation's economic growth was rapidly gaining momentum, while the daughter's accident occurred when it had reached its peak. In both those years, there had been a plane crash.

169

I found a way past the silence by saying, "It was in the plane accident in the bay at Haneda that year that your friend's father died, wasn't it? That friend who was in the hospital there last year, who you visited on the way home from work. The one who lay in bed feeling as though the plane crash was somehow his own fault. How is he now? Is he better?"

"He committed suicide," Yamagoe replied. "He became quite happy once he left hospital, you know."

Nothing followed this. The sun's rays suddenly grew stronger, and the wood on the far side of the green lawn took on a midsummer look. Here and there the deep green at the crowns of the trees seemed to flare golden and then white with light. The summer before I fell ill, that same hot summer that Fujisato and Sugaike had spoken of together like some sort of password, the crowns of the trees had indeed seemed almost boisterous with whiteness. I may well have been suffering from some kind of problem with the dilation of my pupils. At the time, I had not the least knowledge that my spinal cord was undergoing compression. The doctor told me later that he thought the problem would have been slowly progressing over the years.

"I had the feeling that evil vapors were still emanating from that place." Yamagoe's eyes were on the distant wood, though it seemed he was speaking of the blackened windows of the burnt-out hotel.

"I wonder if it would be possible for some strange chemical change to be happening inside it at this stage? Something to do with microorganisms, or the effects of some waste product gasses from the earth beneath. It could be scary if people ever sneaked in there."

"No, I'd say it was the eyes of those people I felt standing there by the window all this time, accumulating and distilling poison till now it's slowly, naturally, begun to pour out into the surrounding atmosphere. A kind of transparent, scentless poison from which hatred and resentment has been eliminated, a poison akin to pity."

"It would be heavier than air, I'd guess. I imagine it creeping out low to the ground in all directions. It would be pretty powerful. But it wouldn't have any effect on the majority of people, you know."

"No, it certainly wouldn't," Yamagoe said with a laugh. "Here's a dream that I heard the friend who committed suicide had. He was told it was an old folk tale from somewhere. Some time past midnight, the people of the town get up and stream out to gather in the square, where an emanation from heaven strikes them all down. In no time, the place is transformed into a scene heaped with corpses. But when the first cock crows, one by one they rise to their feet and return to their homes. When the sun rises and they wake up in bed, they remember nothing. This is repeated night after night. He wondered whether it was the fury of heaven or the blessings of heaven that did this, and as he was wondering he awoke, before he managed to ask. I wondered how the people looked as they stood up when the first cock

170

crowed, whether they seemed rather abashed, and at this he rolled about laughing. And then he died. This happened about two weeks earlier."

As I sat there on the bench in the pouring sunlight, beginning to be enveloped by the stench of sweat that had begun to pour quite as fiercely as the sun's rays, I marveled again at the youthful life force of the young. Then, within the stench of sweat I sensed the swelling of another scent, darker and sweeter.

"Are things back to normal at last?" I asked, just as if I were enquiring about the death of a relative.

"Yes, I had a strong connection with him one way and another. I went to the police, and stayed overnight in a temple, and took a couple of days off work. Torizuka came along to the temple too, and helped out."

"Is she well?" I asked, repeating a question I seem to have asked at some stage previously.

"Yes, she's finally feeling the urge to have a child," Yamagoe replied.

· · · · ·

A few days after the start of the rainy season, I was invited to a friend's mountain villa in Chichibu outside Tokyo, and had an opportunity to hear the famous summer cuckoo calling. The lone bird would call for quite a lengthy period in the morning and at dusk, apparently defining the boundary of its territory as it slowly moved about over the gentle slopes that descended to the basin. It was a voice I hadn't heard for ten years or more. If it were about twelve years, I calculated, it would be the same length of time as that since the hotel had burned, and since Yamagoe's father, who was two years older than I, had died. Then I realized that my own father had died in the same year. I'd never counted up the years since my father's death, in hearing Yamagoe's story. My memory of his death was anyway rather prone to year shifts, and if I weren't careful, I could misremember it by several years either way.

Listening to the cuckoo's sporadic call, I pondered that perhaps those who had died old were liberated from their death year within the passing time of the still living elderly. I had since lost my sister and brother. My father died at eighty, but my brother and sister had both been in their fifties, which seemed to me now a youthful death. My sister had been younger than I was now. And I have grown old in the interval, I thought, weighing the weakness evident in my knees as I trod the rain-fresh mountain earth and the cuckoo sent forth its call again and again—yet it seemed to me that the peculiar weakness that suffused me in the instant I heard that call, or rather in the instant when it had died, was exactly as of old. The moment of that call was equivalent to its moment of ceasing. With each call, the boundary of time was removed. Was this perhaps what Fujisato meant with his expression "it's ended"? Each time, the call has ended, the listening person

171

has ended, and that person longs to send back an echo from the hollow sense of relief within himself.

Like a fresh welling up of life, the vague memory of an old haiku rose within me: *The child on my back / mimicking the call of / the mountain cuckoo*. I spread my arms like an infant giving itself up to the universe, and made an experimental call in imitation—a call that sounded uncannily similar.

By the middle of June, my wife's father was losing the strength to swallow food.

Then, at the end of June, some time past eleven on a summer night that was over thirty degrees, the telephone by my desk rang. I took a steadying breath, and answered.

"It's Yamagoe. Something weird has happened," came the voice abruptly. I hadn't had the television on since noon that day. When I heard the words "poison gas," I recalled with a strange serenity the wet rubbery stink of the gas masks in their round cylinders that were in each house during the war. Even when I learned that there were many dead and wounded, for a while I didn't quite make sense of it. When places began to burn from aerial bombing raids, these masks were deemed useless and consigned to the corner of the air raid shelter; I had not the least thought of a mask as I rushed out to escape the flames. There was generally only one mask per household, and I remember the sense of helplessness at the question of who would be the one to wear it when it came to the point. Yamagoe was astonished that I knew nothing of what had just happened. In a calm voice, he relayed all the details that had been reported to date, and then added something odd.

"To tell the truth, the instant I heard the news I had a feeling I'd been hearing a rumor that this was about to happen for some time before. I couldn't for the life of me remember where, though. It's not possible I could have actually heard such a thing."

He was talking as if he hoped I could help with the answer.

"It wouldn't have been that evil gas you spoke of emanating from the hotel ruins?"

"That would surely be altogether too much of a leap."

"You can't recall a face?"

"What face?"

"With this sort of thing it's often best to locate the memory by vaguely recalling an expression on the face that would have told you."

"I don't get anything, not even a face."

"Even a voice would do."

"I don't get any voice either."

"It wasn't that friend who died?"

"He wasn't the grim sort."

"Why did you ask me?"

"If you ask anyone close to you about this kind of thing, they're likely to be immediately infected with your own feelings, and start to believe they have a similar memory too. That's why I've gone to someone more distant."

I smiled grimly at the admission in that "distant." Still, though at my age I can tend to get things wrong, I decided to try to be helpful.

"They do say these things happen, it's true."

"You mean feeling that you've heard about it before when you hear of something happening?"

"Terrifying things seem to smash the boundary between what came before and after them."

"I guess premonition is something that would occur after the event, then? Still, even if it does come later, I felt like I'd experienced a real case of it. When I had the feeling I'd heard rumor of this already, for a moment there I felt something close to absolute certainty."

"There are always various voices unconsciously penetrating us, aren't there?"

"I'd actually be relieved if there really is a law that premonition always occurs after the event."

"I'd say that law holds on the whole. But ..." I stopped, thinking that I should refrain from further impertinence before this wise young man, since I hadn't even fully grasped the evening's events myself yet. But then I continued, with a sense of responding to some interrogation. "In the year the war ended, there was a middle-aged man in our neighborhood who repeatedly maintained from a month earlier that there would be a large-scale air raid not long after the twentieth of May. He went so far as to state that it would be on the first fine night after that date. And that's exactly what happened. But then, about a year after the war, this man discovered where we were staying and came to call, and when my parents fondly recalled his premonition and praised him, he was astonished. He had absolutely no memory of it. We reminded him in detail of what he'd said when, and he gradually began to recall it, but he was intensely embarrassed. He said he'd been swept along by unfounded rumor and shouldn't have spoken."

"He'd managed to guess right, eh?"

"That's it. Years later I went back over the dates leading up to the big air raid, and you could certainly have made some sort of estimate from them."

"And yet he was still embarrassed?"

"He went bright red."

"People whose prophecy didn't eventuate are embarrassed, surely?"

"No, you're more embarrassed if you get it right."

I was surprised at the strength of my assertion.

"He was like someone who's been caught doing something wrong. He sat there huddled over, and he kind of stank. From time to time he slowly raised his eyes and looked back over his shoulder, sort of cold in that bright midday midsummer room. 'I've really gone and done it, I'm despicable,' he muttered...."

"Hello, are you there?" Yamagoe was saying loudly.

Two days later, the parliamentary cabinet changed again. Every time I saw the new prime minister's face in photographs or on television, I would scratch my head in disbelief that everyone was saying what a good fellow he was. Back just after the war, someone once softly tapped on our window just on dark, and when we opened the door we found an old man there in the shadow of the hedge, his eyes swiveling to and fro as if something had surprised him. He was an old peddler from the country, selling minced fish and fish cake, but even though this was a punishable offence under the current food restrictions, he was still remarkably fearful and edgy. "We're not black market folks," he said, but nevertheless he kept a worried eye out. My mother remarked that he charged a lot for someone who came across as so honest.

When summer came, I was always awoken when the temperature in my east-facing room rose rapidly to over thirty degrees once the sun was up. Around four on the second morning in July, when I woke as usual soaked in sweat, the telephone in the living room was ringing. When I picked it up, my wife's mother told me, in a tone that still hesitated whether to speak of it, that her husband's condition was worrying. The women of the household gathered in their pajamas and discussed plans for the day, and then my wife set off.

The fierce heat continued. Four days later, my wife returned, reporting that her father was suffering from being unable to get rid of mucus. Those watching over him could hardly bear to watch. I'd seen my own father having mucus removed when he was dying, though in my mother's case she died too quickly for it to be necessary. The men had been sent into the corridor, in the case of my sister. My wife's father also had kidney failure, and the doctors gave him a week or so. My wife lived with her bags packed from one day to the next.

Three days later came a message that his blood pressure had dropped early that morning, but was up again, and that evening our eldest daughter went up there.

The next day, I went out for a walk in the park just before noon, and paused for a while by the pond where a pair of spotbill ducks were swimming, to watch a tortoiseshell cat that was asleep in front of the pond beyond the netting fence. Not long after one o'clock, a call came through from my daughter, followed by one from my wife's brother, to let me know that the doctor estimated he would die that night or the following morning. My wife had just seized a spare moment to slip quickly off to the hairdresser. At two thirty she returned, and immediately began to prepare to leave. At this point, the doorbell rang. It was a parcel delivery of refrigerated food, a beautifully fresh half of bream plus the head, that was a summer gift from a friendly fishmonger in the city who had sent it straight over because it was such a fine specimen. My wife took a look at it, then put it in the refrigerator, washed her hands, and hurried out the door. I noticed that haste made her movements clumsier these days.

The next day was also hot. Just before seven in the morning, my daughter called and in a still tearful voice told me that her grandfather had taken his last breath soon after six. An hour later there was also a call from my wife. She had gone back to the family house late the night before, but woke at four thirty and couldn't sleep, so she had left the house and walked alone all the way along the road to the hospital, and was in time to be present for his death.

14

BEFORE NOON

The hot summer arrived. At the end of July, I received a formal announcement to the effect that Fujisato had retired—"having attained the traditional retirement age of fifty-seven," it said. It went on to say that his working life had been a total of thirty-four years and three months, and there was mention of the full year's leave he had taken. Back in April, he'd said he intended to try taking it easy and doing nothing for two years, but evidently this way, he'd decided, he could put a stop to the rumors that had him taking an indefinite rest. After all, he himself couldn't predict with confidence how things would turn out.

With the announcement came a letter hastily scrawled on a single sheet. Now that he was spending all his time at home, he wrote with joking formality, he would be following the lead of one who had long pursued this path in life (meaning me). It was his turn now to sit back there diagonally behind and back of the head of someone he admired.

Recently, I had begun to find that when I received a letter or even a postcard that dealt with anything personal, at first I couldn't manage to make complete sense of the contents. Looking back over the formal notification Fujisato had sent, my eye was caught by the part that said "having turned my attention back to my long-neglected home environment and set things around me more or less to rights there, I now aim to become a new man again." Though the contents of the letter were far from stiff and formal, yet on the whole it stayed well within the accepted conventions of such letters. This was the one place where a more personal note was evident. Nevertheless, this talk of "a new man" struck me as recklessly bold, though this may have been the effect of the summer heat on my judgment. And depending on the way you read it, wasn't that phrase "set things around me to rights" in fact a little moving, and did it perhaps leave a slight aftertaste of envy?

The handwritten letter ended by referring to the summer heat, and remarking that it reminded him of his fifth year in the company, back in 1964, when the summer had been so scorching people had spoken of "the Tokyo desert." He had almost made up his mind to leave the company that sum-

176

mer, he said, and now at last the time had arrived.

Turning once more to the formal letter, the part that had struck me as odd before no longer did so. The personal note in it was redolent of what would undoubtedly be deep feelings shared by other men his age. When I thought about it, those "things around me" that he wrote of setting to rights were indubitably the various depressing matters in his life such as his still-unmarried daughter, the question of whether or not to live with the son and his family when they returned sooner or later from abroad, and the question of what to do with his aging house. There was nothing secret about any of this. It was simply that I was still struck by the impression I had gotten, when I went to the house that evening back in April, of father and daughter as two people holed up together with scarcely room to breathe, locked into the confines of mutual relief at finally having weathered a crisis. Under these circumstances, the phrase "become a new man again" held strange shadowy depths, while also momentarily suggesting a happy brightness.

Fujisato's house had seemed meticulously tidied, with a subtle tension in the careful placing of each item of furniture that seemed to me to express the equilibrium of relief that father and daughter sustained between them, a tension that even subtly affected the movements of the guests. Yet in my house too, around the time of my father-in-law's final illness and death, when my wife and two daughters had managed the days in such a way that one of them was always off staying with my mother-in-law, while things hadn't exactly descended into confusion at home, there had certainly been an unusual atmosphere about the house. Somewhere or other there was always the evidence of preparations for a journey—since there was only a brief period between their return and setting off again, only half the bag would be emptied, the bag's contents would be left ready beside it, and even if things were put away, there was an air of haste and disorder to them. The washing machine would sometimes be on late at night; the women would sit talking together, almost nodding off in a state of exhaustion. For another month after the invalid had begun to weaken, the fierce summer heat continued.

Watching my wife and daughters during the period after he had died, it struck me that the tradition of the first forty-nine days, when the soul is suspended between one incarnation and the next and sutras are performed for it, also applies to the living who were close to the dead person, who shared his blood. For the dead, it is the period between one life and the next, but for the living too it is a period between lives, though in their case the lives are both in their present body. It isn't that they depart from this world—quite the opposite, in fact; they are locked more firmly than ever into its haste and bustle. Such bustle is in fact the ultimate experience of the everyday, the essential "here" of the act of living. And yet one thinks, Where is this "here"? It is not the head that thinks but the body, and it does so even in the midst

177

of rushing about. Indeed, it's only through such dashing hither and yon that the question can be thought. To be pressed by things to do and to press after them, busily fixing one thing and moving on to the next—and in the very act of doing so to be face to face with that place, directly ahead, at which life's limitless proliferation of demands in fact comes to an end, and the point at which one stops being of use comes into view. At the point at which one stops being useful, it's easy to lose one's bearings.

When the house was all tidied, and one of the women was doing some last minute repacking on the verge of departure, a kind of earnestness manifested itself in her body. There was an urgency to the placing and removing of things in the case; objects piled up around her. At such moments, she would develop almost a little girl's attachment to trifling things. When the case was finally packed and ready and she tried to lift it, it was so heavy she could barely walk. She would remove half the contents again and spread them one by one on her lap, and now her hands as she worked, pulling out and repacking, instead of moving rapidly in fact became extraordinarily languid. She seemed suddenly struck by sorrow, at a loss, gazing at the objects around her with a bewildered lack of recognition.

The heat made my body go slack and loose, so several times a day I doused myself with cold water, to revive its tautness a little. It was in the early period of my wife's absence that I first noticed how remarkably slowly the water was draining away. If I left this unattended to, the problem would probably get out of hand, so before I started work in the morning I removed the bell-shaped cover from the drain and thrust my hand in as far as I could. I hauled out some clotted pieces of hair, and assumed that this would solve the problem, but when I poured more water down the drain, the flow was still almost as slow. In danger of losing my temper with it, I quickly gave in and took myself off to the manager's office to arrange for a plumber to call in. Two days later, no less than three plumbers arrived. They checked the flow of water, declared that the problem didn't seem serious, and poked various things down the drain, but it still remained blocked. In the end, they resorted to inserting a steel cable, pushing it down and drawing it gently back by degrees. Down it went, deeper and deeper, while they scratched their heads in puzzlement, until at last it seemed to have met something. They twisted the cable back out, and there at the end of it was a shiny black object—a great ball of hair the size of a sea cucumber.

· · · · ·

Late that night there came a phone call from Sugaike. I asked how he was doing, whereupon he blurted out the news that he'd been up in Kanazawa walking about the streets in all this heat. "Kanazawa has hot summers too, doesn't it," I said, and inquired whether he'd gone there for work. "No," was his strange reply. "It was sleeting up there." Then he added that he'd

178

only gone in imagination, and he drew breath and continued. He'd been working outside the office that afternoon, and had discovered himself with a bit of unexpected free time, so dropped in to visit a friend in hospital who'd been on his mind for some time. The friend had suggested they go to Kanazawa together in November. He'd agreed, and somehow or other had wound up staying on at the bedside until the hospital meal arrived. The reason his friend had chosen November was that he'd spent some days in Kanazawa during that month about ten years earlier, and apparently had happy memories of the stay. The more he talked, the more details emerged, and they found themselves discussing the intimate ins and outs of various little lanes about the town. Sugaike was more than able to hold his own in the discussion, having spent a lot of time there with me in his youth, wandering about the bars to kill our boredom, and also been there numerous times since for work and, of course, after-hours pleasure. Yet when he supplied more details at his friend's urging, describing the way a place used to be, the friend then recalled some further small thing and asked about it. He knew the place, the season, the shifts of sky through a typical day, and the oddly melancholic mood that a patch of fine weather produced, as if he had lived there. The feel and the look of the town in his friend's impressions made Sugaike nostalgic for the Kanazawa he had left long ago, despite the fact that the city the friend had visited a decade before had already changed considerably. Sugaike remarked that the man's recall of the place from a single stay was astonishing, whereupon his friend confessed that he'd also been there long before, when he had eloped, a very outdated thing to do these days. Sugaike suddenly recalled having overheard something, about ten years earlier, about that marriage and the problems it had caused. On the fourth day of the elopement, he told me, the woman had apparently seen what was in store, and left after breakfast to go back home; he had stayed on there three more days, spending his days and nights aimlessly walking the town. He'd walked in and out of every little backstreet in the old district of the town. The memory of each of them remained vivid, but even at the time he'd had little sense of continuity as he walked—it would be fine one moment and sheeted with rain the next, thunder rolled about the sky, sleet fell white on the street about him, then it was sunny again, he came to a three-way crossing and couldn't recall now where he'd been or how he'd gotten there, nor what had happened on which day. He did remember that on some street corner he'd stood talking to a woman with an umbrella and wooden *geta* sandals on her feet that were capped against the rain, but he had no memory of what they'd talked about. All in all, he'd gone missing for a week, but everything settled down and was virtually forgotten within a year or two.

The hospital room faced west, and the sun was sinking toward the horizon, but the blind was firmly in place and the air conditioning turned on, so the room was neither glaringly lit nor stiflingly hot. And yet, as he sat with his sick friend in the bright room, Sugaike's eyes went to the window with its blind behind which the summer lay, and though he was aware that he was on the ninth floor, he found himself imagining washing on a roof outside reflected in the window's frosted glass. It seemed pointless to hang washing out on the roof under cover on a rainy day, but if left there all day it would at least dry a little. This was in a time before washing machines were equipped with a spin drier. It was a rainy weekend day, and it would only be depressing to try to go out, so there in his lodgings after lunch he'd spread out his futon and gotten back into bed—but the boredom only intensified until finally he leapt up and rushed out, and set off quickly walking aimlessly about among the dark little streets. It was a dream, but in the dream he was beset by a far more depressing sense of fruitless effort. This was what he was recalling. And suddenly, there in front of his sick friend, he was disconcerted to find himself overwhelmed by a thought that rose up in him, bringing with it a flood of feelings—I too have had a time like that in my life, when I was aimless and at loose ends. His friend had cancer. The fact wasn't kept hidden from him. Sugaike had heard that it had metastasized, but he didn't know much else. The friend had grown thinner, but there was no sign of the sternly drawn features of someone in the later stages of the illness. Though he could speak of future pleasures, he may or may not recover....

"It was a strange afternoon. Oh yes, and Fujisato seems to have resigned, doesn't he? What did you think of that letter he sent around?"

"Well, I guess it was a pretty relaxed sort of communication, wasn't it. Of course no one's going to be surprised, at this stage."

"He talked of coming back a new man, didn't he."

"That struck you too, did it? A little audacious, I thought."

"People do say that sort of thing on these occasions, in farewell speeches and so on. But in his case it seems to mean something a bit different."

"He said back in April that he'd probably change, didn't he. He said he was aiming to change, that this was the reason for his optimism."

"He may just do it, you know."

The words "do it" hung between us, undigested.

"At least that's probably what he thinks," Sugaike corrected himself.

"His first concern would be for his daughter's welfare," I found myself saying in a light, admonishing tone, as if talking to some other person altogether, and realized that with these words I had dispelled some feeling in myself. There was no telling the ominous from the auspicious. All I knew was that the thought of a man his age speaking of intentions to change struck me suddenly as an alarming project. Surely in fact it could not be anything like a project?

"She's going to get prettier, you know," Sugaike said with a laugh. "It's going to be a while yet before he manages to marry her off. And I'd say she's had a long, oppressive history of being so close to her father that they were almost one."

He sounded cheerful.

"I gather Fujisato has been through some kind of physical danger," I said questioningly. "I must confess that when I went to the bathroom that time at his house—before the wine came out, remember?—I found myself standing out there at the bend in the corridor listening in on your conversation."

"Yes, he did," Sugaike replied. This was all he said. There followed the kind of silence that would seem fatally frozen to those used to the ways of the world.

"That evening, after you left, he said something of the sort to me too," I finished lamely.

"He was apparently in the midst of some very risky process," Sugaike reluctantly continued. "There were a number of people involved in various ways, I imagine. I'm not in a position to know much about it all. I don't think I was able to grasp the situation from what he told me. And as for whether the expression 'physical danger' is fitting or not ..."

"Of course I'm sure it's all in the past by now."

"He said he relaxed his guard around spring of last year. He'd apparently been out of the picture for some time before that, but this talk of being on his guard is another matter. I've never had the experience of being on my guard so much that I could speak of relaxing it, I must say."

"It must be pretty serious."

"It would be all very well if it was just the one person involved. You can get used to almost anything. But even if your family doesn't know what's going on, they suffer from the oppressive atmosphere. And Fujisato's only family is his daughter, of course. There in that house together. You could say it was stupid of him not to realize that she'd caught on, but it would be inevitable, really, I think. The way he sat out there on the veranda in the summer night—well, of course, it was partly because he couldn't sleep, but it would also have been in a spirit of stubborn lone exertion I think. And all this was perfectly understood by her—that thought was too much for him. It was apparently when he realized this that he began to go to pieces. Well, at any rate he did realize it at last."

I wanted to ask next about when exactly it was that he'd gone mad, or been believed to have gone mad—Sugaike would have seen this in his own inimitable fashion, but I felt that it would be difficult for him to answer, so instead I kept the topic to the letter about his resignation.

"It would be a rather taxing business to work out how to let people know that you were retiring early but didn't intend to find new work, I imagine."

"Yes, he did a good job of that part, didn't he? If you put on a halfhearted show of intending to keep working in some way, things are quite likely to be more obvious to everyone, after all."

"It could look better to everyone if you put in a quick mention of the household?"

"Yes, if you write 'my long-neglected household' or some such thing, we'd all recall our own circumstances and nod in recognition, you see."

"People wouldn't envy him, then?"

"I should think there'd be people who tended to feel relief when they read the words. It's a good thing, you know, to make people feel relieved."

"Would he really have been so intense?"

"No, he isn't the type you'd call 'intense,' exactly. But after all, he took everyone's resentment onto himself, and think of those rumors that spread that he went crazy—a kind of compassionate, saintly person, you might say."

"Those rumors would have died down long ago."

"Well, it's a funny thing. Another rumor's sprung up recently, in fact. And what's more, it's exactly the same one as all those years ago. Fujisato's been in an important position at work all along, the story goes, and he's had to shoulder all those unspoken criticisms that came his way through the period of the economic recession, and finally he either went mad or pretended he did, and has retired."

"So the old rumor's been reborn, with new dates attached."

"I guess, but the thing is, the same people who whispered the old rumor are now whispering the new one with a look of amazement, as though they'd never heard it before. Anyway, Fujisato's not around any more; he's made his escape. It's as if he's thrown this rumor like a candy over his shoulder as he left. I find this talk of setting things right around him and coming back as a new man rather cool and nonchalant, don't you?"

"Cool, yes, lovely and cool in the midst of a hot summer."

"Actually, you know how I ran into Fujisato about two weeks before we all met at his house back in April, and we decided we should all three get together? Well, when I saw him again at the house, I was astonished at how suddenly youthful he'd become. He looked even younger than when we'd first met more than ten years earlier. Of course, I don't know what he was like before that. Even apart from the rumors, I'd say he'd had a wretched time of it. He seems to me to be well qualified to be able to take on whatever the future brings."

Sugaike's cheerful tone never wavered as he spoke. There was an element of pleasant irony and banter to it, but the greater part seemed to come from sheer good will—he appeared to be delighting on Fujisato's behalf over the fact that he'd managed so neatly to retire from work. I thought to myself that this would be something I wouldn't really have been able to understand.

"What's that noise?" Sugaike asked after a pause. "Is someone doing repairs there, at this time of night?"

"That's right. Ever since the hot weather started they've been coming around at night and digging up the local road."

"It sometimes sounds a bit like a beast howling. Or like a huge bird, with a long neck ..."

"They seem to be at it long into the night. I wake up soaked in sweat and lie there listening."

"It sounds like hell. Do you catch the smell of oil and sulphur on the air? I had the same nightmare experience one summer myself."

"It's an odd thing, though. I don't mind it much. I just lie there thinking how hot it is." "You wake up in the night, but you have no problem going back to sleep again."

"And as the days go by, the work gets further and further away down the road, too."

As I said this, I focused on the sound of the road repairs, trying to recall how loud it had been back when they were working right under my window, but even though it was so recent, the experience felt strangely distant.

In woods that lie quiet under the noonday heat, there is a slight stirring of the leaves somewhere in the continuous canopy of the trees. At first it seems that the leaves are merely trembling under the sun's force, but slowly the movement swells until the branches too are swaying wildly. You watch the strange scene as if from a great distance, and then, long after the movement began, a wind comes blowing past you and the wind grows a little stronger. And yet the small red dragonflies that flit about over the grass in the equestrian riding ground that lies in front of the forest seem not to be touched by any wind. Then all is locked again back inside the still heat.

Once there was a woman who suffered badly from the heat. She was a hard worker. During the morning, she rushed breathlessly about at her work, then once the lunch had been eaten and tidied away, she would retire to a corner of the kitchen and prepare for herself some cold rice with a few leftover pickles, pour some cold water over it, and mix it through. As she did so, the color was draining out of her, from her neck down to the tips of her fingers and toes. The old folks in the house would laugh about how she turned into a ghost in the afternoon. At length she retired into a small room. Going along past the back garden, you could peep in through the slightly open window and see her there, her body placed where she could feel the slight cross-breeze from the window to the paper doors opposite, on the corridor side, that were open still further; she lay curled there with her forehead pressed to the wall. At first you thought she was asleep, but then noticed how her shoulders heaved with rough breath. The calf of her leg, the only part flung out exposed on the tatami matting of the floor, showed blue veins. If by chance some man were to sneak in and take her there, she would experience it as no more than another kind of oppressive heat—this image came to me now, overlying the other memory, which was from so long ago that she would now be on the verge of old age, I realized.

When the gust of wind had passed and the air had grown still again, the momentary slight relief from the heat produced an ooze of sweat. I waited in a state of saturation, the drops oozing gently, my eyes on the distant canopy of the woods to detect the next tremor in its leaves. And yet, I thought to myself, I seem to be sweating quite easily this summer. My pores prickled painfully in the daytime, and glancing at my arms I sometimes saw sweat breaking out like fragments of glass beads—this was during the fierce heat of the summer four years earlier. At night, as I began to drift off to sleep, I would feel a pain like a light pinprick on my shin spread slowly along until my legs were bathed in cold sweat from the kneecaps to the ankles. The tiny movement of air that nevertheless flowed through this sealed room caressed my shins unpleasantly. I waited, oppressed at once with heat and cold, until the wave of sweat had passed and my body had grown slippery with it. Then I got up and bathed in cold water. Sometimes I was so soaked that I had to change into fresh pajamas. My legs were smeared with sweat and pale. It seems my nerves were already ill. When winter came and I began to have trouble walking, my body would suddenly flood with heat in the chilly night, and I wouldn't sweat. Rubbing my legs, I felt no moisture there. By early spring, when I went into the hospital, my limbs were rough and dry like an old man's skin whenever my body was aflame with heat. Sometimes they took on a weird and unpleasant purplish brown sheen. For the three years since then, though, we'd been lucky enough to have cool summers.

Now I would take my walk before noon each day, and pause to sit on one of the benches in the bleachers by the riding ground, gazing across the green grass to the woods that stood quiet in the midday sunlight. I had done the same thing often four years earlier too. Looking back on it now, I realized that in fact I had paused here like this because my legs were growing heavy, though I hadn't felt this at the time. The reason I did so now seemed to be from the recent urge to picture myself as what I have in fact been for some time, a man of leisure. Waiting there for the touch of a wind about me that responded to that faint stir of the distant woods, I momentarily became such a figure. At the same time, I was a gasping invalid. I could only sit there a bare five minutes, in fact; once noon was past, I had a raft of work to attend to each day. Brief snatch of time though it was, however, while I sat there measuring the rise and fall of wind in the movement of the trees, from the concentration of my senses came pushing forth a sighing murmur—there's nothing more to do today, it's all done, indeed there's been nothing more to do for a long, long time. I felt as if I could stay sitting there for half a day, that in the end my breath would become one with the breath of the forest, a sense of release rose up in me, and I realized that I had in fact been muttering just these words, without realizing it, at the time of my illness too.

There had been others before me, men still not quite old who had sat here at this time on a summer's day as I did, gazing at the woods as if testing their eyes; some of them would already be dead by now. It would be close to twenty years since I began to notice such figures. I could still recall the face and eyes of one of them, though it was about ten years ago that I used to see him. He was a man who had just retired. He sat here following me with his eyes as I walked swiftly by just below him. I noticed him as I was in the act of passing, turned a little and acknowledged him with my eyes, saw his flustered greeting in response, and hastened on until I had reached the other side of the riding ground and the bleachers had grown small in the distance; there I recalled his figure, trim and youthful, hair freshly trimmed, and suddenly wondered at the way he had watched my thoughtlessly passing figure with a somehow resentful and suspicious gaze. Six months later, he was dead from cancer.

Here on these bleachers four years ago, too, I had recalled this man. As I thought of him sitting here following me with his eyes, my eyes too began to follow my own figure passing below, and I felt an emotion like resentment stir and linger a while in my own breast. Then, watching that figure hastening along on its way, heedless of the oppressive midday sun, unaware that it was about to suddenly be blotted out in the white light it was entering, resentment was at last replaced by pity. Very soon I would stop sitting there on the bleachers, and in autumn, delighted at having gotten through the fierce summer heat, I would make a month-long journey. And as winter arrived, my body would take on renewed vigor.

"I'm in a T-shirt and shorts, you know, and a pair of sandals. If I have a mesh baseball hat on my head and sunglasses, I give a fine impression of coolness. If I do a round of the park, come home soaked in sweat, and douse my head in cold water, it clears away the sluggishness of the night before. By the time I settle down in front of my desk to work, it all feels a little absurd."

This is what I found myself shamefacedly saying when someone rang one afternoon about work and was astonished when I told him I'd missed his earlier call because I had been out walking. "Under that fierce sun?" he exclaimed. In fact I didn't always dress in quite such a stripped-down way to stay cool on my walks, but the next day I determined I'd do as I had described. I was just rounding the edge of the riding ground, in high spirits at how pleasant it all felt, and setting off towards the woods with the wind blowing round me, when I realized someone was leaning down from the bleachers above me to look at me. It was Fujisato.

I came to a halt in the sunshine and blurted out my thanks for the evening at his house.

"You're looking very cool in that get-up," he said, continuing to gaze.

He had one bare foot propped on the bench below, and was rolling up his trouser leg to the shin. I climbed up beside him, and observed that he'd thrown off shoes and socks, and that a hand towel was balled up in the straw hat that lay beside him. His close-cropped salt-and-pepper hair was wet. He told me he'd done a round of the park, and when he reached the drinking fountain he couldn't stand the heat any longer, so had thrown water on his face and then over his head. As I listened, I saw that his face was glowing as if he'd just emerged from a hot bath.

"The turtles," he said oddly as I seated myself beside him, "hold their heads up above the surface and come plowing rapidly through the water, you know, paddling left and right with their flippers, no, I suppose it's their forelegs actually, but they open them out on either side of them just like flippers. Charming to watch. Over there, see, beyond the woods."

He stretched out a languid arm and pointed at the woods, and though the direction was wrong, I realized he was talking about the pond in the park. He went on to say that if someone stands on the bank the turtles come over. There were turtles of various sizes there, and I'd also noticed how on sunny days in the rainy season they would be out of the water, perched on rocks here and there around the pond. Each had its own place, and would sit there, neck stretched out in the sun, busy drying off its shell. But I hadn't known they would come when they saw someone on the bank. I asked whether they come *en masse*, doubting it when I tried to imagine the scene, but he replied that he had only seen one do that. No one else had been about, and there had been this turtle, swimming towards him for all it was worth, from quite a distance away. When it arrived at the shore, it clung to a rock at the waterline and stretched its neck out towards him. It was a shiny iridescent neck. As he gazed back into the turtle's face, a sorrow came over him. He realized that a silly habit he'd had for many years had finally found a use. Fujisato then began to search in his pocket in a worried fashion, and finally produced a little flat packet containing two slices of what looked like hard oily rye bread. The pack was torn, and most of one of the slices was gone. A smell rose from it that was mixed with the smell of human sweat.

He began to talk then about something that seemed quite irrelevant. Back when he was close to forty, one day in a foreign city he'd paused on a bridge on his way from one job to the next, and as he glanced at the shining river, he was suddenly overcome by a strange sensation of starvation. He'd gone dizzy, broken out in a sweat, and felt weak in the knees, but he realized it was actually a nervous hunger that had resulted from a recent excess of nervous tension and that whatever he might try eating or drinking, his stomach would probably not be able to handle it. Leaning there on the railing of the bridge, searching foolishly in his pocket, his hand came across this little snack pack of rye bread. He'd apparently slipped it into his pocket at the breakfast table of the hotel. His weak fingers fumblingly tore it open, and as he brought a piece up to his mouth the rich smell struck him, and he felt his gorge rise. He paused to let the feeling subside, then took a tiny nibble, and held it in his mouth as he dealt with another surge of nausea, chewing slowly. He chewed till tears almost streamed from his eyes, desperately intent on not vomiting, then, eyes fixed elsewhere, gently swallowed. If I don't eat I'll die, he thought to himself. But though he managed in this way to get down two or three bites of the bread, with the next mouthful his mouth refused to move, and he fished the bread out with his finger and threw it into the river. Things went on like this until at last the nausea had largely retreated, and a melancholy sweetness spread over his tongue. At this point he noticed a flock of seagulls circling in the air just beyond the railing. When he threw a piece of bread out, they would match the instant of his movement by flying around underneath to catch it in their beaks. He and the birds together threw and caught, threw and caught, and in no time the two slices had disappeared.

Six months after he returned to Japan, he discovered the same product in an imported food shop, and he took to slipping a packet into his bag on days when he was likely to miss lunch. Generally, he carried it back home with him, but there were occasions when he made do with the bread to see him through the day. It was particularly useful on days when he didn't feel hungry, he said. He'd just nibble at it, a little at a time, and chew. If he took his time and ate one and a half slices, that would get him through the afternoon. It seemed to soothe his nerves, too. It wasn't an activity he was inclined to let people see. Late at night, when he was having a drink, he'd nibble at the bread as an accompanying snack. It helped him sleep. There had been a time when he'd depended on it quite a lot, at a stage when even a meal felt like too much of an effort. Then these tasteless black lumps of hard bread, compounded out of the need to eat and the poignant sorrow of the act of eating, had been perfect for him. Eating, he would think only of the strange way that the rich taste rose out of some desolate place as he chewed, but while he chewed it he had the feeling he was deep in thought. In fact he'd been thinking nothing at all, but afterwards, things had somehow become a little easier for him to do.

Once he had offered the bread to the vagrant in the park by his house as an accompaniment for his drink, and the man had devoured both slices at once. His jaws had seemed to work happily as he chewed, and after he'd swallowed it he remarked, "This is good stuff. I feel like that was really eating. I'll be able to sleep for three days on this."

That morning, Fujisato had remembered something. Apparently the student who had jumped from the roof had had in his pocket a half-eaten roll of the kind they used to sell in those days. As he ate breakfast, he wondered why on earth he should suddenly remember such a thing now, after all these years. He thought sadly that there was no knowing how the boy's feelings might have changed if he'd eaten just one more mouthful, and a mournful sense, not of the boy's life but of his own forty years since that day, came over him. Once his daughter had gone out on an errand, he hung around the house for a while, then decided he too would go out for a walk. On his way out, he slipped the bread into his pocket. He was rather surprised at himself, knowing that his daughter had suggested he wait at home as she was returning at one and would make him iced noodles for lunch. But he was glad now, having met the turtle.

"And is your daughter well? I had a call from Sugaike the other day, and he was singing her praises again."

"She gets better every day. I can scarcely believe I'm seeing my own daughter. These days she goes trotting along the corridor, singing. It's all thanks to that visit by the two of you, you know."

"Ah, well ... Hey, I read that letter you sent around when you retired."

In a slight gap in the unbroken canopy of the trees, where the top of a taller pine poked through, the leaves began delicately to glitter and shift. All the red dragonflies hovering over the grass of the riding ground suddenly lifted lightly up into the air.

"There was a time when I was crazy," Fujisato said with a dry cough.

And then a wind passed over, and that cracked voice seemed to spread, flowering out through the light-saturated air around us in a yet whiter circle.

15
Bell Crickets

Late at night, crickets sang somewhere in the house, a soft, lonely little "tink tink." The name I've known these creatures by since childhood is "bell cricket," but this is the sort of thing that one could be wrong about all one's life.

There's nothing odd about the fact that they made their way into the house to sing toward the end of August. My home is in an apartment building, but it's only on the second floor, and crickets of various sorts do sometimes come in. However, the place where these bell crickets could be heard was in the little section between the toilet and bath that is the most sealed-off part of the house, with no means of access front or back. The song came from one part of the ceiling, but no one ever laid eyes on the creatures themselves.

Bathroom ceilings in modern buildings have no unlit areas, and there's nowhere for an insect to hide. Toilet and bathroom do each have a ventilation opening, and the two ventilation pipes no doubt meet behind the ceiling. However, the fan is directly behind the hole, and it spins constantly. Could an insect really manage to get into such a place?

Yet I couldn't think where else an insect might be able to hide. It occurred to me that perhaps the crickets didn't actually mind the fan, since it turned quite softly. Perhaps there were insects living permanently in there beyond the ventilation hole, mating, spawning, and somehow managing year after year to hatch their young. But occasionally, sometime past midnight, I also heard a cricket up in the corner of the ceiling in my study. I of course never caught a glimpse of it, nor was there ever any little corpse lying fallen to the floor in the morning. No pipe connected this ceiling with those in the bathroom area. Being well over twenty years old, the building was now aged and decaying, and I thought perhaps a long crack may have formed in the concrete connecting the bathroom and study ceilings, through which an insect could crawl. The thought made me a little fearful, but years had passed without it developing in my mind beyond the level of vague imaginings. I had first heard the crickets about five years earlier. It was a clearly distinguishable song, no mere auditory hallucination or ringing in the ears.

This year, when I heard the bell crickets sing again, a strange thought occurred to me. I had first heard a single cricket singing between long intervals in the ceiling above the toilet and bathroom. I was at the desk in my study at the time, and it was past midnight. The song moved gradually in the direction of the living room, then finally it came from outside. I went out onto the veranda and confirmed that this was where it was. But when I returned and sat down at the desk again, a bell cricket's clear "tink tink" began again from the bathroom. The two insects, one inside and one out, were calling and answering, though with long intervals between. Of course, as they were both males, this calling and answering was not done to attract a mate; separated though they were, they could hear each other, and these were assertions of territory. Yet it struck me as strange that though the cricket outside hardly changed position, the one inside was constantly shifting about.

I then slipped into the bed that had been set up in the study and turned out the bedside lamp, and as I lay there waiting for the sweat to stop oozing and drowsiness to settle over me, I heard a crisp "tink tink" in the corner of the study ceiling. It was just like a little bell being struck. Then some distance away, from outside the window, came a tiny response. The song in the room ceased, and only the distant cricket continued to sing.

It was only then it occurred to me that perhaps in fact there weren't insects singing inside the house—it may be that from time to time a song from outside was somehow picked up and echoed by something in the house. Perhaps, I thought, a closed space distant from the outside, like that between toilet and bathroom, would be a particularly good resonator ... but at this point I paused to take account of the considerable distance between the clump of grass where the insects sang and this apartment, second-floor though it may be, and the thickness of the separating concrete, and my musings struck me as absurd fantasy. I tried once more to tell myself that even a single cricket's song might reverberate right through a concrete slab, but the suggestion only induced a blockage of thought.

· · · · ·

"There was a time when I was crazy," Fujisato said. He gave a soft cough, though not one that hinted at any inner turmoil, and narrowed his eyes against a passing gust of wind. When it had died down and the midday heat closed in around us once more, he gazed levelly at the distant trees as though he hadn't spoken. I too settled my eyes on the woods, aware that I had not the slightest desire to take up the conversation. Those few words were enough for now. They were an essential fulfillment of an act of communication, I thought, going back in my mind over our few brief exchanges during the last year or so, and the almost forty years of complete lack of contact that stretched before. What struck me as strange was rather the presence of those two young men back there at the far end of this long period of non-communication. No doubt in six months' time he would say a little more.

Yet I surprised myself by asking, "When would that have been?" Fujisato's gaze became thoughtful. He didn't seem to be hesitating over whether to speak or not. It seemed he was genuinely trying to recall when it had happened.

At length he replied, "No, it wasn't then, not during that hot summer four years back. I rode it out. Things became a lot easier after that. More than six months went by, then around the beginning of spring the following year, one day I suddenly couldn't speak. Language simply left me."

He was at a meeting, where he had to give a report on some important matter, although the matter had already been more or less settled. All those present had been involved in it in various ways, so everyone was well aware of the general outlines of the case and indeed some people knew more about it than he did. A final decision on the matter had come from higher up, and what now remained was the business of persuasion and compensation. The difficulty now was the long-standing feelings of those involved, so words had to be chosen carefully. On the other hand, he wasn't there to soothe feelings, so he mustn't speak in a way that sought to elicit people's agreement. Above all else, accuracy was required at this stage. Yet accuracy was no simple matter, for there was a delicate balance to the whole affair, and it could be rather risky to lay it all out in detail again at this stage. It was hard to talk about a situation that the audience knew so well; it could happen that, depending on how things were phrased, listeners might find themselves unable to comprehend things that they already knew.

However, Fujisato had not been feeling particularly tense at the prospect. He was thoroughly aware of the difficulties involved, but he felt that he was well prepared for any contingency. All one had to do was be on top of the points that required particular accuracy, and for the rest, it was better to bumble along quite dully; it was better to be under– than over-prepared. This was indeed how he began, and things went more or less as intended. As he continued to speak, there was on the whole less and less need for forethought, and he reached a point where the crux of the matter was fairly safely dealt with. His audience listened calmly, quietly supporting him by being prepared to fill in the gaps whenever he stumbled over the particulars. He saw a few people nod encouragingly to indicate that things were clear and he should move on. By now, the remainder of the report should be an easy downhill slope. No further difficulties loomed ahead, but still, he mustn't rush—if he hastily cut corners at this stage, he would give the impression of being on the run. He had made it through the report so far, but now was the time to suggest to his audience that he was at something of a loss as to how to draw it to a close. Each listening face now held an individual variation of a wry and sympathetic smile. Perhaps it was the relief this sight provoked that made him suddenly lose his words. Outside the forty-second–story windows, the sunlight of early spring was flooding the air with a kind of haze. That light is also falling on my garden at home, he thought. He saw the figure of his daughter crouching in the garden. Before he knew it, the words had died on his tongue.

Here Fujisato's expression became one of quiet bewilderment. He lifted his right hand upright in a posture of one-handed prayer, and gently moved it to and fro before his mouth, continuing the gesture for some time without speaking. There was nothing weird in the impression this produced.

He felt no agitation or dismay, he said. The spring sunlight continued to flood his head. He did feel an urge to entreat those around him, but although he was in the awkward position of being speechless, he was without a sense of panic. He could detect no perplexity in the faces in the audience. They were all maintaining their wry smiles, increasingly relaxed. Seeing this, a shiver of fear did at last run through him, but only for a moment, and it was quickly drowned in the sensation of pouring light. Things resolved themselves before people began to be actively concerned for him. He turned to his boss, sitting beside him, and bowed, and the man immediately accepted the gesture. "Fujisato's exhausted," he remarked easily, "so let's declare his round finished, and I'll step in and take over for him." So he brought everyone together in good-natured laughter and smoothly finished things off.

Afterward, his boss remarked to him that it was actually a good thing he'd come to a standstill at that point. It had helped everyone's feelings to settle. Of course, he didn't interpret the event as a straightforward matter of having lost his words. Fujisato had remained unable to speak until the meeting had ended and he found himself alone with his superior and tried to thank him. Up until then, he had stood at his place and silently bowed to each man who passed on his way out the door. He was told later that he had kept smiling throughout.

It wasn't the same sort of thing as alalia, the pathological loss of speech, he continued. He felt no strain, either physical or nervous. His head simply felt like a blackboard that had been wiped clean—such a wide expanse, such a lack of any presence, that it was meaningless to ask what, or where, or how anything had ever been written there.

"I guess you couldn't say you were mad," I said, and it wasn't just an idle remark to help things along.

"No, no, I was mad, there was no hiding it. Everyone saw it. It can only have been this occasion that set off all the rumors."

"That may be how others saw it. What about you yourself?"

"Well, I was mad," Fujisato repeated, almost happily.

He had to work late after that meeting, too, but he managed it without incident. Late that night, he was heading across the park on his way home when the vagrant on the bench called him over, and he stopped to chat. He told the other man, admiringly, that he looked like an intellectual. No, the man replied, he hadn't even gotten through his basic schooling. It was just that he was good at pretending he knew a lot. If he found himself a single magazine, he could talk for ten days on what he had learned from it, and he had a nose for locating good books. While this conversation was proceeding, Fujisato found that the time he had lost his words in the meeting had seamlessly connected itself with the present, where he was conversing effortlessly with this man. The intervening nine or ten hours could not be said to have disappeared. He could feel his way back over the intervening time quite clearly when he tried; it was as if the single chronological thread was joined together at both its separate ends, and the intervening period was now dangling there, quite dead. No, that wasn't it, either. It wasn't dead. It was alive—in fact, it was flourishing. Whatever he might say was said wholeheartedly at that moment. It was just that at the same time another and different self was looking on, watching with a heart sodden with tears. Here, as he exchanged this foolish talk with the vagrant fellow ...

"That happens quite often, I'm told," I began in an attempt to break in, but my voice was hoarse, and it sounded almost as if I were speaking to myself.

"Yes, I'm sure it must," came Fujisato's amiable reply. Nothing else seemed to be forthcoming. Then, after a pause, he went on, "It's just that I'd lived all those years till then with time being connected up. If time isn't neatly connected together, you have no way to apply your judgment from one situation to the next. You don't just judge things from the context of the event itself, you know. You have to begin from a sense of your own chronological continuity, or the whole thing falls apart."

"I wonder if you were approaching that feeling of 'it's over' that you spoke of, the thing you always felt when you were driven into a corner."

"Yes, that's right." Fujisato's voice emerged in a tone steeped in nostalgia, almost a lamentation. "It's when the only possible conclusion to draw is that this is willful arbitrariness, a kind of self-abnegation. You withhold all judgment, you just wait there, ghostly pale, with the next step before you a meaningless blank. Sometimes you can't just wait in silence. Even in the midst of some tense, difficult dealings with others, you go on waiting. During this time, that sensation that it's over will descend always just in the nick of time. Everything's over. It's been over for a long time. And then, somehow, ever so tenuously, the sense of time's connectedness will begin to return. You know how when something's ended and irretrievable, you'll find yourself setting to work attending to this and that demand, quite irrelevantly. And while you work, deep inside, your body is registering the calm that comes after an ending. This absolute calm links itself directly with everything you do, lending it a temporary feeling of something like necessity, you know? Well, the sensation I'm speaking of is very like that."

193

"Couldn't this recent experience be the same kind of thing?"

I was aware that envy stirred within me as I listened to Fujisato speaking in this tone so fully accepting of the idea of everything being finished and over.

"It was some days later," he went on, ignoring my question. His tone had gone back to being so bright and happy that for a moment I was confused as to what event he was referring to. "I woke up early in the morning. The weather was good. I stretched in bed and lay there beginning to go through the day's plans. I carefully checked each item against the items that had been set out in the final decision of the day before. It took some time before I realized that a day had intervened between then and now, and it wasn't necessarily one of those calm and uneventful ones."

"So which day's plans were you going over?"

"Actually it was the plans that I had made the day before and then revised after various things had happened in the earlier part of the day."

"It's interesting that you could still check them against the plans of the day before that so well, then."

"It all connected up neatly for a while. I'd spent half a day putting a lot of effort into getting things to connect, you see. The new version of the plans tied in well with the flow of events from the day before. Still, comparing present plans with those made two days earlier inevitably produced some discrepancies. But in fact it was before any discrepancies came to light that I discovered I'd skipped a day. Suddenly, the image of myself chewing surreptitiously away at that rye bread popped into my head. I'd gotten caught up in things and missed lunch, so here I was, past three o'clock, finally eating something."

I smiled, attracted by the picture of him. "It's the sort of scene that might make a girl exclaim, 'That's so sweet!' Apparently girls do love it when old people do things like that."

"Probably because it's a childish habit, huh?"

"But you realized while you were lying in bed, didn't you? It's a good thing the truth dawned on you so soon. It would have been a different matter if you hadn't realized till after you'd gotten up, particularly if it wasn't till you were at work. That would really have made things difficult. You were in a dangerous situation there."

"But you see, I'd gotten to a point where I didn't consider that sort of thing to be dangerous any more."

He spoke heavily. I pricked up my ears, sensing that he was at last approaching the crux of the matter. But a little smile creased the corners of his eyes for a moment, then again, and then it spread irrepressibly over his face, which glowed now with a faint flush.

"I had this sensation of bliss," he said, as if appealing for my understanding. "It continued after I got up, too. It insinuated itself into every movement

194

and action. It was there in the water that flowed when I turned on the tap. It was there when I went to stand on the veranda, in every stem of every plant that swayed in the breeze. I spent a whole hour with my daughter over breakfast. Not talking about anything in particular, you understand. I just wanted to point to everything I saw and ask, 'What's this?' 'What's that?' She sat with me the whole time, too. The feeling didn't entirely leave me even while I was at the office. It remained faintly with me all day. Next morning when I woke up, there it was again. Now it's moved backwards into my past, and colored everything retrospectively."

Though the sky was utterly cloudless, a shade seemed to brush me, and I thought the distant sea of treetops flamed white. When the wind had passed, sweat was seeping from my back again.

I responded to his words in a similar vein. "Yes, recently I find that I can sometimes be swept up for no reason in a kind of ecstasy." As I spoke, I remembered that these were almost the exact words I'd heard from Sugaike's mouth the previous autumn. "It might be a voice instructing you to age comfortably. I have a feeling it may go on for three or four days."

"It never really came to an end," Fujisato replied, picking up the socks he had taken off and tossed on the bench, and beginning to put them on. "When I woke up each morning, day after day would have passed me by. Naturally, I no longer tried to make it all add up in my mind."

"And the bliss would return?"

"It wasn't quite as strong as bliss. It was a strange ease that enveloped everything."

"That it was all finally finished ..."

"Though it struck me as odd, since nothing was really finished. And yet there was this ease. Very odd. Sometimes I'd find I was connected back to a much earlier self, with the intervening events erased. But that didn't disturb me at all."

"You wouldn't be able to mix with people in everyday life while you were in that state, I imagine."

"You know, that actually got easier."

He had now put on his shoes. He planted his feet firmly, put a hand on each knee, and seemed about to rise to his feet. I also felt inclined to bring the conversation to a close. "Well, at any rate, it doesn't seem as if it was such a bad experience."

"You couldn't say it was madness, no."

"Perhaps there's a similarity between madness and consciousness."

"Maybe I was mad, maybe I was becoming more conscious, how could I know for sure? But during that time I did catch a glimpse of myself as crazy quite a few times. It would suddenly become apparent when I was among people. In this situation, you find yourself looking and acting in quite inappropriate ways. For instance, your hands might sort of float out in front of

195

you, not particularly held there, not particularly dangling. They're earnestly saying something entirely different from your eyes and mouth. Or your feet might be moving ever so quietly, as if you weren't walking among this bustling crowd. The kind of movement that makes people want to ask where on earth you're going ..."

I was staring in amazement at the broad smile that was again suffusing his face, like the smile on the Old Man mask worn by a No actor. It was a smile that could easily be mistaken for pitying sorrow, but that was in fact an expression of calm bliss.

"These are some of the things inside my mind," he finally apologized.

"Don't you find yourself pulled into them?" I asked, touched with apprehension on his behalf.

"I have this feeling that I'm standing about three feet behind my real self, looking on. Sometimes there's the sensation that I'm a breath behind my actual movements, following along like a sort of aftertaste of the moment itself. The long and short of it is that I feel as if I'm a presence radiating out behind myself. It's hard to say whether I'm pulled in or possessed, the whole thing's topsy-turvy. And it's not some perilous ghostly presence, either. But when I'm spending time quietly at home, sometimes I see my own figure still coming and going down the corridor where I've just been walking as I wandered aimlessly about the house. It throws me a sideways glance as it tiptoes along, in a flowing gait—yet it doesn't feel as if there's only one person wandering around in the house, there seems to be enough bustle and activity for a whole crowd. But at the same time, I push the whole thing away, telling myself it's not the sort of thing I would do. But then I look up, and my daughter is standing somewhere nearby, watching me. One evening, we were in the act of studiously avoiding each other's gaze when suddenly we both burst into laughter. I have no idea which of us started it. I remember pointing to my head and asking, 'Have I been odd?' and she rested one hand on a pillar, convulsed with silent laughter."

"What a hopeless father, huh! And what did she answer?"

"She told me that for a while there I was coming home each evening with a very different face. It was a long time since I'd brought a guest back at night. She meant my own physical face."

"I remember that vagrant once said to you that you no longer looked as if you were fated to die by the sword. Was it that summer ..."

"I told you about that, did I? Perhaps Sugaike mentioned it too. That danger had dissipated from early on, actually. It couldn't be said to be about anyone in particular any longer. In every sense."

"We met in the park with the hackberry tree last April, right? Would that have been somewhere less than two years after that look of yours disappeared?"

"That's right. The chances of our meeting like that were amazingly slim, you know."

"Yes, it was after about forty years, wasn't it? You know the saying 'wait a hundred years for the right moment'—well, maybe our forty years have been still longer."

"Yes, they certainly have been. I'm impressed that I could still recognize your face. But you know, even when I first noticed there was someone standing under the hackberry, I believe I had already realized that it was you."

"I thought to myself for a second, here's some white-haired old man coming striding up to tell me off for something."

"My legs started to move before I thought of addressing you. I imagine I might have hurried those first few paces in quite a fluster."

"And also, you know, this was a complete illusion on my part, but just before that I had seen a house—there was a stone wall beyond the park, with a two-story house above it, and a feeling that a scary old man's face was peering out at me, and the next instant he seemed to be running down the stone steps. But of course there's no such house."

"A house with a stone wall in that area—" I thought Fujisato was about to laugh, but instead he paused to think, and a light shone in his eyes. "I don't think there was one, but of course it's a hilly area. It may well be that the different levels were clearer in the old days. Sometimes you can find yourself in the grip of an illusory memory, if you've spent many years living in the one area. Yes, come to think of it, it was forty years ago that I moved there."

Still apparently sunk in thought, he put on his gardener's straw hat, wound the little towel around his neck, and stood up.

"And it certainly is strange, isn't it, that we should meet up after forty years." He cast a final glance at the wood from under the brim of his hat. Then he added, oddly, "It's like another crazy tale, really," and set off without waiting for an answer. It was more than thirty minutes past noon.

We parted at a telephone booth just outside the park, where Fujisato paused to wait for the person using it to finish so that he could ring home to say he was coming. When I arrived back at my house after a brief walk, the place was empty and the telephone was ringing. I ran to get it. It was Fujisato's daughter, asking whether her father was by any chance at my place. I told her to put down the receiver, because her father was trying to call her at that very moment, and she did so, with a short 'all right.' I noticed then with surprise how tensely I had responded, as if some crisis was in the air.

In no time the telephone rang again, and his daughter apologized and informed me in a laughing tone that her father had indeed called as soon as she replaced the receiver. I thought to myself that there was really nothing to feel relieved about in all this, and yet, alone in the house again, the heat of the sealed rooms suddenly wrapped around me, making my skin clammy. Though I had left the house empty for a bare two hours in the midsummer heat, a faint moldy smell hung in the air. Then the song of a bell cricket began to rise through the stale air. I must have been mishearing.

It felt later as if Fujisato's daughter had already let the phone ring for a long time before I heard it as I opened my front door.

. . . . .

I was just thinking to myself that the crickets really did seem to be singing from some hiding place in a crack in the concrete, when suddenly, right before my eyes, outside the glass window, someone fell. The subway train had pulled into a quiet station platform just right at about dusk, and the last scattering of alighting passengers had just dispersed. I remembered hearing somewhere that you should always be alert if somebody falls with apparent weightlessness. The man collapsed flat onto the platform, rolled over onto his back, and attempted to raise his head. Then his face took on a strange expression and he lay motionless, all strength gone. Two platform attendants rushed up, lifted him by the elbows and knees, and ran off to lay him on a nearby bench, struggling to support the slack body that hung sagging from their hands. From moment to moment, a clay-colored pallor intensified over the man's face. It was the face of one who is at the exhausted extreme of illness; his age was impossible to guess, beyond the fact that he was elderly. The skin around his closed eyes was deeply wrinkled. But then the eyes suddenly snapped open, he began to lift his head again, his limbs grew firm, and slowly he sat himself up. At length he was sitting upright, looking no different from someone who has just sat down on the bench for a brief rest as he searched for something in his coat pockets. When the two attendants came running back with the stretcher, he stood up, revealing himself now as quite a tall man, and stood smiling and bowing and apologizing deeply to them. Finally, he rested a hand on the stretcher, as if offering to carry it.

"Ah yes, I know just how he feels. I've been feeling exactly the same myself every day recently. It's almost a miracle I walk without falling. I'd love to take three minutes or so like that to faint on a platform bench."

The voice came from down the carriage as the train left the station. I didn't turn to see who it was, but the firm voice was of a man much younger than I. Though we were now well into September, the spate of extreme heat had continued unabated. But it seemed that the hot air already held a certain coolness, for the skin was brushed with chill even as it gasped in the heat and oozed with sweat. When I touched my skin, it did feel cool, though it continued to stream with sweat. Then I began to feel weak at the knees. When I came up from the subway onto the street, the sun had not yet set completely. Only a soft glow still lit the edges of the clouds, but the white hair of the passing elderly men took on a faint red tinge from the light. I was aware of constantly passing couples dressed in mourning clothes, and for a while I was beset by a premonition that from out of their midst at any moment Sugaike would come up to me, looking surprised, and say, "Well, well, fancy meeting you here."

After the tenth, rain fell at last, and the temperature immediately dropped. From then on, the weather remained rainy. On street corners here and there in the area near my house I found myself noticing, too, a number of notices of funeral wakes. When the stark whiteness of their paper struck my eye in the gloom of the now-cool rainy evening, it felt to me as if summer lingered only there, a summer suffered through by one racked with illness.

Exhausted from the summer, I slept heavily each night, and a slightly desolate feeling accompanied my wakening. I recalled Sugaike saying there had been a period when he dreamed of his childhood life every night. He would gaze at the scene overwhelmed with sorrow at their poverty, almost weeping with despair and desperate to do something about it. As he did so, he would begin to feel puzzled and realize that the family quietly eating their meager meal before his eyes was his own present-day family, not his childhood one. It had been quite a while ago that Sugaike had told me this, when we were both in our forties. They were apparently dreams about falling on hard times, he said, adding with a laugh that for him then the threat of hard times was too close to be merely dream material—he had recently changed jobs yet again. Looking back on it now it struck me that he was much too young to be dreaming of himself dying and looking back at his bereaved family. Yet it seemed to me, as I thought about it, that the scene of his gathered family eating in silence might well have been such a scene. I sighed again at how busy he had been all this time, perhaps since his late thirties.

Soon I too began to find my days filled with work, for all that I was at home, and the nearly two hours I had spent in conversation with Fujisato under the fierce summer sun of midday already felt distant. Day in and day out, the rain kept falling and I slaved away at my desk. It was only as evening fell that at last I paused to wonder in passing how Fujisato was spending the same hours at his home. One day, an image floated into my mind of Fujisato on his dimly lit veranda before an easel, daubing oils onto a small canvas with a palette knife. His clear gaze was cast out over the rain-soaked garden, but the canvas was filling with red swirls of color. And yet he sighed with peaceful relief—how white, he seemed to be saying, how white and calm. I hadn't heard that Fujisato ever painted pictures.

By the time the Buddhist ceremonies to mark the forty-ninth day since my father-in-law's death were approaching, our house had returned completely to normal. Finally recalled how the pipe in the bathroom had become blocked while they were away, and the plumber had poked at it until he produced the ball of hair, and I told my wife the tale. She was surprised, and responded that she'd always been careful to remove any hair

199

left floating after a bath, to which I replied with a laugh that after all there were three women in the house, so perhaps it was inevitable. As I spoke, I counted up the days since her father had been taken to the hospital, and realized that it was three months later that the pipe had become blocked.

They say that early autumn is a time when invalids begin to register the taste of food again, and indeed I found myself impressed from time to time, with the image from Sugaike's dream in the back of my mind, at how deeply absorbed my own family could become as they quietly consumed the evening meal.

When the Higan Festival of the Dead holiday came around, my wife and daughter set off for my wife's mother's house, to attend the ceremony for the dead. That morning, on my way home from doing a bit of shopping near the station as part of my walk, I ducked down a little side road that ran along one side of a high concrete wall. I had always walked past this wall without pausing to wonder what was on the other side, but this time I noticed that a little steel entrance door in it was half-ajar, and when I stopped to peer in, I found that the walled-in area beyond was crammed with graves, and incense filled the air. I recalled that until a few years ago—three perhaps, or five, or even ten—there had been a lower wall here, and as I passed I used to gaze over it at the tops of the mass of wooden grave markers beyond. There had originally been both temples and graveyards in the area; indeed there was an impressive temple not far from here, with graveyard attached. But this separate patch of land was separated from its temple by a road. It had been enclosed by walls, then encircled by new buildings, and now only the graves remained, without any temple building attached.

I did no more than gaze for a while and heave a sigh of surprise. I don't care for the sight of someone gawking in from somewhere, so I very soon went on my way. And yet as I turned away I had glimpsed the figures of people, most of them elderly, moving about among the graves, tending them for Higan. Until that moment, though the vivid colors of the flowers placed on graves here and there had disturbed me, I had felt that the place was completely deserted. As soon as I was aware of the people, all surrounding noise was blotted out, and then a sense of gazing deeply came over me. I was not staring, yet the depths of my eyes registered how the flowers placed before the graves echoed and spoke back to the flowers blooming in pots on the balconies of the high-rise flats beyond the wall.

Making my way home, I said to myself that registering only the place, unpeopled, was like a scene from a dream, and did not bode well. The rest of the day passed in work, and then that evening, Sugaike telephoned.

"The cool has settled in," he began, "so why don't we console ourselves for having suffered all that heat with a belated drink?" He fell suddenly silent, and after a long moment I heard a trembling breath.

"I've had a strange dream," he began, his voice shaking with laughter.

"It was you and Fujisato and me. One of us had died, and we'd all met up. We were eating some dried shredded cuttlefish and drinking saké."

"Dried cuttlefish and saké would make it autumn, even in a dream," I responded, and then I carefully went on. "But that's peculiar, isn't it? I'm dead, and you and Fujisato are there, okay. Fujisato's dead, and you and I are there. Fine. But if it's you who's died, then who is dreaming it?"

"Don't panic," Sugaike replied. "All three of us are there together. We're all in good health. That's what's so good about dreams. One of us has died, and we're all there together to celebrate it."

"Aha, I see. And did it strike you as odd in the dream?"

"It sure did—in fact, it was so odd I went and woke myself up. One had died, and there were the three of us. One had died and there were the three of us," he repeated, and burst into helpless laughter.

"Hey," I said, "if you've had such a crazy, mixed-up dream, does that mean you've actually managed to visit the family grave this autumn?"

16

An Inn at Nakayama

"What about going to Nakayama this Sunday? The day after tomorrow, I mean," Sugaike asked me.

The autumn horse racing events at Nakayama had wound up the previous Sunday. It was a full two weeks since Sugaike had called to propose that we go drinking to cheer ourselves after the rigors of the summer heat, now finally over with the advent of Higan.

That evening on the phone we had both found ourselves in a playful mood in response to that dream of Sugaike's—not, we trusted, an ominous one—and had even considered following its suggestion and getting together with Fujisato, but the conversation had ended only with a vague promise to meet soon. Later, when I picked up my old and trusty watch, which had seen long years of service, I discovered that it had come to a complete halt. Apparently it was simply at the end of its life. The following day, a Saturday, I set off in the rain to the Nakayama races.

I told Sugaike that the races were moving to Fuchu as of the next day. "Is that so?" he replied. "But I distinctly remember going to the Nakayama races late one October, just around the time when the persimmons on the trees were coloring up." In fact, it was ten years since there'd been races through October at Nakayama.

"I guess that's what happens when you let yourself get out of touch with things," he said regretfully. "Well, well, so they move to Fuchu these days, eh?" I sensed that he was experiencing a sudden nostalgia for that distant memory of the atmosphere at the Nakayama racetrack, something I could well understand. I also felt in his voice a certain faintheartedness, so I stepped in with a counteroffer. "Why not go to Fuchu instead? Come on. I'll come too. The racetracks there are still the way they used to be."

But Sugaike surprised me by responding, "No, it's not that. I can't go anywhere on Sunday till around sunset. I just thought that if you felt like going to Nakayama for the races for a while, we could meet around there after it's over. It would have to be Nakayama, though. I have to catch a plane from Narita on Monday morning."

. . . . .

I asked whether he was tied up with work at a hotel near the airport all day Sunday, and was intending to head off to nearby Nakayama that evening when he was free. But no, he said he had taken an inn at Nakayama itself. These days, traffic conditions had improved so much that it didn't take much extra time to get to Narita from where he lived, but when he had such an early flight, he found he couldn't face it. On the other hand, he didn't care for the hotels around the airport. Nakayama was a compromise solution, but that was what he liked about it. He'd been told about the place years ago, and once or twice a year ever since, he made use of the same place when he had an early flight to catch. Nakayama is an old town that grew up around a temple, so no doubt there are still some old-style inns in the area, but the place he stayed in seemed to be in a separate area. It wasn't run as a full business any longer, and seemed only to put up regular guests who'd been coming for years, and those they brought with them. It was apparently on a road that led to the racetrack, but he couldn't recall going to the races from there in the old days. Of course he usually arrived after dark, and his memories of the place had no connection to his race-going days....

He seemed to have reached the end of what he had to say. I began to inquire whether in that case he was going there from his home on Sunday, but then I stopped. If I wasn't going myself, I felt I had no right to be so inquisitive. Instead, I asked, "Are you off for a long stint of work this time?"

"It would be good if it was all over quickly," he replied. "But in any case, it won't be long," and he chuckled at his choice of phrase, with its overtones of one dying.

"Can you sleep when you're traveling?"

"I don't have any trouble sleeping, but I do wake up during the night, no matter how tired I am."

"You have the experience of not knowing where you are for a few moments?"

"Yes, I don't know where I am or who I am. But I just set that question aside."

"Ah yes, the business of who and where one is is just idle explanation at the time, isn't it."

"Sometimes I simply go right back to sleep again. There are times when I get up in the morning and vaguely recollect that I was awake for a while in the night, as if it was someone else's memory. There's a novel called *Metamorphosis*, isn't there? The protagonist was a businessman who traveled all over, as I recall. Some mistake happened when he'd arrived somewhere."

"There are certainly times when you don't want to get up, aren't there?"

203

"No, I'm a man of excellent intentions, I always want to get up. It's just that my body won't move. My policy is to wait patiently. I wouldn't want to force myself out of bed and turn into something bizarre. It only takes about ten minutes of lying there. But once that's over, my clock starts ticking precisely."

"Do you let the alarm go on ringing on while this is going on?"

"My arm reaches out of its own accord. I don't like it—I feel as if it's acting from some ulterior motive."

"It's a shame, you know. The races were still at Nakayama last week. There was a really good one on Sunday, too."

I myself had gone to Hokkaido Sunday evening and only just returned late last night, Thursday. While I was in the hotel in Obihiro, the place had been rocked by an earthquake. The building's steel frame had creaked and trembled for what seemed a long time. I woke up close to dawn, with the impression that a great crowd of people were rushing about inside the room—I'd apparently fallen asleep with the TV on, and the flow of breaking news continued as I slept.

"The yearend races are still at Nakayama, aren't they?" came Sugaike's somehow distant voice. "I remember in the old days the end of the year was when they held the Grand Steeplechase."

"It's a special chance to meet," I replied, "so I'll go there regardless. I know the way by subway. It'll make a nice change to go to Nakayama on a Sunday evening when there are no races on."

After I'd spoken, I remembered how the previous evening on the monorail coming back from the airport, I had been aware of a slight but painful ache lurking deep in my lungs.

．　．　．　．　．

As I stood at the bus stop near my house that Sunday evening, I wondered why Sugaike should make a point of staying in an odd place like Nakayama on the night before his departure. If it were me, I thought, I'd prefer to spend the night at home, even if it meant getting up at 4:00 a.m.—I didn't care to leave home on a Sunday evening, for a trip or for any other purpose. Aside from the time of my youth, my life had been a largely sedentary one, and a departure on a Sunday at this hour was generally associated with unpleasant events. In the crises of my father's and my mother's illnesses, both had been taken to a hospital not too far from my house, and on both occasions it was late on a Sunday afternoon when I had set off to visit. In my agitation, I had decided against taking the local bus and instead strode wildly off to walk the couple of kilometers to the hospital, bewildered at my own haste, while the evening set in around me. When my sister was ill, the hospital was not within walking distance, but in this case too it was after sunset when I arrived. Each of them had welcomed me with a strange look when I walked into their room on those Sunday evenings. And each time, I had been chilled at the thought that they may have read some evil tidings into my unexpected arrival at this hour, and decided that I should avoid turning up on a Sunday evening that way in the future. But the pressures of my weekday life always meant that I would find myself repeating the mistake the next time.

But then, three years ago, in early spring, it was my turn to spend time in the hospital when I had the surgery on my spine, and from the time when I had to lie faceup on the bed with my neck immobilized, my elder brother took to dropping in to see me on Sunday evenings just after the radio broadcast of the horse races was over. He would seat himself by my bed, not really talking but generally reading a magazine he had apparently bought along the way, and when he finished he would leave it with me and go. Later, it occurred to me that as my brother moved away from the hospital he would no doubt have felt forlorn at the thought of me left back there in the ward as the evening drew on; then at some point, it became instead him who struck me as forlorn, this man on the verge of retirement who left his house after midafternoon on Sunday, spent some time by the sickbed of his younger brother, then returned home along a darkened road. Even after I left the hospital, I wondered whether my sense of forlornness had to do with the fact that so far that spring the weather had worsened every Sunday, but then, within six months, my elder brother died.

"What about Fujisato? Should we invite him along?"

"It would be good to see him, but perhaps we should treat him carefully for a while yet."

"Yes, he seems to have settled comfortably into his new life as a man of leisure, doesn't he, so maybe you're right."

"So let's make it that he's the one who's died, on this occasion. Though in fact he's the healthiest of the three of us. I thought the same thing in my dream, you know."

With this, Sugaike returned to his odd dream of the three of us together after one had died, and we ended our conversation with a laugh. The weather on Saturday was cloudy, and though it cleared temporarily on Sunday, a cloudy gloom descended again in the afternoon. The distance between my neighborhood and Nakayama seemed far on the map, but in fact I arrived at Nishi-Funabashi Station inside an hour, after a mere five-minute bus ride to the subway station and a single change of trains. Thanks to the rapid expansion of the public transport network in the last twenty years, one could travel under the center of the city from near the western edge of Setagaya across to just this side of the Arakawa River, but no matter how many times I made the journey I couldn't seem to come to terms with the fact; whenever I set off for the afternoon races and the carriage emptied after Shibuya and Omotesando stations, a bored drowsiness would descend on me, as though I had lost all sense of both time and place. It was not far to the station where

I had to change trains, so each time we stopped I briefly opened my eyes to check, and as I gazed out through the open doors at those quiet platforms in the heart of the city, emptied of people in the weekend midday, my eyes closed with an image of my own back leaving the train, drawn impulsively to step out there. Eventually, having walked the long distance to board the next train, the same thing would happen again once I was in it. At that stage, I felt as though it was late at night.

Opening my eyes to stare at a still more deserted station platform, I wondered whether perhaps my mother had once taken me by train late one Sunday night to some distant place. We had arrived at Kiba Station. A momentary sureness dawned in me. It was when I was very small. My mother was still young. She wore a Western-style dress. We were sitting in a corner of the dark private railway line carriage. My mother sat with head bowed and eyes closed, while I sat quietly, well-behaved, beside her. I had a feeling I had been crying. All that rose in my memory now was a vague view of the inside of the carriage, but my nose also began to recall the smell of the town where we had finally gotten out. There was also a scent of stagnant water.

But that was as far as I could remember. The doors closed and the train moved off. Very occasionally in the twenty-three years since my mother's death, this recollection would rise in me on some chance prompting, but there was never any hint about what had happened on this occasion. It carried a whiff of false memory about it. Our house had been in the western suburbs along a private line. If we ever caught a train after dark, no matter where we were going it would no doubt seem to my child's mind that we were traveling a long distance. In no time it was late night. But I knew it was Sunday night. There was never any change in the fact that it seemed a false memory, and that it was Sunday night.

My mother died not on a Sunday, but soon after nine on Saturday. I spent the entire Sunday by her body.

"Ah, the poor thing," a voice said. I felt it came from the carriage in my memory, but from its tone I realized that the words came from my uncle, who had come running from their family home deep in Gifu Prefecture when he received the news. He was bewailing the fact that she had died at just sixty, after three long months of hospitalization. His words would no doubt have included pity that the hardships she had endured during and after the war had not been sufficiently rewarded. These words, that had lain hoarded inside this distant brother, sank deep into me. Suddenly my mother seemed a young woman. And truly, for some time after her breathing had stopped, her face had been a young one.

My uncle also died not long after. This memory of mine seemed to be a shadow thrown by an amalgamation of various formless memories that had crystallized together inside me around the nucleus of his pitying words. Over this shadowy projection hung that voice—no longer his own, indeed no longer even a voice, but merely an atmosphere. But then, even given that the memory was mere insubstantial shadow, whose voice could it be that muttered these words in the scene of that memory? These were not a child's words. It could only be that they emerged from my mother's mouth. Perhaps one night at the height of the fierce air raids during the war, she had gazed at her child of not yet eight years old, and pityingly declared that it would be better if I had never been born than that I should die such a terrifying death. This was the only situation in which I'd ever found myself sorrowed over and pitied in this way, either by parents or by others. Or at least I had no memory of another such experience.

It sometimes struck me that my mother's words were in fact spoken in pity for herself, a young woman caring for a child, and when this idea occurred to me it provoked a little shudder of regret. Then from that dim shadow again I would see the child's face, oddly meek, gazing up at the passenger straps swaying above him in the gloomy electric light of the carriage as he sat there dangling his short legs from the seat, and the thought then came that of the four children it was only myself, the youngest child, that our mother had taken along with her at such an hour.

Very occasionally it seemed to me that the voice in the dream was not the voice of a person seen in a dream, nor yet was it the voice of the dreamer; it was the compassionate voice of the dream itself. Yet I was not a vessel capable of resounding with such a voice as this, even if only as the shadow of a memory. A wry smile at last emerged from these thoughts as the train shot out from underground. The last light still lingered in the sky, and a moment later, gazing down as we crossed the bridge over the Arakawa, I saw that the grey stretch of water at the river mouth upstream held a red light from the cloudy sky above, a light that was not reflected back into the dusk but instead pooled into thick ropes of flowing color here and there over the river surface, with sometimes weirdly jasper-tinted veins of water threading the current, pouring down and away in a sinuous surge of water.

In the instant after the thundering from the railway bridge ceased, my ears rang with what seemed an auditory hallucination of the cry of a child. It seemed to me a sobbing that continued all night long, emanating from the ground floor of a large wooden building.

. . . . .

"Well, you've got an early start tomorrow," I said, preparing to leave, and then I glanced at the clock and saw that it was just after nine. It seemed surprisingly late for the hour. Each breath I took was still redolent with the scent of incense, though it must have long since burned itself out. Within this scent was another, that of warm human skin.

"Come on," replied Sugaike, "all I have to do is stroll downhill with a bit of light luggage on one shoulder. It's just a matter of taking the slow train

207

or the express, whichever comes first, from Higashi-Nakayama Station, then waiting for the special express at Keisei Funabashi Station, and I'll be at the airport in no time."

The sloping road of the next morning rose before my eyes. I had arrived in the early evening, however, so my sense of our exact location in Nakayama was hazy.

It must have been before eight that evening. Our meal trays had been removed from the room, and now Sugaike laughingly produced from his bag a bottle of what he identified as wine from Bohemia, and ordered a couple of glasses from the young girl in casual clothes who waited on us, apparently the daughter of the establishment. After some time we hear slow footsteps ascending the steep staircase, and a pale old lady well over seventy, who seemed to be the mistress of the inn, appeared. She exchanged leisurely greetings with Sugaike, then set about arranging things on the low table. "I'll do it," she said in a youthful voice, then moved to sit before the alcove, facing it. From her back, she appeared to be going through the process of lighting some incense; then she slowly got to her feet, and in her wake there rose, from the incense burner sitting alone in the plain little alcove, a faint thread of smoke.

The old lady was as mute as timelessness itself. She sat beside Sugaike, who likewise said nothing, vaguely watching as he pulled the cork. Then, when we two men had replaced our glasses and looked at each other, she spoke.

"I thought we'd be seeing you here before long. I put out the incense burner in readiness for you. We have your incense here waiting, of course."

Then she fell silent again.

"You have a fine memory," Sugaike said to the old lady, then he turned bashfully to me. "It's terribly like something we know, isn't it?"

Apparently, it had all begun when his eye happened to light one day on some Indian incense whose name he recognized, selling cheap in a shop in the city. He bought it, threw it into his bag, and had forgotten all about it when, one night at this inn while he was having a drink before sleeping, he was groping around in his bag when his hand came across this little box that had somehow got mixed up with his other possessions in there. He opened it up, propped a cone of incense on the ashtray, and managed to light it with his cigarette lighter. At this point, the old lady came upstairs in her nightclothes. "I wondered where the scent was coming from, and here it is," she said, and sat down by his bed. She remained sitting there, on and on, absorbed, remarking what a lovely scent it was, and how she seemed to recall smelling it somewhere when she was young. "Did the smell really reach you on the ground floor?" Sugaike asked wonderingly, and she replied, "I scented it quite clearly," using the elegant old expression "to scent." She then floored Sugaike by going on to add earnestly, "If that weren't the case,

I'd have to be here after sex, wouldn't I?" And then she added softly, "You're a serious sort of person, aren't you, sir, to be burning incense at this hour."

Sugaike said he had absolutely no knowledge of incense, but he found himself trapped by her admiration. Whenever he was planning to stay here, he would remember about the incense the way a fool will repeat his one joke, and sure enough, when he quietly lit a cone in his room there late at night, up would come the old lady. When the chilly weather arrived he worried that he'd be getting her out of bed in the cold, so he set about lighting the incense directly dinner was cleared away. and the old lady stayed kneeling there neatly for half an hour or more, her eyes silently following Sugaike's hand as he sipped the brandy he'd brought along. When she went downstairs, she said, "Please burn another cone before you go to bed, it will make me sleep better." In order to be sure he never arrived without the incense, he left it with her to look after.

She would come up the stairs at the appropriate moment, place the incense burner on the table, and wait there patiently for him to get around to lazily lighting the incense between drinks. Apparently her gesture of going to perform it herself at the alcove was a special expression of politeness toward me as Sugaike's guest.

"Isn't that so, ma'am?" Sugaike said at this point, turning to the old lady. She had been sitting there throughout, listening with the same happy smile to whatever was being said about her, and now her smile broadened to a childlike beam. I turned to look at Sugaike, realizing that she was rather hard-of-hearing, and he nodded back.

At this stage, I decided to break in, so I said, "Still, it's a rather erotic scent, isn't it? Kind of candid and rich. No doubt it's of vegetable origin, but at its heart this has the scent of the warmest part of an animal."

"That's probably right," Sugaike replied. "I'm always rather astonished at how inappropriate it seems for the night before an overseas business trip that is completely devoid of eroticism, but then it strikes me that imbuing myself with this sort of scent might actually help me put up with all that bleakness."

Our talk returned to the desultory conversation we'd been having before the old lady's arrival. Sugaike remarked that for a number of years now this sense of bleakness had accompanied his business trips abroad, and it wasn't because the work grew more difficult with the years, and more boring. Nor was it necessarily the result of the fatigue of increasing age, or personal exhaustion. He felt that it was rather the tiredness of the Japanese people in general, manifesting itself in him. Whatever it was, there was a sense that there'd been some failure of firmness at a critical point. The moment of opportunity had slipped from grasp at this point, in procrastination and expediency, leaving in its wake a gaping wound. Nor did the tension of any sense of crisis arise. Instead there was a deceitful ease. Language no longer functioned properly; whatever was being discussed, the debate never moved much beyond repeated assertions of the same thing. We were racing our engines and going nowhere; our wheels were bogged, spinning gaily in place. He could manage not to feel all this as long as he stayed inside the country, but when he left it he was forced to rely on his poor grasp of English. Handicap though this was, he could generally manage to get through the business at hand; but when it came to the question of whether the other party understood his own position, though he might get a certain degree of confirmation, there was no sense of a firm response. It seemed strange to him that things nevertheless proceeded to work out, at least for the moment. To be honest, this was a relief, yet he also felt negligent, and in the end he was beset by a nameless fear. This was more likely to overwhelm him when matters were going smoothly than when the negotiations had become mired in misunderstandings.

"Didn't you once say that you felt like a busy ghost?" he asked, and then his eyes went suddenly to the ceiling behind me, above the alcove, as if tracing the last wisps of rising smoke.

"I don't remember that," I replied, "but it's true, when I'm really busy I do begin to feel as if my shadow's getting thin." Drawn by his gaze, I listened for a sound behind my back.

Sugaike's eyes returned from the ceiling, and he resumed the conversation, in a voice slightly more tense than before. "It really is quiet around here, don't you agree? On those trips I come back to the hotel late at night, you know, and these days if I'm tired I'll jump straight in the shower, toss back a drink, set the alarm, and flop down on the bed. But in that time I'll have followed a detailed series of steps. At times like that, there's nothing like being painstaking about trivial things. If you're a bit distraught or mad, you see, it can emerge the next day as some quite unimaginable mistake or other. It's actually a fine piece of economy to hum along some mindless little tune, and do your best not to stir up your jangled nerves at this point."

Suddenly I had the urge to ask him, "Could it be that you're actually watching yourself when you're doing this?"

"You hit the nail on the head," Sugaike replied simply. "You watch and you say to yourself, Well done, my friend, you're a serious fellow. You're a serious ghost."

"Ghosts are serious things."

"You're serious about sleeping with women too, you tell yourself."

"Aha, that's good. But which is the watcher and which is the watched … you've arrived from some far place, or rather, you're headed somewhere far away."

"I just have a gut feeling that someone's watching. So it covers both, I'd guess. They're one and the same. And then the room fills with the scent of this incense." On both our faces was a look that seemed to be seeking the

210

origin of this scent.

The old lady suddenly took charge of the conversation. In a thin, high voice, she remarked, "That's right." Then she continued in a singsong voice, "It's the incense for the laying of souls."

I shot Sugaike a glance that said, "Hey, maybe she's heard something," and he too twisted his head disbelievingly. The old lady had a distant look in her eyes, but it was clear she was listening to something in the direction of the ceiling. She seemed to be intending us to notice it too. Sugaike turned to me and gave a brief grin. At last I too began to make out, coming from the ceiling behind me more or less above the alcove, a woman's soft intermittent sobbing—now swelling, now dying away again.

"For some reason it carries from two rooms away, and collects there in the ceiling just above the alcove," Sugaike told me.

"Couples sometimes stay here, you see," the old lady added by way of explanation.

. . . . .

"Let's call a cab for you, so you can ride as far as a handy station down the line."

"No, walking will give me a chance to clear my head after the drink. You just follow the road from in front of the inn, right? Once I'm out in front of the temple gate, I know the road. You just go on down the hill. I seem to remember there were quite a few branching streets before the gate, but I'll sniff my way along like a dog."

"They've marked off the boundary of the graveyard these days, so you won't find yourself in there by mistake. I wonder if our hostess has gone to sleep. I must light some incense for her."

It was well past ten. I calculated I ought to get up and leave once we'd reached the half hour, and as I thought this, my mind pondered the long way I would travel home. I decided that, since I was in this part of Nakayama, rather than take the same train I'd come on earlier that evening it would be better to go back the long way around that I used to take whenever I came to the racetrack here until about twenty years ago. That way there were less changes of train to have to negotiate, and I could sleep better.

A little earlier, I had asked Sugaike about himself. He hadn't exactly confessed, but his answer had been fairly detailed, and he mentioned that these were things he hadn't told anyone else. When his tale was over, I found myself asking, "Are you okay?" and was surprised at my own rather exaggerated reception of his words. "Setting off on your own after having told someone all this," I added rather lamely. But Sugaike seemed to have understood my mind. "No, it's better to be open about what needs to be open. It was in danger of becoming a kind of vacant space in me otherwise," he replied. And now I was the one who felt a difficulty in leaving.

211

"I remember it well," the old lady had said softly, her expression unaltered, her listening eyes still turned to the ceiling. "It was a rainy autumn evening. He was standing in the entrance hall, dripping wet. I knew immediately that he wasn't just someone on his way home from the races. The little red *higan* lilies were in flower, though it was past Higan, I remember. But he was coming back from visiting a grave. I could tell, because he smelled of incense. Sometimes there are people who visit a grave on their own after dark, you know, some days after the Higan period is over. Anyway, late at night when it was all quiet upstairs, this sweet smell came drifting down, and when I tiptoed up to see, there he was, burning this incense, just sitting there gazing at the smoke."

When her words faltered, Sugaike, who had been listening silently, signaled me with his eyes, then bent over towards her and asked clearly, "So when was this?"

"Ah, well," the old lady responded smoothly, "it would have to be forty years or so back by now."

I nodded. "We would have been about seventeen or eighteen," I said. She seemed to be responding when she came in with, "Yes, that's right. And since that time every year, sometime after Higan, he comes here to light incense. I rely on him for it these days. It's a great thing for a woman, you know, a dependable man." Having said this, the old lady lapsed back into muteness with a look of one who has not spoken, and the three of us sat there listening to the small voice above the alcove.

At length the old lady turned to me and made me welcome with effusive politeness, then stood to leave. She assured me that I must stay as long as I wished, since her daughter would be staying up late and could see me out when I came downstairs, and urged me to call anytime I felt inclined to stay the night. Then, leaving me in Sugaike's care, she went off down the stairs, walking perfectly firmly. I was left with the impression of surprisingly able speech and bearing.

"She seems to be attached to someone from back in the past," I remarked. "I guess at your age there's no sin in silently taking on the role she's projected onto you." When the old lady's footsteps could no longer be heard below, the ceiling above the alcove grew quiet as well. It seemed to me almost as if the embodiment of the old woman had risen and lodged there as a voice, or rather as a scent.

"It's a fine thing to be at an age when it's no sin, I must say," Sugaike said with a rueful grin. "That old lady has sniffed me out."

He began by explaining that it had only been for the last five years that he'd been coming to the inn. Then he suddenly came out with a confession. "It's not yet thirty years ago that a woman I knew died, you see. She had been diagnosed with cancer in her youth. A cruel thing. I stayed in the hospital with her for the last two weeks. I resigned from work to do it. For three whole years after she died I stayed single and unattached, a young man of around thirty, and didn't touch anyone."

As I listened, it was those long three years, rather than the tale of the woman, that fleshed themselves out inside me like a crazed lustfulness.

"This didn't involve the time I spent in Kanazawa when we used to drink together," he went on, beginning to be drawn back into the past. The woman was married at that time. When Sugaike returned to Tokyo he happened to run into her, and by then she was divorced and had been living alone for a year. She'd had some major surgery, and couldn't have any children. They stood talking for a while, then parted without exchanging addresses, but arranged to meet again in a month with the proviso that if something came up for one of them the other would forgive them for not showing up.

"I had a strong feeling she wouldn't come, you know. The place where we ran into each other was on the way back from the races, on the road leading to the temple back there, so the old lady's mistake isn't all that far-fetched, in fact. It wasn't a rainy day, and I didn't know about this inn. But actually a red *higan* lily was dangling from her hand."

I pondered the sense of distance in his calling her simply "a woman." Sugaike's story was now drawn back to the present. The old lady had begun mentioning the incense for the laying of souls that first time when she had come up while he was burning the incense, but Sugaike had diverted the conversation by wryly recalling a comic turn that was based on the same sort of thing. But when he'd been performing his incense ritual for her with no more than a vague sense that he had been partaking of some shadowy memory of hers for about two years, maybe on about the third occasion he'd been there he realized that she had grown to see him as someone dependable, perhaps from another generation, who was there to light incense in mourning for a dead woman. There was no grim fixation in her delusions when she spoke of them; she seemed to find ease in the fulfillment these private ideas provided for her. He, meanwhile, had come to a full realization of her misunderstanding only in the process of fitting himself naturally to the way she spoke, taking things slowly, and finding himself at one with her feelings, so his final realization came as no great surprise to him. He had only agreed with her gently that he was indeed a dependable, loyal sort of man. Even now, when her feelings deepened and she sought a response from him in the grip of a powerful emotion, he responded in this fashion.

"Yet although she seems to be slowly losing her grip on reality with the passing years, she never forgets about me, or about this 'dependable man.' As for me, I'm as busy as ever, and less and less able to think clearly, but I don't forget to come here and light incense. That's astonishing, you know," Sugaike concluded with a laugh.

The talk had begun to revert to light chat on other matters when I took up this earlier remark with the words, "But this woman …" For a moment

213

I wished I hadn't spoken, but it seemed to me that this question must be asked, as the fruit of the confession I had heard from him. "You say you stayed with her in the hospital till she died, but does that mean you would have taken care of everything after she died as well?"

"I performed a solitary wake in the hospital morgue from past midnight through the following dawn. In the morning her younger brother rushed in, so I handed things over to him and went home through the blinding sunlight. And that's the end of the story."

He showed no sign of being inclined to say anything further, and I fell silent, to let him know that I would ask no more. A yet-deeper calm seemed to descend over the room, from above the ceiling of the alcove.

It was Sugaike who broke the silence. "It takes lighting incense to recall her to my mind all these years later, so I couldn't say I come here to mourn her, but if the old lady chooses to see it as incense for the laying of a soul, then that's what it is. If she interprets it as the repentance of a man whose wrongdoing caused a woman's death, then I can be numbered among such men, I accept that. If that's the way I'm seen, that's how I come to feel. I begin to sense that it's not really such a mistake. Still, meaning no harm to the old lady, it does occur to me to wonder—if this really were honest-to-god soul-laying incense, whose soul would it be that was called down that long path as we offered this incense up to the gods and buddhas? Personally, I don't have the kind of quiet room inside of me that could welcome such a one. All I've managed in that way is the night spent by her body in that underground room; that degree of quietness is beyond reach in my life, and in the world in general. The awful clamor simply goes on increasing. When I light the incense here, you know, I think to myself that I've lived clamorously too, just like all the rest. And there's even something clamorous about such a thought. There's no escape."

Then his eyes slowly widened. "And yet every time, every single time, I feel somehow that I've all along been making the same excuses to myself. When the old lady is sitting here beside me, things grow calmer, ever so slightly. I've learned that there's an erotic quality to being a dependable man."

I saw in my mind's eye the frugal form of a man in the shower of a foreign hotel late at night, hoping to ensure a good night's sleep by letting the chilly water pummel the back of his neck, on and on. Then suddenly this figure disappeared, and all that was left was the sound of the falling water and the sweet scent of incense in the air. And it seemed as I gazed that the calm quietness hung there until it overflowed backward into the past, year upon year.

Brushing aside this vision, I turned my attention to a sound outside the room, and remarked, "Isn't that a drum out there somewhere?"

Sugaike listened too. "It sounds like a sutra ceremony. This area has a lot of temples, you know. It seems to have been part of a temple complex," he said. "We would have heard sutra drums off and on all evening if we'd been listening, you know."

"Now that you mention it, perhaps there was a sound earlier."

"It's not beating any more, though. When the sutras finish, the drumming ends with a bang. You notice the final drumbeat, and that's when you realize you've been hearing it."

After a pause, he murmured, "Apparently there were nights here in the old days when you could hear the sea."

"That woman spoke of hearing the sound of the sea when she was in hospital, too," he went on. "'Hold me,' she'd say, 'make love to me. I can hear the sea.'"

17

Vermillion Women

At the edge of the forest, I picked up a three-inch twig with seven or eight berries attached. The berries looked like they belonged to the *iigiri* tree, but no such tree was visible in the vicinity. A wintry wind gusted through. The previous evening, the wind had been mixed with rain, and a gale had been blowing till dawn. I placed the twig on the palm of my hand and held it to the light that filtered down between clouds, watching how the round berries changed color from vermillion to crimson. They were no larger than the little beads that decorate traditional combs, but they felt comfortable to the touch, I thought as I gazed. When the sun was shadowed, the vermillion receded into their depths. I found I couldn't simply throw them away.

When I carried the berries home and looked at them again indoors, the color was much duller. I put them on a far corner of my desk. As the afternoon deepened towards evening and the temperature began to drop, it seemed to me that occasionally from the corner of the desk the vermillion would flash up again. My winter-sensitive body eagerly sought out that subtle warmth. When night came, I put the twig up on the bookshelf behind me. Then, before dawn, I had a dream.

I was climbing a road at night. It seemed to me that the road climbed straight up toward the south from Yamagoe's house to Fujisato's. It's true that the two houses are within walking distance, and Fujisato's house is on an elevation, but the two are off to west and east of each other, and there could be no sloping road directly connecting them. A private railway line does run between the two. I was muttering such thoughts to myself as I climbed rapidly on and on, and the steeper it became the heavier my footsteps grew, as though the slope were indeed a real one. Then a woman slipped past me and went on ahead. A rich scent pooled in the road, and her back, shining a bright vermillion even in the darkness, drew me on as she walked before me, her loosened gait evidently nursing some pain that afflicted her lower back. I wondered whether the purplish coat she wore was somehow reflecting red from something around her, but as she drew away the vermillion only grew stronger, and seemed to swell about her like a gown. I was puzzling over the

216

strangeness of it when another woman slipped past me and moved ahead. The two backs were exactly the same. They both walked on up the road, almost merging, only the rhythm of their paces maintaining a subtle difference. I frowned to myself, thinking that it wasn't a very pleasant dream, and at this point another woman moved ahead of me, virtually brushing my side, so that now three backs walked before me. I felt a fourth approaching, and a shudder of *deja vu* ran through me, but I could not turn to look back. It seemed to me that there was some admonition against seeing that face. The slope at last evened out to become the top of an embankment, and I seemed to have been suddenly tumbled into the mud below, from whose darkness I watched the seven or so figures of the vermillion women climbing strung out against a whitening sky. By the time the woman in the lead had paled and disappeared, another woman had joined the rear of the procession, a shape still more brilliantly vermillion. Each time this happened, a dark, inhuman laugh echoed from somewhere beneath the earth.

. . . . .

Sugaike's woman had appeared on the road from the temple dangling a red flower. Sugaike did not mention whose grave she was visiting, and nor did I ask. I also avoided inquiring whether she had been buried in a grave there. Silence intervened. I thought of the distance of time that caused Sugaike to refer to the woman he had sat beside until death simply as "the woman." Sugaike lifted the lid of the incense burner that he had moved to the table after the old lady left, breathed on the dying embers of the incense, and gazed until a thin thread of smoke rose again. I guessed that as he gazed, in Sugaike's mind might be an image of the woman, red flower hanging downwards from her hand, standing still on the temple road, perhaps because the man had called to her, perhaps because she had noticed him. When he closed his mouth abruptly after mentioning that a red *higan* lily was dangling from her hand, I had clearly sensed regret there. It didn't sound as though he were suggesting if it hadn't been for this the rest would not have followed. Rather, it seemed to me that his later regret was that, given what happened subsequently, he had not made love to her that day.

A month passed, and there was no contact from Sugaike. He should long since have returned, but it's true he had said the trip would be a long one. He had mentioned that this time he would be in a rather difficult position in the job he had to do there. Apparently the work involved the organization of a flexible team including various internal and external medium-sized companies, as well as small companies and independent individuals, to undertake a one-off job. A section of Sugaike's own company was taking part, so he was being sent to ascertain a number of details, but there was no clear sense of precisely where he should go to complete his mission. It may well be, he said, that setting off like this was quite useless. Furthermore, if he found himself engaged in real negotiations while there, it was unclear whether his position would be that of a representative of his own company or an employee on loan to an outside organization. He began to explain the details of how this would put him in an anomalous position when he came back to Japan and returned to work as usual, but then he realized that he was broaching areas quite outside my understanding, and ended by admitting with a laugh that though he felt he had an excellent grasp of the matter, when it came to explaining it to an outsider for whom the technical language was incomprehensible, he began to feel he that he himself was out of his depth.

I can hear the sound of the sea, the woman had said. Hold me, make love to me. But had he responded to her plea? This question returned to hang in my mind again and again, and each time I brushed it away with the thought this it was pointless for a third party to consider such a thing. I belatedly amended my thoughts by telling myself firmly that these were wild words muttered from the midst of a delirium, at a moment when her suffering had eased. I saw eyes fluttering lightly as with laughter as they faded and grew distant. Sugaike would have nodded. The sound of the sea is always audible, wherever the hospital may be. I too almost reached the point where I could hear that sound. This was not that occasion three years ago, but when I was fifteen. I had begun to see before me an expanse of shining blue. It was in a hospital that stood on the edge of a dirty canal. At Nakayama, in fact, the sea had once been not so far away. Perhaps the valley that spread out to the south had acted as a kind of sound box to funnel in the faint sound from the sea. I imagined that perhaps on quiet nights sharp ears could detect not only the sound of waves but the horns from passing boats. Or it may be that even now, when this area that once held the sea's sound had become separated from the coast by ten or twenty kilometers thanks to landfill, it still retained its nature as a reverberator and held somewhere below the level of hearing the agitated voice of the ocean.

Yet, ever since Sugaike had spoken of the night he had spent alone with the corpse in the mortuary room, the thought of water had been in my mind. The subject of the sea had not yet appeared at that point. What I was aware of was not a sea sound, but the sound of falling water striking a hard floor. I could only conclude that Sugaike's wry mention long before of taking a lonely shower late at night in the hotel room had somehow leapt the intervening space and connected itself inside me with the hours of quietness in that mortuary. Yet though I had had a similar experience in the hospital mortuary when my mother died, I could recall no sound of falling water there. Nor had I heard the sound of water from downstairs while Sugaike and I talked. It was just that within me water incessantly fell and struck the floor. And with its incessant sound, all sense of human presence disappeared.

What was it that Sugaike had done as he sat there beside the dead woman? As for me, I continually gulped down the bitter tea that the nurse had left me in the teapot with the thermos of hot water. When my stomach rebelled at the bitterness, I added hot water, pouring it as if it were sake, as I sat there cross-legged, my head jutting forward from a curved back, watching the incense slowly burn down. From time to time, a chilly drop of water would splash onto the back of my hand from the tea cup I clutched, and I realized that I had dozed off as I watched the incense stick shorten. It was a short snatch of sleep, in which my body barely swayed, but apparently it would suddenly slip deeper, and when I awoke I would sometimes have an erection.

At last the tiny window grew whiter. I was in a small wooden building that stood apart from the hospital wings, and already I had become aware of quiet movements of people beyond the window. I listened half-dazed to these movements for a while longer, then, when the room had grown paler, I stood up abruptly, sensing a breath in the room. I turned off the naked light bulb, lit a fresh stick of incense, and went to stand in front of the window that let in a little light just level with my head. Outside, I could see the road climbing up from the hospital's rear entrance, a sunken area beside it filled with dwarf bamboo, and there, up to his thighs amongst it, a white-haired man wielding a sickle was for some reason culling select bamboo stems. I stared calmly out at him for a long time. As I stood there, the man straightened himself and looked up suspiciously at the window where I stood. Then he slowly turned his eyes away, his expression continuing to suggest he had caught a glimpse of something, cut one more stem of bamboo, then turned his back and made his way out through the thicket, turning once at the top of the slope to look back.

During this time, the body that lay behind me felt to me more than my mother—felt that of a female parent, of a woman. In the instant when I turned back from the window, that figure seemed to me to lie there with hair drenched, and on the patch of flesh exposed at the neck where the collar of her fresh gown neatly crossed to form a *V*, I registered a faint remaining glint of wetness.

There are times when I spend my days feeling as though all communication with friends has ceased, though on the face of it nothing between us has changed, I realize when I pause to think about it. One day, I found myself thinking with a wry grin that it's as if all these friends were dead, or, closer to the mark, as if I myself had died. It's perhaps another kind of self-sufficiency, I thought, and indeed, the sort of person I am could attain no finer self-sufficiency than this.

There was no communication from Yamagoe for almost five months after the end of June. This was understandable in a young person, whose interest in someone his parent's age might all too naturally cease, but I found myself recalling him whenever occasional guests in my busy and reclusive life made some passing mention of the connection between the poisoned gas attack at the end of June and a certain new religious group. One guest told me about a representative of the police authority concerned with the case, who firmly asserted in an interview with the press that such a thing could never happen again, and when asked why he could speak with such confidence, more or less replied that he left that up to our imagination. When I heard this, I had a premonition that there might be a phone call from Yamagoe even the next evening, bursting to ask me what I thought of this—but when I checked with my visitor, I learned that in fact the interview had happened more than a month ago.

At this stage, Yamagoe's "Hullo?" at the other end of the phone seemed almost to come from inside me. It wasn't the first word he spoke, but something he said after we had been talking for some time. I was in the middle of describing to him a man hunched as if caught in the act of some crime, a dark stench rising from him, who from time to time turns a slow chill glance back over his shoulder into the midsummer, midday room, when my voice suddenly hoarsened and I ceased to speak. We were talking about premonitions. Yamagoe had cut in dubiously with the comment that anyone whose premonition proves wrong should feel humiliated, and I had spontaneously responded that in fact it was the true premonition that should cause shame. Aware that what I proceeded to say did not provide any evidence for this assertion, I launched into a detailed account of a childhood memory, then words failed me when I found myself overwhelmed by the vivid image of the distressed man I was describing. I had reached the point where I explained how he had shamefacedly muttered the words "It's despicable," but as I spoke this long-unheard expression, what I tasted was not the man's own shame but rather the blame of others.

At length, I heard Yamagoe's "Hullo?"

I must have passed it off with a laugh, changed the subject, and made a quick end to the conversation, but I found I had completely forgotten what was said before we hung up. I didn't feel I needed to concern myself over this slip of memory, since the conversation had happened five whole months earlier, yet I had an unnerving feeling that somehow I had simply hung up after Yamagoe had spoken.

On the other hand, I could also hear Yamagoe's voice from the midst of that gap of time, when I had surely hung up, continuing to speak. "It's Yamagoe. Something strange has happened," came the voice, a kind of double delusion that made me wince at the realization that it looped endlessly back to the beginning of the evening's conversation.

Yamagoe phoned near midnight that evening to tell me that when he had heard the news he was wracked with a strong sense that he had already heard somewhere that such an incident would occur. He spoke as if hoping that I could supply him with an answer to the conundrum of how or where this might have happened. Listening to him, I thought of the ruins of the Akasaka hotel. Its tragic frame still stood to this day, unaltered since that day twelve years earlier when it had burst into flames and killed so many. Yamagoe had once spoken to me of how eerie he found that skeleton. He felt a chilly sense that people were gazing down on him from the scorched and blackened windows of those floors above, he said, and he wondered whether some evil gas was not flowing again from those windows. A gas, he said, composed of the aggregate of all the hatred and vengeance that for long years had gathered and distilled itself in the eyes of those dead who stood at the windows, until it overflowed and began to hiss softly out into the atmosphere.

But perhaps rumor of that incident had indeed been around somewhere before it happened. Still, I found it hard to imagine that a young man of barely thirty, with the power of memory of such a youth, could fail to recall where he had heard such a rumor. Perhaps some new and nonexistent crime had managed to become tangled in with all the criss-crossings of the various rumors predicting this and that calamity that floated about in the world, or if not tangled then hidden somewhere within as a possibility. There was surely a dark desire that yearned to enmesh itself with precisely the images of crime that one recoiled from, which everywhere became the fertile ground from which rumors were born, or generated them retrospectively after an incident had occurred. Undoubtedly, what lay within Yamagoe as he saw those eyes pouring poison down from the ruined hotel windows was one such example. Perhaps, too, he had felt down his back a shiver of horror at the feeling that he had not only heard rumor of this incident somewhere, but had somewhere spoken of it himself.

Recalling Yamagoe's "Hullo?" it now felt to me as if it contained a slight hint of rebuke. If it happened that the eyes of those sacrificial dead looking down on Yamagoe from the blackened windows, those eyes whose twelve years of hoarded rage had flowed together and distilled itself at last, also contained the eyes of Yamagoe's father who had died of cancer the same year, then my thoughtless words would surely consititute a kind of sacrilege.

A poison like pity, Yamagoe had said. Then he had added with a laugh, Not a poison that has any effect. His father had from time to time cursed the world for its decadence, so his mother said, and Yamagoe had passed this information on to me. No doubt this had been the aversion of fastidious youth. He had chosen to give up his precious job, in an age when finding work was a difficult feat. Then he began to live with an older woman, and the exigencies of life had forced him back into the work force, where he had continued to be employed until struck down by illness. I guessed he was an earnest man who had been impelled by a woman to lead a normal life. But he chose to see this woman, who as far as I could tell was nothing but reliable and submissive to him, as belonging to the decadent world. Three children had been born in quick succession when they began living together. I had no idea how long his uncompromising attitude continued, but then he lost his eldest son at six to a car accident. Two years after her father's death, his daughter chose to leave home while still a student, and at the time she spoke resentfully to her little brother of her belief that their father could not have delighted in their birth as a normal father would, and that someone who secretly so loathed the world could not have loved his children. Hearing this, the boy had privately been struck by her harshness. Then, three years after his death, this sister had died in another accident. Eight years later, the previous year, the last remaining child, Yamagoe, had begun to share the house with a woman who moved from her own apartment to help him look after his sixty-one-year-old mother. During her illness, his mother had told this girl in more detail the things about his father that she had only spoken of in a fragmentary way to him over the course of many years, or at any rate this was the impression he had. Despite this feeling, however, he apparently failed to ask or could not ask these details of the tight-lipped girl. But no, it was over a year ago that I had heard all this from him. They were a young couple in a physical relationship, and since they were still together, all this had surely been cleared up between them long since. Yamagoe had mentioned in June that she was now inclined to have a child at last. The fact that he still referred to her by her family name was no doubt just a habit of speech when talking to me, or perhaps it was a sign that where I was concerned time did not pass.

Still, the memory of his muttering "The dead are truly stubborn" stayed with me. He told me that, in a world that was prepared to compromise any principled stance for the sake of material gain, his father's obstinacy was such that, when circumstances coincided to reveal it, seemed quite autonomous. At this point I retreated into humor by jokingly bringing up the subject of ghosts.

That passage of time that Yamagoe had seen in the skeleton frame of the hotel building was also the twelve years since his own father's death. I was all too painfully aware of this fact as I counted up the years. If the dead are stubborn, how much more stubborn are the living. I instantly sensed that the obstinacy exposed in that skeleton surely was one that I too shared. Yet I fled. As Yamagoe pursued me with the statement that it seemed people were gazing down on him from those high windows, I sought an escape route to the plane crash that had happened the same year, by asking after the friend whose father had died in that accident and who was now ill. But Yamagoe's answer blocked my way. He committed suicide, he informed me.

A silence had intervened, then Yamagoe said, his eyes turning to the wood that flashed wildly white in the sunlight, "It seemed to me that perhaps some bad gas was flowing out of that place again now." This would have been at he beginning of June, less than a month before Yamagoe had telephoned after that incident occurred. We were sitting side by side on the bleachers in the park, some time just before noon on a day reminiscent of the fierce heat of summer. Two months later, also around noon, also gazing at the hot summer forest from the same place, Fujisato told me he'd been crazy. He had a feeling of bliss, he also said. Remembering now, it seemed to me that then too the crowns of the forest trees had flamed suddenly white.

And hadn't the same scent also hung in that air, two months later though it was?

. . . . .

On a cloudy day, an elderly man was flying paper planes in the park. It was the latter half of November. The previous day had been beautiful weather, with a soft breeze, but today the clouds hung heavy over the sky, the breeze had ceased, and a quiet chill had descended. In the pre-noon Monday park, the only sound was the noisy calling of birds; no other human figure was visible. The man now stood on the rough-hewn table where on fine days picnicking families would spread their lunch; earning himself this extra height, he proceeded to take out from the paper carrier bag one after another, not little paper airplanes but structurally sound hand-made paper gliders, and launched them one by one planing out through the air from shoulder height. I stood to watch in the shade of a tree some way distant, so as not to disturb his pleasures.

Retired men also turn up in the park during the daytime. I sometimes came across a man playing the bamboo *shakuhachi* flute under the pergola by the path round the pond. Sights such as this were wonderfully redolent of days gone by, but there were also many photographers. They weren't taking mere snapshots. They used tripods, and carried professional bags full of all manner of lens, and they waited patiently for the right light to photograph the scenery, or plants and flowers. Whenever I saw such men, I thought of the urges that had never been fulfilled in youth but instead were lost in the busy pressures of later life, and was made aware of the fact that I belonged to the same general generation as these men. I also sometimes saw a man practicing the saxophone along the avenue leading to the park, with a breathlessness that spoke of a gap of forty years in his playing. Nevertheless, what he played was swing jazz.

When a white glider was launched from his hand, it would slip along stably through the glimmering air until, due to the lack of wind, it would make a sharp dive ten meters or so away; but unexpectedly it then swerved again suddenly, seeming to be borne up on a faint air flow just above the ground, and described a beautiful arc to right or left. Sometimes one would lift lightly into the air again to come curving down in another long arc. I watched, transfixed by the instant of landing, thinking that no doubt there was a skill to the timing and moment each one left the hand, yet even so, what elegant flights they made. As I continued to gaze, I began to feel as if I too could faintly register that slight, almost non-existent current of air that flowed just above the ground. At length, about ten gliders lay motionless here and there on the lawn, and the man got down off the table and slowly gathered them up. He was neatly dressed in coat and leather shoes, and as he departed, crisp clean paper carry-bag hanging from one hand, he might have been someone who had dropped into the park on his way home after doing some morning shopping in the city. I thought again of that precise figure standing on the picnic table, paper glider poised at his shoulder, testing the breeze.

Walking through the wood, I saw that the ground was scattered everywhere with twigs of red berries like the one I had picked up and carried home, and ten days earlier thrown in the rubbish bin when I came across it, now withered and wrinkled, on top of the bookshelf. They gleamed on the forest floor with a still more vivid light in the cold pale sunlight. From evening, rain began at last to fall. Late at night, I thought at my desk that that kind of paper airplane was the work of a third year student in the national school system during the war—the gliders fourth year students made were a more realistic model. I went on to think that my own third year had been the year after the war ended, and in my second year in fact my schooling had been frequently interrupted and more or less brought to a halt by the constant air raids. My thoughts were just drawing me into a lazily relaxed state of mind, when my mind flashed suddenly awake again with the sensation that a long-stagnant pool of time had suddenly begun to flow once more, a sensation that repeated the feeling earlier that day as the white glider had arced swiftly on the breeze.

Fujisato poises his upright hand loosely before his mouth as if in one-handed prayer, and waves it slowly to and fro, a gently bewildered smile on his face. He goes on waving his hand, while all eyes gather on him. The hand is remarkably gnarled and impressive. Seeing him, the faces of the audience break into the same smile, and the tension falls visibly from backs and shoulders. They are relaxed in the silence, no longer awaiting the next words. You've just died, they seem to be saying, let us take on our share of this with you for a while. Outside the window, the spring sunlight pours down. It falls too on the fierce wind that still moans shrilly against the wall, melts the shudder of horror at that fall, and shines also over his daughter as she squats low in the garden. And that same light pours as well over the figure of the man who stands two years later beneath the blasted hackberry tree, his gaze traveling up the broken trunk all the way to its canopy of twigs, summoning some dark memory.

Standing beneath the hackberry, I looked over into the little children's play area. I dislike invading places in any way. On that occasion, there was definitely no sign of anyone in the park. When I finally became aware of approaching footsteps behind me, at the edge of my vision I thought I saw a house above a set of stone steps, and saw a figure coming running down the steps. I later thought it odd that the illusion involved a longer stretch of time than the instant I must in fact have entertained it, which backtracked from the moment I became aware of the sound of footsteps. But it seemed not all of this experience was illusory. I had felt since before the footsteps became audible that someone was running towards me from somewhere. When I turned to find the old man standing in the middle of the park, bathed in sunshine, his tense expression made me wince at the thought that he may have disapprovingly detected my fantasy of a moment earlier, of a couple engaged in breathless sex.

This summer I had made a rather tasteless reference to the old expression of "having to wait a hundred years for the right moment," and Fujisato had replied with a heavy earnestness that our forty years had indeed been longer. When I registered that someone was standing at the foot of the hackberry, he told me, I already knew it was you. This was no mistake, of course, but was the I that he saw precisely this I? In the instant he recognized me, had he not come running, to glare at that figure of forty years of death?

Yet we two had met three times in the year or more since then, and on each occasion Fujisato had seemed filled with calm relief, and had spoken of how he allowed the madness in himself—I was the one who afterwards worried belatedly over the crisis that had already passed for him, and on occasion had felt myself an empty room, in which only the imaginative impulse toward another had now fluttered in the air, now disappeared—and when at last I felt in the paper glider's swift arcing motion that time had long ceased to flow in me, I saw before my eyes Fujisato's face, with the hand waving gently to and fro before the unspeaking mouth.

It was odd that, although all these memories were directly from the last one or two years, they now passed through me filled with a sense of distance.

. . . . .

Past midnight, I heard the crying of a baby. It came from below the stairs. The crying continued till dawn whitened the sky. I was in the two-story mortar-frame hospital that stood beside an oil-rank drainage canal. I had lain in the second floor ward unable to get up since two weeks earlier, when I had been carried to the hospital for surgery, so I had no way of imagining the layout of the place when I heard voices.

The mother squatted hunched over and weeping by the ticket gate before the stairs to the underground connecting passageway. What's the matter? the girl asked, and she replied that she was sad because she had lost her ticket. Then, leading the boy and girl by the hand, she had gone down the long passage, and leapt from the station platform in front of a train. The mother died instantly. She was suffering from tuberculosis. The little girl lost a leg, and when she arrived at the hospital she seemed past saving from loss of blood, but she was fully conscious, gave her name and address, and before she fainted she explained clearly that the three of them had caught the train to the terminus where the event had happened. She also explained what had happened at the ticket gate. Perhaps her mother had told her there, or perhaps it had been before they left home, but she knew that they were to die together. She was five years old.

The three-year-old boy had been thrown back onto the platform, where he had rolled like a ball.. He had lost consciousness, but suffered only bruising. The mother had held her daughter in one arm, but I heard that at the last moment she had thrust her son back with her other hand. He was carried to the same hospital and left in a separate room after treatment, where he slept deeply, then woke long after midnight and began to cry for his mother and sister. I don't know whether he cried continuously till dawn. I myself was moaning all night. I had complications from peritonitis, at that time considered almost certainly fatal, and from early evening I had been wracked with pain. Exhausted from my own groans, I sank into a heavy aching sleep, to wake from time to time, a moan echoing in my ears, and hear the child crying. For a brief time I would feel that my own endless pain had floated me out the door of my room, and it was myself crying downstairs. I had been carried up those stairs on a stretcher after my first surgery, my lower body anesthetized, so I knew that there was a landing half way up where the staircase turned, and that the steps creaked. The following evening, I was carried down those stairs, which did indeed emit a dark creak. Before this second surgery, my parents informed me that the worst may come to the worst. I was fifteen.

It was only ten days after it happened that I learned of the tragedy. Then, one day, a little boy was standing at the door to my hospital room, dressed in a white and indigo cotton hospital robe, his little head held at an inquiring tilt. He fearfully checked my complexion as I sat up in bed, then finally gave a happy laugh, and ran into the room, his head still to one side. The old lady in traditional trousers who promptly pursued him into the room told me that his head was still a little tilted from the aftereffects of the bruising. I learned that she was spending her days living at the hospital with him, and that she wasn't his grandmother but someone who'd had intimate dealings with the family for many years. Her elegant features suggested that she had been a great beauty in her day, but the upper lip bore the signs of a faint scar, which made the head doctor at the hospital remark admiringly that it showed considerable medical skill for its time. Apparently long ago at the very same station she had tried to throw herself under a train, but when she came to her senses she found herself instead running along with all her might beside it.

Little by little I also began to notice the lean figure of the gentle-looking father who sometimes called at the hospital. He had the habit of coming along the corridor and then pausing at the child's room to remove the regulation hospital slippers before he went in, which made him seem extremely diffident. The boy himself was growing round and plump. He had very fair skin. He quickly grew familiar with me, and was always wanting to play, which I began to find quite annoying.

One day, as the head doctor watched the boy with his tilted head pattering happily up and down the corridor, he told her that the lad should recover completely if he could manage to put up with a little more time spent in traction.

I rather rudely broke into the conversation at this point to remark that if the boy survived without aftereffects, he would surely make it to forty-five, and I wondered whether there really would be no permanent damage to the bones of his neck ... and then, something white went arcing swiftly through the darkness, days had passed since that quiet cloudy afternoon, the late night train stopped at the station before my own, the doors opened and a cold wind blew in, and as I stretched my neck to stop myself slipping off to sleep, there on the seat diagonally across from me, as if poised waiting for this moment, a young woman was bowing in my direction. Before I could make out that it was the woman who lived with Yamagoe, a vermillion-tinged confusion rose up in me. She mildly acknowledged my hastily returned bow, then turned to look ahead of her again, apparently pondering something, a smile flickering on her lips. I thought I detected reddish patches on her pale face, and looked more closely, wondering if perhaps it was the face of pregnancy, and at that moment another woman of about the same age went out the door, as she did so casting a quick firm glance diagonally down at the seated woman. That serene, somehow distant profile, that lost itself in the crowd beyond the window, reminded me of the expression of Fujisato's daughter after she had looked carefully at someone.

As the train drew out of the station, Torizuka, still facing forward, gave me an open smile.

18

Before the Earthquake

Toritsuka greeted me formally just outside the ticket gate, where she arrived a moment before me. "How is Yamagoe these days?" I asked in reply. I hadn't heard from him in six months. "Well, thank you," she responded, then lowered her eyes and drew her elbows in against her sides, as if surprised at her own thin clear voice. There was nothing more to be said. Our mutual "Good night" as we parted to the left and right seemed to glow redly as it hung in the air somewhere beyond us.

I stood waiting in front of the lowered railway crossing gates, and just before the roar of the approaching train drowned it out, my ear was drawn by a man's voice behind me saying, "Looking back on it, the wound when I fell wasn't as deep as you'd expect." "You'd think something would have to come of it all, but perhaps it doesn't, eh? The thing just drags on for years," another man responded, and the first replied, "Four years it's been now. I just kept busily opening up the wound again." "You were being driven into a corner, and the worse it got the more extraordinary you became, didn't you? No memory of when you slept or when you ate. You don't want to call yourself a sacrifice of those 'bubble economy' years, but still ..." and at this point the voice was overwhelmed by the roar of the train. It passed the crossing and drew up at the station platform, and as it did I heard, "But he's lasted four years, hasn't he? It makes you pity him to think of it, really. But just you wait and see, there'll be odd things happening all over the place, things won't be able to hold together." At this point the crossing gate lifted, and when I turned to look as I crossed the chilly tracks, there was no sign of the two men whose voices I had heard.

As I set off for home along the dark road, I wondered if it had been a voice talking to itself. Perhaps someone had been taking both parts of the conversation, I thought, and I even seemed to see the distressed and wrinkled face, but just as I was about to look back once more towards the crossing, I was prevented by a quick patter of footsteps approaching from behind. I sensed a scream within the sharp high clatter of the footsteps and slowed my pace to let the person pass, imagining a woman hastening home, afraid of the cold shivering night road, but my own male legs still strode ahead of hers, and though I heard the breath along the frozen road, the footsteps approached no nearer. I now began to sense something grim in my own alertly expectant form ahead of her, and the puzzling thought occurred to me that if I were a man who found all escape blocked in life, at this moment I would be in a great flurry of emotion, perhaps not even aware of how the sound of those footsteps exposed my own physical state. And then the footsteps ceased. The person seemed to have turned off into a side street.

Now only my own footsteps echoed through the quiet of the single stretch of road I walked. The sound was perfectly firm and even. Walking like this along a cold and windless road just before the symptoms of my paralysis of the limbs had become evident, I had listened to the strange decorousness of my own footsteps. Something was growing clear and transparent inside me with these steps. I had no premonition that any disturbance would soon appear in my gait. Yet, turning the corner at the end of the road, suddenly my feet had stumbled weirdly. I glanced down, half expecting to see a hollow that had caught my foot, and walked on. This was four years ago.

I rounded the corner in a long gentle curve, to avoid any repetition of my stumble, and registered again the strange firmness of my knees, when from the dark of the little park on one corner of the crossroads a pale face floated up, and there was Torizuka, slowly bowing to me from beneath the dead cherry tree.

. . . . .

"I have a favor to ask," she said, walking straight over to me. "Could I ask you to keep a secret?"

I looked into her face, noting the expression of determination. For a moment I imagined being asked to take over a baby.

"Would you be kind enough to listen to my story?" she asked instead.

"Be kind enough to listen," she repeated, her eyes wide with tension. "I'll go home after this, and tell Yamagoe that I met you in the train. I imagine that it won't be long before he gets in touch with you by telephone. If he asks you then, please tell him I said all this. If he doesn't ask, please keep it hidden inside you. He's bound to ask sometime. If by chance he doesn't telephone and you don't hear from him for a long time, please forget what I've told you. I'll be forever grateful to you."

Here her shoulders drooped, and she started breathing faster. I gathered that she had run after me, then come round ahead of me via a side street.

"When you say 'a long time,' how long do you have in mind?" I asked. I privately compared my sense of time with that of a young person.

"Not long," Torizuka replied. "About two months. If you haven't heard by the end of January, please forget everything."

I was startled at the unexpected shortness of the time, and wondered what it was all about.

"But is this a good thing for you, and for Yamagoe?"

"Yes, it's something I want to do before we get married."

There was a gaiety in her voice, and I was silenced.

"I believe you," I said at last, moved at the words I had heard so often before.

"Please do," she replied, her eyes beseeching me.

"Perhaps," I said, broaching the conversation, "it has to do with Yamagoe's deceased mother?"

Torizuka nodded. A calmness emanated from her. The nod was something that proceeded from deep within her.

"It's probably enough just to hear that that's what it's about. I'll keep the contents safe and secret as a blank."

Torizuka gazed at my eyes, which were filling with sympathy, and shook her head. She shook it calmly several times.

I decided that if I were to break that gaze and hear her tale, I must first move the situation beyond the present-tense moment. I looked around, and my eye lit on the red glow of a cigarette machine on a street corner a little way off.

"I'm going to go over there and get some cigarettes," I said. "I'll take my time. Please think again while I'm gone, and if you feel the slightest hint of regret about all this, just run away without a word."

"I will," replied Torizuka with a nod.

I had turned my back on her when I looked back to say, "There's a road out onto the main street from that corner. I may run away myself." She twisted her body a little, and smiled.

It's true, I thought as I set off. The moment I buy the cigarettes I may just forget the whole thing. And as I walked away, I felt my back give off an aura of old age.

·　·　·　·　·

It seemed that Torizuka had kept the story completely to herself till now. I settled down to listen, assuring her that I would ask no questions, and she thanked me and began. She spoke with the gingerly care of one who is handing over a delicately wrapped object, intent on preserving it intact; she spoke with moderation, with nothing stiff or grim in her tone, her words wrapped in the warmth of an emotion long nursed.

"To begin with," she said, "I should say that Yamagoe's mother told me quite a lot about her earlier life when the two of us were alone, but I must admit that at the time I understood nothing." Here she looked carefully into my eyes, gauging my reaction, and when I nodded, her tension fell away. "I haven't been able to completely dispel his suspicion," she went on, "that my

230

silence is covering for his dead mother, for the dead members of the family, and that I really know the truth. Even if I can do away with it for the most part, he still remains racked with suspicions that we two women must have talked together in detail, so if he asks you what I've said, please tell him I said this, and then I'm sure he'll accept it."

She went on to defend him by pointing out that in fact, he had good reason to be suspicious, since she had felt in two minds about things for quite a long time after his mother died. After his mother had taken to her bed, she had called Torizuka to her a number of times when her son was out, and confessed to her before she joined her dead husband that in fact there had been a mistake. Her husband had seen it all along, and had devoted himself lovingly to his oblivious wife, and taken on the task of preventing her from slipping any further into error, something he could not bear the thought of happening. She had been thoroughly scolded, and she believed that he had forgiven her without her saying anything in response, so she had worried no further about it. She said that she even forgot that such a mistake had ever been made.

At that stage, the mother was saying quite a number of odd things, so Torizuka hadn't really taken all this in fully, apart from an initial surprise at hearing it. It didn't sound as though she had had a wild youth, and the expression "a mistake" suggested that it hadn't been a frequent problem, so Torizuka thought it not really surprising that she should have forgotten the event. Yet she didn't doubt the veracity of the story. The sick woman held Torizuka with a clear gaze as she spoke. Drawn in by that earnestness, Torizuka in turn listened earnestly. She didn't nod, but she told herself that while she was listening she must be willing to believe what she heard, and she must not disturb that gaze. It turned out that what the sick woman wanted to communicate was that she had been happy to have met her husband and spent her life with him. Although it would have been not much more than twenty years that they spent together before he died, she repeatedly spoke of thirty years.

The story was told over a number of occasions. It always began with the confession of the mistake, and because the sick woman soon grew tired, it never proceeded very far. She spoke of how she had spent her life innocently relying on him, but even though he had forgiven her everything, he had never believed her. She went on tearfully that though he hadn't believed her, he had looked after her well and had been truly kind to her.

She also spoke of how all his life he had been conscious of the decadence of the world, something beyond her own ken. Since he must look after a family, it was necessary to abide by the ways of the world, and he undertook to observe its rules precisely; this responsibility he fully accepted, but all the while he watched in silence. He never complained, nor excused himself for anything. He watched his children grow with sorrowing eyes. He always said it was a wonderful thing.

When he lost his six-year-old son Sakae in 1966, he cried aloud that this wasn't the way it was supposed to be. The mother broke down and wept, lamenting that the automobile should have sped crashing so deep into their lives. But the father groaned in reply that it was all his own fault, he who had made the child in the first place, and then he fell silent. He never spoke another resentful word about the event. The mother wept again on the seventh night after her son's death, declaring that it must be accepted as fate and that they must dedicate themselves to looking after the remaining children. From the following morning she set herself to be strong, and set to work single-mindedly to ensure that nothing happen to her other children. Then one Sunday morning, some time after the hundredth-day anniversary of the death, she noticed her husband to one side gazing at the two children who were squatting down playing in a patch of sunlight in the living room. His eyes were full of pity, and he himself seemed lost in darkness. Seeing him, she felt suddenly that today she had at last recovered from a long period of being so distraught with mourning for her firstborn that she left the childcare to him. The four-year-old daughter Megumi pretended she was unaware of her father's gaze, and continued to play. Little Hitoshi, a year younger, sometimes glanced in his direction with an embarrassed smile.

"And then both of them …" the sick woman began to murmur, but here the thought trailed off. Torizuka took it to mean that she was thinking of the fact that first her eldest son, then her husband had died, and then three years later her daughter was killed in another car accident. She sat stroking her till she slept, her hand registering the quiet sobs, but the words "both of them" bothered her. She asked Yamagoe about it later, and he replied with a laugh, "It means I'm dead too. I've even known her to number me among the dead to my face, in fact."

But on another day, when she was again confessing her "mistake" to Torizuka, she suddenly said gaily, "My married life was a happy one, you know. I had three children by him." Yet even then, not a shadow of the later loss of two children darkened her tone. It was now some time since her hospitalization had begun, and she was growing weaker. She spoke of how happy she was when her husband remarked on the pretty innocence of children. He had often been amazed at what a strange thing a woman's womb was. Sometimes, after an episode of fierce criticism, he would say at the end of an evening when he had treated her with great gentleness, "We've had children, you know, three of them. I remember it."

As the sick woman's voice grew weaker and hoarser, there was an increasing brightness to whatever she talked about. "Oh, I was a shameless woman," she might say regretfully, but there was a sense even here that she had just awoken from a happy dream. "I'd just clean forget again, you see, as soon as he forgave me and was kind, no matter how he'd berated me, and how I'd cried and apologized at the time. 'You're a blessed woman,' he'd say to me. It wasn't irony, either. Just the other day he gazed at me and said, 'You really are blessed, you're fecund …'"

There was no way to grasp the chronology of the stories she told. Torizuka often could not follow when an event had happened, or from the midst of what memory she was speaking. At the slightest break in her words, the topic could swing through a period of up to thirty years or more, including the period after her husband's death. At length it all came to be something that had happened in the last few days. The sick woman spoke feelingly of being denounced by her husband just last night, or this morning, and then told happily how he had been so gentle with her afterwards. The essential story was repeated endlessly, but each time a little more detail emerged. There would be a scene that Torizuka hadn't heard before, a little more filling out of the background. She began to feel she could see the surrounding objects. Somehow, she said, she still didn't feel inclined to tell anyone these things. Not that there was anything particularly interesting in the scenes …

It was quite some time after Yamagoe and Torizuka began to take turns staying at the hospital that his mother finally died. Of course they had no clear idea of how long it would be, and both were still working, so they were close to the end of their stamina several weeks before her death. For this reason, it was not in her normal frame of mind that Torizuka listened to the woman talking. What she heard sank into her without passing through any thoughts or responses to it. In it went, and it stayed with her as she went about her life, day and night. Her state of mind was far from one of worrying whether to believe it all or not. When she half drifted off on the train home from work, she realized how strained she had been, for all her intentions to remain relaxed. She wouldn't be able to cope with that now. She had simply let everything come flowing into her. Half awake, she nevertheless managed to get off at the right station and set off walking down the dark road, needing to think no further for the moment, since the house and the hospital lay in the same direction. Sometimes she would meet Yamagoe ambling along from the other direction, with the same leaden walk as her own. She would pass him, hearing the bare information that he was dropping down to the local shop. Sometimes they would walk silently side by side past the hospital and on to the house, which grew moldy after a mere day's absence, and manage to spend perhaps a half hour alone together there.

One evening, as she was changing before going off to spend the night at the hospital, she remarked to Yamagoe that she was going about the world all day barely half awake, and he had replied that a woman in that state can get pregnant just by brushing up against what's around her.

This is the state she was in as she listened to the sick woman talk. It wasn't simply a formal problem of not having sufficient energy to distinguish between what may be true confession or delusion, but rather, when she was moved by what she heard, the response rose up in her without any thought of untangling the ins and outs of the story or considering results. It rose, and she let it die back down of its own accord. She found she had to go clopping up and down the corridor constantly.

Thinking about it later, the story she heard from the sick woman didn't really contain a lot of content. Nevertheless, she was woken numerous times in the night. She would come awake with the sound of words spoken in sleep or the husky voice talking at her ear. Even as she slept, she was aware somehow of the invalid nearby. Though in fact she never heard these stories in the middle of the night, her feeling afterwards was that she had done little else but listen to them. Or perhaps it was that since there was never any promise of an ending to what she heard, even as she listened she had the feeling that it had been going on continuously. Sometimes she would suddenly be overwhelmed with the smell of Yamagoe, who had slept there the previous night, and the smell would linger for some time. He had told her that he was sometimes mistaken for his father. He added with a laugh that sleep generally intervened before the error was discovered, but she wondered which of them it was who fell asleep, and which of them failed to discover the error.

The night before she died, the sick woman somehow found the strength to suddenly raise her head as Torizuka was settling down into her low cot by the bed, call her name clearly, and look at her with the light of sudden sanity in her eyes. Half sitting up to look up into the invalid's face, Torizuka thought that she was perhaps about to be asked to bring something from home, and even imagined running down the dark road to the house, shaking Yamagoe awake, and together going through the cupboards and chests of drawers in search of it—but instead the woman stared hard at her body, as though she were naked, and said, "Nothing will begin unless you have a child," after which her head sank back onto the pillow and her breathing immediately told that she was asleep again. Torizuka held her awkward pose for some time. She had the odd thought that perhaps one could become pregnant from a scent.

After she died, Torizuka continued to keep those talks private inside her, without thinking much about them. Exhausted from their long endeavors, the two slept whenever there was time to spare. She would wake and find herself planning her preparations for the trip to the hospital. When this drowsiness had finally abated, and they had time on their hands again, Yamagoe would sometimes become obsessed with his mother's past. On these occasions, he would seek answers from her. She didn't intend to hide things from him, but she was unsure of her own judgment, so her answers were always vague. She would say that she really didn't have any clear idea, and he would quickly withdraw. It was as if he was stepping hastily aside in avoidance.

This went on for about six months, during which time Yamagoe was convinced that what his mother had said was the truth. It seemed that for a while he wondered whether the "mistake" was the first child who had died at six, but he finally seemed to convince himself that she wasn't a deep enough person to have hidden such a heavy secret from her adult son all her life, even if her husband had known about it, and in fact there had been no hint of such a thing. Therefore, he said, it was not something he should bother himself over.

He told her that he had witnessed the way his dying his father had returned to berating his mother again, more than twenty years after he would have forgiven her for her past. His mother was strangely meek and submissive, but he had seen how she suffered. But as the years since his death accumulated, her memory of him had undergone a purification, and since his sister's death, this process had been unobstructed. And with his own accident, the figure of his father had taken on more than realistic dimensions for her. In the end, she told the grim tale of how he had berated her and she had confessed and been forgiven, as if it were some honeymoon memory. He always listened to this in astonishment, but after she died he realized that until he was twenty his own memories of his father had been tinged with his mother's self-sufficient confession. He had been unable for a while to think for himself about his father. He would laugh, then, and remark that it could be said his mother had managed before she died to settle things wonderfully well for her remaining child.

Later, he thought that perhaps, seeing the beginning and end of the whole story, it came down to a man being obsessed with the wife's past. Perhaps it wasn't so much that he was jealous of another man as that his own present life—of loving and caring for a wife who at an early age had been tainted by the world he loathed and loving the children they had together—constituted in itself a kind of jealousy, yet it was undoubtedly a blow to have his eldest child killed, he said, and he mused about why his sister had so hated her father, and pondered that perhaps he was insensitive.

During this period, Torizuka continued to repeat that she really didn't understand very well just what she had been told by the sick woman. But as she demurred she found herself tending to accept the story at face value, since this is what the woman's own son was inclined to do. Yet when Yamagoe began to talk about his father, she would be filled with a vague fear and find herself beginning to prevent him speaking further. Then his eyes would plead with her to tell him the truth. He in fact seemed unable to finally be convinced one way or the other about his mother or to believe that Torizuka had gained a sense of the real story from her. One evening, she surprised herself by saying to him, "Really, nothing happened, you know." She hastily went on in confusion, "I mean, nothing really clear between your mother and me." Yamagoe apologized for pushing her for answers, and after that he didn't broach the subject again.

It was more than six months after this, when the first-year memorial service had long passed and the spring leaves were fresh on the trees, that she told him she now felt that what his mother had spoken of had probably not in fact happened. She was simply saying what was in her thoughts, as she frequently did these days, but when he turned to look at her she went on to explain simply that when she looked back on it she couldn't sense that there had been any man in his mother's life other than his father. Hearing herself, she wondered in surprise why she had never until now thought such a perfectly obvious thing. Her habit had been to tell herself that she mustn't doubt the confessions she was hearing, and this habit had apparently persisted for a full year since her death, and only now finally resolved itself.

"It's true," Yamagoe responded equally simply, "there was no sign of any man, nor of any place where such a thing might have happened." Then he turned over on his back and remarked that they were falling behind in the arrangements. By "arrangements" he meant the formal registering of their relationship. It had been decided that they would do this before the first-year commemoration service for his mother. "We've both been too busy," Torizuka replied. It had indeed taken more than a year for both to feel they had made up to their workplaces for the time they had taken at the expense of their colleagues during his mother's illness. "We're tired, is what it is," Yamagoe said. And it was true, at last they had relaxed, and the exhaustion had revealed itself.

Yamagoe murmured that perhaps they wouldn't get around to handing in the paperwork until she was pregnant, just like his father. "Still," he continued, "I wouldn't really mind ..."

A further six months had passed since then, and still they remained unmarried.

· · · · ·

The year drew rapidly to a close while I waited for Yamagoe to telephone. I couldn't plan beforehand just what I would say to him, yet as it was put off from one night to the next, the thought of it became like a wall before me. I didn't think about either Sugaike or Fujisato, though occasionally the face of Fujisato's daughter would rise before me. Perhaps it was owing to the amount of time I spent sitting at home, but the year's end seemed to pass quietly as I gazed at the slowly withering leaves on the branches of the oak trees. By the twenty-eighth of December, I had decided that Yamagoe would not be phoning within the year. That evening, I finally got around to writing my New Year's greeting cards. I wrote to both Fujisato and Sugaike inquiring how they were, but, recalling Torizuka, I decided not to send anything to Yamagoe. Then, past nine that night, there was an earthquake. It was an unusual one that thrust suddenly up from below and was followed

236

by no further shaking, though I waited with breath held. I strained my ears toward the horizon, picturing to myself the old canal road snaking quietly through the landscape.

From the wine shop on the corner opposite the vending machine that stands at the edge of the park, a road leads off to join the canal road, and if you cross it, turn another corner and climb a small slope, you reach a ward office branch. From in front of Torizuka I traced a route that would take young legs only ten or so minutes to walk, even coming from Yamagoe's house, and thought of the exhaustion of the young man and woman who had dragged themselves over that short distance. Perhaps when a sense of the geography entered the story, a dawning understanding appeared on my face and this conveyed itself to Torizuka, or perhaps she felt that since she was the one to broach the subject she must talk further and not waste the opportunity—her breathing slowed, her eyes closed, and she grew pale.

Then she broke her silence and began, "Yamagoe said he could only think that if something had seemed natural for so many years, it must be true. I took his hand then. That was six months ago. Even now, he still questions me wordlessly. I have no way of answering any more."

Then she went on, her eyes fixed on me as if asking whether she was speaking too wildly. "I was wrong. I'd been uncertain myself all along, and perhaps I shouldn't ever have answered those questions of his …"

She managed to control her breathing and finish, "I love him, you see." I nodded. The light in her eyes softened, she lowered her head a little, and I thought I heard her say faintly, "Thank you." Then in a firm voice she added, "Please tell Yamagoe simply that you've heard the story, when he asks. That's all that's needed. Then we can go forward."

"I understand," I replied.

. . . . .

A New Year's card came from Yamagoe. He had added the simple message, "I'll invite you out again soon."

Cards also arrived from Sugaike and Fujisato, the first I had received from either of them.

Fujisato's had a note saying, "It's six months since I retired, and I find I'm surprised by something every day. My daughter laughs at me and tells me I'm as young again as Urashima in the fairy tale who peeps into the magic box. Those thirty-five years spent working away from home feel like a dream."

Sugaike had written on the card in a small hand, "I went into a telephone booth three times to call when I thought of you. Once I had no coins. The second time, my prepaid card had run out. The third time the phone was out of order. Each time was on a different street, on a different work trip." He added that he'd been sent overseas three times since October as a

237

"messenger," a system that was surely quite pointless, but it seemed they sent people just to test whether this was so. "It seems Japan's nervous breakdown is rushing about the world carrying a suitcase, and yours truly is well on the way to becoming a ghost. By the way, it would seem that the shabby figure from the past that used to hang out broke in gutters after the races and in cheap suburban drinking holes can these days be observed in airport departure lounges. I have another plane trip in the new year, and it looks like I'll have lots to tell afterwards."

Towards the middle of January, I left the house at last after a long period of seclusion. I had arranged to meet with two friends on a railway platform far underground at Tokyo Station that evening. Two arrived at roughly the same time that I did, but we went on waiting for the third for a long time. We were wondering what could have happened to him, when a sudden thought occurred to me. "He lives in Kokubunji, doesn't he? So that's it—the Chuo Line is temporarily out because of an accident. I hadn't remembered till this very moment, and now I couldn't quite recall where I'd learned the information between the subway station and here, whether I'd heard an announcement or seen it flash up on a board somewhere. I did know that it happened somewhere before the train reached Hachioji. Then it came back to me that I'd overheard a passerby saying, "Apparently someone else threw themselves in front of a train this morning." "Now that you mention it, things have felt a bit odd," said one of my companions, looking up the high staircase as if belatedly searching out some whiff of calamity.

Late that night we four piled into a taxi and headed off along the bayside expressway to return to the center of the city. As we were crossing the dark water, one of my friends told us that this was the place where they say a doctor from Tsukuba wrapped his strangled wife and children in bed quilts and threw them in. "He was lucky no one saw him from a passing car," the other remarked. "Well, I must say it's a lonely sort of place. The further you go the more lonely it gets."

The other idly took up the comment by remarking, "I guess maybe he felt so lonely here he just had to throw the bodies in when he'd stopped the car."

"I wonder what he'd really planned on doing," I added, after a while.

When I arrived home to the sleeping house past midnight, my desk looked oddly tidy, and on it was a note to tell me there had been a call. From Yamagoe, I guessed, but it turned out to be from Fujisato. He said it was nothing urgent. When I called him back the following afternoon, he sounded cheerful. After a bit, he said, "You stopped being able to walk four years ago, didn't you?" I had written in my New Year's card that being able to walk was a strange business.

"You wrote that peace and normality had a dreamlike feel, and it's perfectly true," he went on. I had indeed written this. But what I had had in

238

mind was not my present good health, but those six weeks or so four years earlier, lasting from year's end to early February, when I had staggered along through life, ignoring the danger signal of my faltering gait, indeed feeling that my feet were firmly planted in the joys of peace and normality. I had even taken two trips abroad during this period. Yet when Fujisato said this, I did feel the apprehensiveness of that time merge with my present sense of relief. Perhaps Fujisato too, I thought, felt the same merging in that dreamlike feeling.

"At any rate, I'm grateful for the way things are now," I said, and changing the topic I inquired about his daughter.

"Ah yes, she says she wishes we would ask those guests along again. She's in fine form, thank you. But she says ..." His voice had begun on a cheerful note, but now it slowed. "She says that sometimes her neck and shoulders suddenly freeze up and she feels stiff as a board down her back. And on the other hand the tips of her fingers and toes tingle, and this spreads all over her apart from the stiff back, till even the ends of her hair feel almost tingly. And inside her head goes white and tense, and there's a kind of flickering deep inside her eyes. It's not constant, but around dawn it's bad. She wakes up with the feeling that her back is glued directly to the earth, and the whole surface of her body, including her hair, is filled with a tiny buzzing. She says although it's still dark she feels a sort of paleness, almost a glow, around her bed."

"That must be awful."

'No, she's fine, actually. She takes it all quite calmly, and talks about the possibility of some treasure being buried in the garden. Apparently the feeling comes from the direction of the garden, a kind of gold or metallic power."

"It could be a feel for gold, in fact. Women are said to be sensitive to invisible light rays."

"And then, around dawn yesterday, she suddenly leapt up with a cry. Not a loud one. She ran out to the corridor that runs along by the balcony, pulled back the shutters and opened the glass doors to the garden. I went to see what was up, and there she was, staring out, her shoulders heaving. 'Daddy,' she said, 'have you ever noticed this garden looking kind of warped?' I asked, 'Does it look warped?' And she smiled and said, 'No, not in the least.' Then she said, 'It's just symptoms of menopause,' and she went out into the garden and started happily doing her exercises, looking at me. She raised her arms and swung them round her head, smiling happily, her eyes fixed on me."

"Maybe she was remembering that summer when you were sitting out there on the veranda night after night, gazing into the garden till first light. She did say you looked as if you were staring at the garden as though it was warped. She must have been unable to sleep from worry about you, I mean that summer. Still, it couldn't be menopause, in fact, could it?"

"She's almost thirty now, you know."

"Life's too quiet at home, that's what it is. You must be living there to-gether treading carefully round each other all the time. We two guests will have to come along and stir up the atmosphere again some time."

"We're waiting for you."

We ended the conversation on a light note by suggesting we get together for the traditional bean-throwing ceremony at the old Setsubun festival on the first day of spring. The image of the young girl in her nightdress stand-ing in the garden early on a winter's morning moving her limbs gracefully about stayed with me. She may well be more sexually mature than Torizuka, I thought to myself.

One day, my eye was drawn to the richness of the winter morning earth where the shadow of a bare branch fell. It did indeed feel dreamlike. Though it was now mid-January, for some reason the yellow adonis flowers hadn't appeared over the ground, but a scattering of small violets flowering out of season turned their faces to the sun.

The next morning I was shaken awake by my family's cries of, "Something terrible has happened!" I went to the living room, and there on the television screen, with the sun coming in through the curtains behind, was the scene of the wrecked city of Kobe.

It was only hours later that vermilion flames began to leap up every-where there, just as they had during wartime.

19
A Leafless Tree in Spring

When I arrived late next morning at the edge of the wood by the park, the patch of earth with its shadow of bare branches looked as beautiful as it had the day before. No actual frost was visible, but the ground surface seemed parched and dry, as if covered with the grains of soil that were broken up each time the sun rose to melt the earth that had frozen up before dawn. It looked as if it would crunch if stamped on. This earth looked similar to the strangely friable soil I remember seeing long ago under an old house that had been knocked down in the forced evacuation of wartime. As a child, I had wondered why earth that had not been exposed to the elements would be so thoroughly coated in dust.

At ten that morning, Fujisato phoned. He reported that his daughter had been sound asleep for almost an hour. He had been awakened around eight by the clamorous voice of the unaccustomed morning television; going out to the living room, he caught his first sight of earthquake-stricken Kobe, viewed on the screen over the shoulders of his daughter, who was sitting there in an oddly rigid pose. They exchanged a few shocked words, then gazed together at the screen, agog. She had changed from her nightclothes, but was wearing thin clothing for the season. The living room was icy cold. Noticing this, he stood up and turned on the heating, and when he turned back he saw that his daughter's shoulders were swaying slightly to and fro. "We should eat something," he said. She nodded, and turned off the television. But then she raised both arms above her head, remarked how quiet it was, and set about performing some stretching exercises, still seated on her knees. She lowered her upper body to the floor, and her back began to shake with what looked like suppressed laughter, while the sound of sobs escaped from her.

Her father sat beside her, arms folded. He asked what was the matter, but she only shook her head. Did she have someone in Kobe she was attached to? he asked, but she answered this quite clearly in the negative. For more than half an hour she crouched there voicelessly, shivers running down her back, while tears spilled onto the matting from the hands covering

241

her face. When she had at last calmed a little, he went to her room and laid out the still-warm bedding she had recently put away, encouraging her to rest for a while. She meekly set off down the inner corridor, and before she entered the bedroom she raised her eyes to the ceiling and told him that she had had a dream at dawn of a great crowd of people rushing around inside the house and out again, each carrying a sticklike object, and she heard a ringing and clashing in the rafters. But she didn't say any more about it. "A great crowd in this house?" said her astonished father. "How would they have gotten in here, or gotten out?" She replied, "I guess I'm becoming hysterical," and closed the door with a smile.

Each time he opened the door a crack and peeped in, she was sleeping soundly. She didn't look unwell. A faint flush suffused her skin.

"That kind of thing happens sometimes," I said vaguely.

"How did your family take it?" he asked.

"Well, they're all women here too—but no one did anything unusual."

"It's impossible that a single body so far away could register a big calamity like that. Even one tiny fragment of it."

"Maybe she reacted that way because the thing's so big it can't be registered fully. It's certainly beyond the limits of the likes of us."

"If I was still working, I'd have had breakfast watching the television and then headed straight out to work. No, I would have rushed out when she woke me. Someone would have telephoned to call me before that. In that case, this wouldn't have happened to her. Or maybe I would have spent the day oblivious to the fact that she was back there alone in an empty house, lying there crying."

Fujisato's bewildered voice seemed to have followed me in my head till I reached this spot, for I heard it in the sound of the wind moving through the dwarf bamboo beneath the trees. His daughter sleeps. No telephone call comes. The television is turned off. It's unbearable to listen alone to the hushed radio reports. He said with a laugh that it sounded like the announcements the army used to make over the wartime radio.

He told me that on the night those air raids came, his mother wrapped his little four-year-old sister in a blanket and held her to her breast as she rushed out. His sister had a high fever. The two of them ran and ran through the smoke till the little girl was exhausted. Then, with nowhere to turn, she rushed them into a deserted air-raid shelter, hoping her husband would forgive her, since if the fire got in there they must all die. After that, they knew no more of what went on around them, apart from the sound of his sister's breathing. Elsewhere, people would be dying in large numbers, but inside the shelter there was air. But, he revealed then, when morning came, his sister was no longer breathing.

Listening attentively as the wind blew, I could make out not only the rustle of dwarf bamboo leaves but the gentle creaking of branches, and a soft cracking sound from within them. When I raised my eyes, tremors were passing everywhere through the oaks, even the twigs shivering. The shadow of the bare tree stood out against the gently burning distant dawn sky. Its twigs too were trembling. The wind seemed to have died down at that hour, and when I thought back on it, it seemed to me that in fact it was me, the one looking on, whose breath had been stilled.

That afternoon I set to work in earnest, driven by the feeling that I must finish what I had to do as soon as possible. I threw myself into it with particular energy. As I worked, I felt my silent body invaded by the noise of that hushed and urgent voice talking. About once an hour I stood from the desk, went out to the living room, turned on the television and watched for a few minutes, till I could bear it no more and turned it off again. In this way, the day drew to a close. By then the prime minister was facing the cameras with his indecisive response, and the tongues of flame were leaping up here and there in the stricken city and beginning to spread. By evening, when the family was back home and the television broadcast was left to run, the screen was showing scenes of burning cityscapes exactly like those of fifty years earlier—the identical fires left burning out of control sent up white wavering flames that sometimes held an excruciating slowness. Fear fixes your helpless gaze to the fire, and when it grows unbearable, you feel rise up in you a sense of terror at the recognition that this feeling is beginning to shift into a strange tranquility, and that the flames seeming almost to be smiling. The horror of this too remained somewhere deep within me.

At nine came a telephone call from Sugaike, to ask what I was doing.

"I'm wandering about, in and out of the living room with the television," I replied.

"We're doing just about the same thing, then. But every time I come in I moan and cry, which makes the family complain when they see me coming."

"What about?"

"Well, you know. I saw all this with my own eyes fifty years ago. Those old wooden houses, you know, when they fall, there's always a space left inside, no matter how flattened they are. And then I think, there are people in there. I saw someone there, crouching low ..."

"Hey, take it easy."

"I can't stand it! That old lady was rescued. That's all I remember about it. But when this happens, they aren't rescued. I wish I hadn't seen that sight."

"It's been going on for a full day, hasn't it?" I said in an effort to fill the silence, but I found myself wondering when it had been, that sensation of whiteness in the head, and of my hair slowly standing on end. It felt as if it was not so long in the past.

"I was only murmuring to myself," Sugaike went on. "But it serves me

243

right for all those years I've spent comfortably with the television. Doesn't it bring back those days when you were a kid, standing there for an hour or more stock-still in front of the electrical goods shop late on cold days, gazing at the sumo match broadcasts? No, we would have been high school students by then, wouldn't we. We've stopped looking at things like that; nothing engrosses us and transfixes us that way any more. So I end up walking about in my own house, pausing to catch a bit of television, and then wandering off again."

"So you think it's a kind of punishment, to have to watch all the details of a distant calamity while there you are, safe and sound in your peaceful life?"

"And what's more, for all the clarity of what you're seeing, it's soundless."

"Soundless?" I repeated, puzzled. I imagined him watching the scene with the sound turned off.

"Of course people are talking like mad, and you can hear various sounds that seem to relate to the scene itself. But the cries and groans everywhere, they're all eliminated. If everyone would just shut up for even a few minutes, we'd hear them."

"If that happened, we too would simply be overwhelmed."

"Precisely." Sugaike's voice had grown a little distant. "My own memory of fifty years ago is basically the same thing, you know. The more clearly I am able to recall it, the more the sound disappears. Even if I can remember that I heard this voice or that cry, it's not the voice or cry itself that I'm remembering. You told me you'd seen houses burning to the ground. Remember how you could hear at the base of that great pillar of flame that went shooting up to the sky a kind of loud seething hum, like a mob of people suddenly jeering, as the sparks leapt back up again? I remember that. But when I look into this memory, sure enough, it's silent. It's been preserved silently, all these years."

"Well, you were only a very little kid, after all. You wouldn't have been able to survive unless you shut out the sound from your memory, I imagine. Once you get rid of the sound, the image takes on a strange clarity."

"No, I'm talking about thirty or forty years afterwards. That little kid staring as hard as he could to shut out the sound is still there. But maybe it's because of it, whenever I see something frightening now I feel I've had a premonition of the sight. I'm instantly seized with a terror of repetition …"

At this point, Sugaike suddenly said, "Oh, just wait there a moment," and then from a distance came his answering voice, "Right, coming." He returned to the phone and gave a hasty apology. "Sorry, the family's calling me. I'll telephone again soon. Let's get in touch with Fujisato and all meet up again, eh? Who knows what will happen."

I too hurried back to the living room after I hung up. On the television screen, the same flames were still rising.

. . . . .

A line of people carrying piles of luggage was making its way through the rubble along the broken railway line. Many had bags on their backs and in both hands. There were women who were lugging all they could manage, walking as far as they could before pausing to change their grip, then doggedly setting off again. I saw some children too who were hauling part of their parents' load. Apparently they had come as far as they could by train, and from there they would walk four or five hours. Their walk had a firmness seldom seen these days, and their step was that of people who were prepared to bear the rigors of an endless walk bearing heavy luggage. They were bringing necessities into the earthquake-stricken area for relatives there. I was reminded of the long-unheard word "provisions," a word that aroused a sharp and painful recognition that had lain latent for decades. Hearing it, I thought to myself how intent we had constantly been on carrying provisions.

The afternoon of the day following the earthquake, there was a call from Fujisato, apologizing for the fuss of the day before. Apparently his daughter had gotten up again before noon, declaring that she was ashamed at having fallen into such a state when she was perfectly safe and it was others who were much more entitled to panic. She said when the sound from the television disappeared and the house fell silent she had somehow become beside herself, although she could vaguely remember what happened. It had been around dawn that she'd had that dream of a vast crowd of people rushing out through the entrance hall into the garden, and she hadn't had any idea that it was related to anything like this earthquake. She'd only happened idly to turn on the television. When she saw the scene there, she didn't understand at first what had happened. She was sure she hadn't turned to look at her father standing behind her, but she did remember seeing him there. She said voices and sounds had grown a little distant at that point.

She remained thoughtful, remarking that over a number of years she had sometimes had a similar dream of a large crowd rushing in. He reported that she'd gone off to work.

I told him simply that Sugaike had also phoned and suggested that the three of us get together again.

Days passed. I happened to catch a scene on the television of a woman relating how she had heard the voice of someone in her family crying nearby for help. She had been unable to reach them and finally had to flee the approaching flames with the cry, "Forgive me!" As she spoke, a visible shiver began to break through from deep inside her. With a little gasp she managed to repress it, and as she did so, the intense strain brought to her face the faint shadow of what seemed almost a smile.

245

I remembered now when it had been that my hair began to stand on end. It was, as I thought, a recent experience, and happened during my hospitalization four years earlier. It was while my body was still held in a brace from the neck to the chest and I was kept lying on my back day and night; sometime past midnight, my eyes flew open and I couldn't get back to sleep. I lay there listening to the intermittent sound of a distant drill from beyond the wall. It was a very faint noise, so it didn't grate on the ear. I could only imagine that somewhere in the hospital someone was carrying out a late-night job drilling holes in the wall, careful not to go on for too long at a time, out of consideration for the patients. As I listened, I felt the roots of my hair contract. It lasted only a second. Yet my breath quickened. Not only was my neck braced, but my chin was held up from below by a metal support, so rapid breathing was perilous. Once I lost control of my breathing, a sensation of suffocation would flood me and my body would be convulsed with gasps. There was a danger that in my panicky fight for breath I would raise myself up. I lay there trying my best to relax my rigidly supported jaw, and gradually the gasps slowed. In the dark, my struggling face was smiling in its effort. I could see that vague, driven smile on my own face. At last, when my gasping had subsided, I tried to locate the smell of burning iron that had been filling my nostrils until a moment earlier, but there was now no trace of it. "If that's how it is," I said aloud, "we might as well all burn to death."

I was echoing the response of an old man who was hospitalized for high blood pressure and was caught secretly smoking one night when he couldn't sleep and gently reproved by a nurse.

Lying there deep in the night in my hospital bed waiting for sleep to come, I wondered how many years ago I had ceased to have the dream of the burning red sky. I set out to count, as if there were in fact a fixed moment when the dreams had ended, but I hadn't the strength to think back more than a year, and as I vaguely counted on, leaping years from three to five to seven, I fell into the state of mind of one buried away in a dark cellar. I could follow the dreams, repeated at regular intervals, back to childhood, youth, into my thirties, and into my mid-forties, and at this point the minor strain of this mental exertion brought a slight ooze of sweat to my forehead where the bandage swathed it. This was only about ten days after the surgery. Lying in bed, secure in the knowledge that this time it was not a dream, I recalled the way the whole sky burns red overhead, the red strengthening from moment to moment as it flames quietly on, the houses still unharmed, until when the sky's scarlet reaches its peak of intensity and burns to pure white all will at last burst into flame—yet I am looking down at the sloping road, feeling quite unperturbed and normal, and that calmly gazing self at length becomes a sense of premonition, and now for the first time I feel a tremor of fear. There were times when I wondered whether I would repeat this dream throughout my entire life to its end, yet at some stage it had ended, and even when I entered hospital with my uncanny physical symptoms, even when the day of the surgery approached, even in the midst of the weakness and slight delirium that followed surgery, the sky had not burned red, and so it had continued until now. The doctor said that I would be able to sit up in bed in four or five days, and I fervently counted down each remaining day.

. . . . .

Late one night at the end of July, exactly two weeks after the earthquake, Yamagoe called to ask how I was.

"Fine, thanks," I replied. "At my age it apparently takes about four years to shake off the last of the effects, no matter how well I think I've recovered. Just recently, I feel as though my walk is completely back to normal again at last."

"It's exactly four years today for me too, since that day I was hit by the car," said Yamagoe. "Now I only see the night road, never a glimpse of the car." Then he went on, "I hear Torizuka called on you recently."

"Yes, she did speak to me," I responded, then waited to see where things would go from here. In the two months since our talk, my imagination had not sullied what I heard. She had asked me to wait until precisely now, the end of July, and I felt that if he asked me I could indeed pass back what I had been given by her, carefully wrapped and preserved.

But Yamagoe simply said "Thank you," as if the matter was now dealt with. "I'm ashamed that I seem to have put a lot of pressure on her without realizing it at the time. But thank you, you've helped."

"So that's all that needs be said, then?" I prompted.

"Yes, she was grateful for your kind ear. She said she would never forget your generous good will." Yamagoe's response did not stray from the formal, and where to me his words could easily hold an ironic tone, his voice was in fact easy and relaxed. "I hear she came running after you."

"I didn't realize it, but that's apparently what happened, yes."

"She's not normally the sort of woman to behave so boldly. She was already pregnant at the time."

"Was she okay?" I asked. When he replied that all was well, the conversation halted for a moment and I went on to ask how he had fared in the aftermath of the earthquake news.

"Well, that's the problem." Yamagoe's voice was wry. "Around the middle of the month I was just getting ready to call you and report that all was well when the tragedy happened. We both got pretty emotional. I've told you, I know, about how both my sister and I were born in years when a terrible accident occurred. The year I was born there was that train crash and the gas explosion in the coal mine on the same day, a total of 620 people dead. I was born within a week of this. And now here's my own child in my partner's womb, and this time it's the earthquake. I didn't breathe a word of this after the quake happened. We were safe, after all. But then last Monday night, in other words six days after the quake happened that Tuesday morning, things suddenly went haywire."

Late that night, just as he was thinking of going to bed, Torizuka stood up and set about preparing to go out. She said she had to go and take over from him back at the hospital—she was talking about taking over from him when he was standing there in front of her. Her eyes were dull; she'd been dozing by the heater till that moment. "My mother's dead, remember?" Yamagoe said, and the echo of the panicky edge to his voice surprised him. She looked round the room, bewildered, than laughed and said, "Oh hell, how stupid!" He was sure she laughed. Then she sat back down again, her expression dejected. He comforted her by telling her that he also had moments when he found himself muttering, "Well then, I must get back to the hospital." "We really got through all that pretty well, didn't we?" she responded, apparently recalling it all again. But then a little later she stood up once more, went out into the corridor, and began to put on her shoes in the hall. She turned when he called her, and that same light was in her eyes. "I think I'm a bit mad," she said in a small voice. "So don't say anything, just follow me." He expressed concern over the cold outside, but she was still aware that she was pregnant, and wrapped herself up well.

Yamagoe set off, bracing himself also against the cold, and as they arrived before the station he checked his pocket for the wallet he had thrust in there, wondering whether she planned to catch one of the late-running trains and go somewhere. If so, he hoped it was at least a train into the city and not a lonely outgoing one. She went around to the north of the station and took the road that ran along beside the tracks. She walked with a firm, purposeful tread. Aside from her dogged silence in the face of his talk, there was no evidence of anything odd. She must have somewhere in mind to go to, he decided.

It was the same path he had taken the evening his sister had left home; he had carried her luggage to the station with her, and she had invited him to walk with her a little, as far as the next station. She was finally spilling her hatred of their father. "There he was, so calm and peaceful-looking, rejecting the world, and he even kept the pain to himself when a child got taken, but what would he do if another one jumped onto these tracks, eh?" she said, with a ferocity that suggested he was still alive, as she waved a hand in the direction of the railway tracks. He hadn't walked along this road in ten years, since that night. It wasn't a road he usually had any need to walk on.

They went through the railway crossing, walked a little further beside the tracks, then turned diagonally and set off uphill. It was only four years since she had begun to come to his house, and she wouldn't have known the geography of this area, but her footsteps were firm and sure. Native to the area though he was, it was Yamagoe, walking behind her, who felt he had come to some unknown place. When they reached the top, the road entered a residential area. It seemed to be going north, and then at the end, where several roads led off, Yamagoe saw a dead hackberry tree and at last recovered his bearings. Torizuka stopped here, and stood gazing strangely up at the broken trunk. The sound of what would be the last train tumbled out of the air. "Where are we?" she asked. "We haven't come all that far," he replied.

Torizuka told him she'd been feeling physically uncomfortable recently. Until the earthquake, she hadn't been feeling there was anything wrong, and nor was it something that had suddenly happened that day. Two days later, she had begun to find her knees suddenly tending to give way beneath her. She was frightened. She couldn't control it any more. She told herself it was all over now, but there was no way her body understood this concept of something being over.

She told him how she had paused one day at the end of the year along a shopping street to look at a stall selling New Year front door decorations. This is something the man of the house buys, she thought, not the woman. In particular it shouldn't be a pregnant woman. Still, her eyes were held by the pine branch decorations lined up there. I wonder if they'd grow if you stuck them in the ground, she thought. She imagined the thin white roots making their way down through the earth. Then her body grew suddenly painful, as if touching through the tips of those roots some fearful thing. Her knees seemed to flinch, and she felt the child inside her …

As he listened, Yamagoe felt a strange apprehension that she was about to lean forward against the hackberry tree beside her and press her ear to its trunk. He grasped her shoulders from behind, and instead she leaned her weight back onto him. "Did you already know this tree?" he asked. "Yes, I did," she replied. "I knew it, but I'd never been here."

She said his mother at the hospital had told her his father had sometimes come to this hackberry tree. Yamagoe had never heard this before. He thought perhaps it was a delusion of his mother's. Apparently it was in early spring the year he died, when he was in and out of bed at home. He didn't come often. One warm day as the dark drew in he prepared to set out for a walk. His wife was concerned when she saw this, but he responded with a wry smile and said that it was surely okay for him to step out for an evening drink sometimes, so she felt she couldn't hold him back. Less than an hour later, before darkness had completely descended, he came back, apparently quite unweary. "Did you have a drink?" she asked, and he coolly replied, "Ah yes, I did," There was no scent of alcohol on his breath. He was someone who had barely drunk since his marriage.

. . . . .

Then one night, he told her about the hackberry. When he was at the base

249

of the tree, he said, he felt physically and mentally serene and at ease, everything appeared calm to him, he felt he could see the sun sinking in the distance, and when he sensed it go down behind the mountains he turned for home, feeling good with the evening glow on his back, with a warmth that stayed with him into the night. He told her how to get there, but though she had lived there for many years, she knew little of what lay across the railway tracks. But she was comforted to know that his walks had an aim. Then one day, as she was running water in the kitchen, he slipped out of his bedroom and vanished.

He returned home an hour later, saying nonchalantly that he had been to the hackberry. He went straight to bed. She shuddered when she heard him murmur, "I saw the sun set, and I heard a voice in the distance." Then he said with a smile, "I won't go again. It's over." He closed his eyes.

For ten years after her husband's death she would occasionally feel the urge to follow the directions he'd given and visit the hackberry tree; but it was generally just on evening when the idea occurred to her, and she said the thought of the other side of the tracks was intimidatingly lonely, so she'd never gone. Torizuka could have even less idea of the location than she did. But apparently his mother had told her the way in painstaking detail, probably exactly the way she'd heard it, although not with any suggestion that Torizuka should go there herself.

Torizuka told him that when she'd gone to the entrance that evening her only idea had been to go out and breathe the fresh air for a while, since her body felt somehow unbearable and she couldn't shake the strange feeling that had accompanied her earlier misapprehension. But when she turned and saw Yamagoe's face, she heard the voice of the dead father she had never known, saying that if she stood at the base of the hackberry she would feel physical and mental ease. This was when she told him, "I think I'm a bit mad."

She said she felt quite sane as she walked along the road beside the tracks, and wondered whether she had ever walked along here following the dead man's directions before. Crossing the tracks, following along a little further and then turning left, she recalled that his mother's description had suddenly grown vague at this point. She had tried this and that explanation, before finally just saying that a long road climbed up on the right. The hilly ground was on the right, however, so all the roads going in that direction went up. She didn't know how far along the tracks she should go, and there was no sign of this long sloping road. When she reached the foot of a dingy road going diagonally up the hill, she was about to pause and suggest to Yamagoe that they go back, but her feet appeared to recognize the place and set off walking up the hill of their own accord. Even when she reached the top and the road stretched ahead, she seemed to be walking endlessly upward. Then finally, as the shape of the tree loomed larger ahead, almost as if speaking to her, she forgot Yamagoe's presence. When she stood before the tree, a low earth rumble came rolling in from far away and quietly entered the tree's trunk. She asked him where they were, feeling that a long time had passed, and he had arrived looking for her.

"It somehow seems to be a tree that draws in some invisible strength from all around when night comes," she said. "Perhaps in the morning it breathes it out again." She was smiling by now. She didn't say whether the tree had given her the ease she sought, but on the way home she kept saying how cold it was and started to skip along beside him, causing him worriedly to take her arm.

Crossing the railway line, she looked left and right, and remarked breezily that a railway track with no trains on it expanded the spirit wonderfully, then suddenly she told him he should phone soon to meet up to apologize. It was me she was talking about.

. . . . .

He assured me that he was prepared to come anywhere at a time that suited me, and asked me to meet even if only for ten minutes. From his manner of speech, I realized he was doing this for Torizuka. "Come here on one of your days off," I suggested, and he hesitantly replied that they didn't want to trouble me at home, and suggested instead the row of trees in front of the park. It would be a pleasant place to meet up on a warm day, and if it were cold there were quite a few places in the vicinity to go. We decided that we we'd meet the following Sunday, a little before noon, as part of a stroll.

"I'm so sorry for all this foolish disturbance we've both caused you," he apologized once more before hanging up. Yet in fact he had spoken calmly and honestly to me of difficult matters, including his partner's wild behavior. He had spoken on the basis that it was all a result of his own blunders, yet without making excuses, neither revealing too much about her nor saying anything to make me uncomfortable, but simply presenting the aspects of the tale that were easy for me to hear; what he spoke of must surely be emotionally difficult for him, and he had confessed it without distortion, so I too could only accept what he said in the spirit in which he gave it. If he had shown an inclination to excuse himself, it would have been a different matter. Perhaps Yamagoe himself felt that even if he could bear to be seen for the moment in an ugly light, it would be straying from the strict facts. It was undoubtedly wise of him to draw in the tale of his two dead parents, and not confine the story to one about the two of them. I felt it was my part to give no indication of having any problem with what I had heard, when we met on Sunday.

But on Saturday night there came another call from Yamagoe.

"It's snowing," he said. "What would you like to do about tomorrow?"

"Really, it's snowing? Come to think of it, it hasn't snowed yet this

251

winter. I wonder how the earthquake victims are faring," I said. I attempted to count the days since it had happened, and was surprised that I could no longer calculate. "In that case," I went on, "you two had better stay put at home for the day. You're the equivalent of a newly married couple, after all, so you've no call to come out and meet up with some old man on a snowy day."

"Thank you very much," said Yamagoe, a laugh in his voice. In its tone I sensed the sweet-sour scent of pregnancy.

The plan was put off for a week, and we agreed that the following Saturday would suit us both. As he was about to hang up, Yamagoe suddenly muttered, "There seem to be rumors going around that there'll be another disaster, you know," but at the news of the snow a drowsy quietness had enveloped me, and I couldn't summon any immediate response to this. I simply shot back some half-baked reply to the effect that the earth may well still be feeling angry.

Half an hour later, thinking back on this conversation, it struck me as odd that though we had talked with an ease that suggested there was now no particular need to meet up, yet beneath both our tones there somehow lurked a strange degree of concern over the fact that we had called each other out, although to a place very convenient for both of us; it seemed to me that this belated sense of tension in what had been a perfectly easy conversation was perhaps an aftereffect of the earthquake's psychological effect on us who had survived that day in distant safety.

Saturday was fine and warm. It happened to coincide with a national holiday weekend. I thought of flags flying at the gate of every farmhouse among the fields still covered in patchy snow—a scene from a movie I saw in Oimachi as a young child during the war. It was shot from the air. The camera panned on and on over cultivated fields and grassy plains, dotted everywhere with tranquil flags, to the music of the old Nation Day commemoration song, "They Bowed and Fluttered." A few years later, squadrons of enemy bombers passed incessantly overhead as we crouched all night deep in the air-raid shelter. Recalling the scene, I felt its cruel irony.

Out on the street, the wintry bare twigs of the rows of zelkova trees seemed a smoky haze in the soft sunlight. I walked beneath them and looked up, seeing the leaf buds already swollen for spring. As dark drew on into night, young kids came here to skateboard. They hauled things out into the middle of the path to use for jumping over, and these were usually left there lying about afterwards. The steel box that was intended as an ashtray for passersby was crammed to overflowing with bits of paper, empty bottles and pieces of food, which the crows came down to scatter early in the morning. But today the place was clean.

I sat down on an empty bench, and before I had waited ten minutes I saw Yamagoe's figure running toward me from the far end of the avenue. It wasn't that he was late for the appointed meeting, so when I saw the sneakers and light sweater wrapped around his waist, I guessed that he had set out from home to jog here. As he entered the avenue of trees his pace slowed, and catching immediate sight of me he smiled as he approached, wiping the sweat from his brow with a hand.

"Sorry to have kept you waiting like this, when I was the one to ask you to meet," he said brightly as he sat down beside me. I found myself recalling a moment when I was a young man and someone about my present age had suddenly said to me when we met in broad daylight, "I'm guessing you maybe had a quickie with your wife on your way out just now." I had indeed felt for a moment that it was the truth. "Congratulations!" he said to me with a nod, looking deeply serious.

"What a nice place!" said Yamagoe, gazing down the street towards the park entrance as if through the heat shimmer that seemed almost to be rising from the road surface, and his face broke into a smile. "White hair can sometimes look black, don't you think?" he went on.

"I guess I'm white today. When there's a hint of oiliness in the hair, it makes it whiter."

"No, it looks black, actually."

"Maybe it's spring doing it."

"Yes, it's spring. Maybe this bright mid-March weather."

I was intrigued at how the conversation had swerved suddenly from the subject of hair. "What about in your father's case?" I inquired after a moment. "He was two years older than me, but he died before the age of fifty, didn't he?"

"He went really quite white in the space of a year. But now that I look back on it, I realize his face was very young." Yamagoe seemed to be comparing his memory with my own appearance, there on the bench beside him. "Young," he muttered again. "He was always thin, but he got to be skin and bones. Yet all the while, his face grew younger. Wait a moment. I can see him as a young man, from before I was born."

He gazed at the gently swaying shadow of the branches that fell over the road as paler shapes than the shadows of winter days.

"I've just called in on that hackberry tree and gazed up at its broken trunk…." he said at last. "Sure enough, a strange white-haired man spoke to me. And then a lovely woman appeared."

253

20

A Second Banquet

Good heavens, I thought, that must be Fujisato and his daughter.

"Maybe it's strange to call him strange," Yamagoe went on, his eyes narrowing as he stared through the smoky sunlight of the avenue. He didn't seem to have received a negative impression of the man.

"He was a white-haired man, smiling happily. He seemed happy as a child," he went on, tilting his head wonderingly. "At first he stood back in the park, looking at me under the hackberry. I felt like I was being glared at. But when our eyes met, he broke into a gentle smile, and I found myself smiling and bowing back. Then he came over and asked quite familiarly whether I could hear something."

Surely not, that wouldn't be him, I thought, brushing the image of Fujisato aside. But Yamagoe went on talking without any hint that there was anything peculiar.

"It seems, you see, there used to be a rumor in the area that long ago, when the hackberry was a fine tree, you could sometimes hear faint music coming from the treetop. He said he'd just remembered this. He said he had the unfortunate habit these days of saying whatever he was thinking, but I'd been standing there gazing so intently...."

"Strange melodies flowing from some ancient tree ..." I began. I couldn't believe it would be Fujisato. But how old was this man he had seen, I wondered. He spoke of "long ago"—how many seasons would he have seen change? "It seems possible," I finished.

"He also said it was possible. He said under the right conditions it was feasible for a large-crowned tree like that to become a receiver for radio waves and to transmit sound, and that in fact there were some known examples of this. But of course it couldn't happen now that the tree had snapped in the middle, he went on, looking up at it with a happy smile. Apparently it was light music. Some people suggested it could be coming from some distant cabaret."

"The mention of 'cabaret' gives you an idea of the period, doesn't it? But it sounds as though he was quite a scientific sort."

"He was a refined man," Yamagoe replied, looking puzzled again. "You saw me running here, I imagine? I had the feeling that we'd been talking there for ages and I was terribly late. But actually we hadn't talked much at all. I was expressing surprise that a large tree could act as a radio transmitter, when I heard a clear voice calling, 'Daddy.' The girl who appeared had a different air about her. She turned to me and gently lowered her head in a bow, as if she knew me vaguely from somewhere. 'Ah, my daughter's arrived to call me back,' her father said, gazing at her face just as I did. Then up she came, and said to me, 'Please call again,' and she led him away, a hand as it were under his elbow. As I watched the two of them go off into the distance, the thought flashed through my mind that perhaps he was blind. But his eyes weren't the lightless eyes of a blind person."

Yamagoe paused to watch the figure of a little boy running down the bright avenue. He seemed to be at the early stage of walking. He was bundled up in warm clothes, and as he tottered along he gained momentum and began to run, both hands stretched artlessly out in front of him, crying aloud as his little feet pattered along; a little girl of about three came running up to walk slowly beside him in an almost adult fashion, not attempting to help until he seemed to be losing his balance, when she slipped around in front of him and caught him gently in her arms.

"When the child is born, we'll have to come up with a name," Yamagoe remarked, his voice dark in the bright sunlight. Then he said, "Sakae, Megumi, Hitoshi. Why did our father give us names like that? That's what comes up to block my mind every time I try to find a name for this child. Hitoshi isn't so bad, but Sakae and Megumi both have intimidatingly splendid meanings—'prosperity,' 'blessing' … They seem to carry some vast desire for the child's happiness."

"They're good names," I replied. Especially when all three are put together, I was about to add, then thought better of it.

"As someone of my father's generation, would you consider calling your firstborn son Sakae?" he asked.

"Your brother was born in 1960, wasn't he?" I said. For all my recent poor memory, I remembered the year of the year that this little boy who had died in a traffic accident at six was born. "I guess in those days there was a different feel to the idea of 'prosperity.' It would have been a desire in your father, I'm sure."

"I gather that at the time my father felt a deep and fixed hatred for the prosperity of the age, remarkably stubborn for one so young."

"Well, I was inclined to turn my back on society too at that age, though only briefly. At about age twenty I was convinced I couldn't go the way the world was headed. I'd guess your father was much stricter with himself than I was. But for all that, it's all part of worldly desire, really. Rejection is just one form of this desire, perhaps the most earnest one. Desire runs deep, however you look at it."

"But that 'prosperity' was what devoured Sakae when he was still a child...."

"It was the year those planes fell out of the sky one after another, wasn't it? Three in a little over a month. One falls in the evening, the next comes down the following afternoon. I had no children then. I'd never been in a plane. But even I lost someone I knew in one of those crashes. He was the last person to be pulled out of the sea."

"My father must have thought back to the moment he chose the name Sakae, and sensed some invisible threatening force at work. When Sakae was killed, he cried out, 'This wasn't how it was supposed to be!' But then he moaned that it was his fault for creating the child in the first place, and he never spoke another word on the subject. When my mother told me this when I was in high school, and asked if I couldn't understand how a parent would feel like this, I came back with the remarkably adult response that what's made is made and there's nothing one can do about it. I imagine it would have been tough on my sister, though."

"Megumi is a gentle name, don't you think?"

"I guess so. But that's the Megumi who said so bitterly that the children in our household weren't loved by their father. That he had no joy in our birth. She was a year older than me, and a girl, so I guess she matured a lot earlier, and she felt differently from me. Still ..."

Yamagoe's eyes followed the line of trees to the park entrance.

"This is something I remembered just now," he went on. "I have quite a few memories of seeing my father walking alone holding his daughter's hand. She would have been in elementary school, in third or fourth grade. But no—I also feel like I saw her dressed in the middle school uniform of the local school. She wouldn't have said anything cruel or bitter while our father was still alive. When his illness got bad and our mother was at a loss how to cope, my sister was a real support and help. Then, around the time the first anniversary of his death had passed, when our mother began to talk about him as if he were a buddha, my sister's reactions got more and more barbed—I'm not sure why. Still, she didn't say anything really terrible to our mother, it just seems to me that when she was talking to me, suddenly she began from one day to the next to rail more and more fiercely against him. I remember once, when I was a university student, she said something so dreadful that I whirled toward her and asked what she was talking about. Then suddenly she went all weak, and cried and said Daddy was a kind man. But she rushed on to say something strange, that the fact that he'd gone and died meant he wasn't at all kind, really. I objected, saying that surely there was nothing anyone could to stop from dying, but she just went on crying and stubbornly shaking her head. I still don't know what she meant. Maybe she was saying it was unkind of him to die just like that. She

256

said though our father loved his children, the way he looked at them had a pity that implied they weren't loved. 'Not loved by who, for heaven's sake?' I demanded, but she didn't answer. I'm the sort of person who becomes confused as soon as I hear words like 'love.' It wasn't as though he chose to die, surely … But then my sister went and died too."

At this point Yamagoe's voice brightened. I realized that right in front of him the same little boy was running along with a tumbling gait, emitting piercing cries, with the little girl flying after him. I watched Yamagoe anxiously, thinking it might just be too much for him to contain himself if the little girl made the same adult gesture of bending down in front of her little brother to take him gently in her arms as he fell, but in fact she grabbed the little boy suddenly from behind, and her small body heaved him off the ground, his tiny legs kicking as he yelled, and carried him off, scolding.

"As for Hitoshi here, he's got off lightly," said Yamagoe with a laugh. "I never thought of my father as particularly odd or strict, after all. I don't think of him that way now, either. When I think about it, the reason I believe he was a straight and honest man with a hidden severity and guardedness was only because of my perspective on it later; it's not something I ever really knew firsthand. And I certainly never had the slightest sense as a child that I was being rejected. If my sister had any real reason to suffer—and there must have been something to make her hate him so much, after all—I guess that implies that I was outside his influence. As for the rest, well I'm just my same old Hitoshi self, a normal guy, as my name implies. I guess Dad wouldn't have worried about me when he saw how I seemed to just not feel things."

Hearing this, I thought to myself that the calm, bright objectivity about himself that this still-youthful thirty-year-old displayed, this strange old head on young shoulders, perhaps came from some deep-down sense that he had been deserted.

"But here you are, surely, taking on the problem of your father's naming on behalf of your dead brother and sister as well as yourself."

"Well, I never thought till now that they were odd names, really," he replied. "I remember when I first met you in the hospital, four years ago, probably around the time I was waiting for the second surgery, one night toward dawn I found myself slowly waking from the ache in my leg. The painkillers had stopped working, but my head was still heavy from them. I heard our three names in my ears, just a whisper from somewhere, but they sounded so stern, so fierce, so solemn. I thought then, What outrageous names we were saddled with! I remember moaning and muttering that two were gone, but I was still alive. At that point in the hospital ward, with the other patients sleeping around me, I was overwhelmed by a flood of oppressive fear, that a plane would fall, there'd be a gas explosion, flames would spurt from buildings, mountains would crumble … I was both outside this watching it and at the same time inside shrieking. The split was agonizing. I lay there controlling it until the window began to grow pale. The morning chimes sounded, and the nurse came around checking temperatures, so I asked how the weather was, and she told me it had started to sleet outside."

"I see, you felt oppressed by the change in the weather, even though you weren't consciously aware of it. Didn't you turn on the radio and listen to the baroque music program?"

"Yes, that languid music they played as the lead-in for it," said Yamagoe with a melancholy smile. "Anyway, that night, I went back to bed because it was time for lights out, and when I'd pulled the curtains round the bed and was just beginning to doze off, I suddenly got depressed at the thought that I might have the same experience again. I didn't trust my pain to stay quiet, so I got out of bed and went off in my wheelchair to sit quietly in the dark common room, and then lo and behold in you came, pushing your walker, and abruptly asked me what year I was born. And I answered just as abruptly, and from then on it all slipped out smoothly without your asking, about myself and the problems at home. When I went back to bed I was amazed at myself for talking like that to someone I'd never spoken to before."

"Were you okay that night?"

"Sure enough, I had an image of my father. He was standing at the corner near the scene of the accident, looking at me lying there. His expression said pityingly that there was nothing to be done. But it also told me there was nothing to be afraid of, I'd get better. It didn't strike me as cold and unfeeling. No, it was no hallucination. I didn't see any such thing when I had the accident. I don't have any recollection of the accident, after all. It seemed that it was an image that had formed inside me in the hospital, two full months after the event. But I felt that that face, that figure, that scene was something I'd witnessed while he was alive. You know how the narrow winding road goes off southeast from the old highway, cuts across the expressway, continues on past the vicinity of my house, and comes out at the three-ways right by your apartment block? Well, it was at the crossroads where the road first divides. I have no memory of going anywhere like that with my father. Even today it's a lonely, deserted place at night."

I was worried that Yamagoe was in danger of falling under the spell of place, so I broke in and said, "There's something I never thought to ask before. If your accident happened at that crossroad, why were you taken to a hospital so far away?"

"The ambulance took me to three different hospitals before morning," he replied. "That hospital was the third place they took me. They promised to save my right leg. All I cared about was avoiding amputation."

"That's amazing!" I said, astonished. "Who was with you?"

"Torizuka came running when I was at the second hospital. She may have been the one to force them to do as I wanted, in the end. Apparently I was beginning to give in at the second place. I was barely conscious."

"It sounds like she was very brave."

"She was always there whenever I opened my eyes. But during that time, I'm not sure exactly when, I thought of my father. I thought how he hadn't, not once, ever voiced any criticism of the world. And just as I thought this, my whole body kind of shrank and dwindled, as if a terrific wind had blown over it, though nothing moved. I thought I was dying. Thinking back on it now, I find it hard to understand how I could be swept up unawares into such calm and relaxed thoughts, when the situation I was in was any-thing but calm and relaxed. And I'm not at all sure whether my father really was as I remembered, or whether I simply didn't recall any scene of him denouncing the world."

"No, that's what you thought, that's how you reacted at the time, so I'm sure it's true. And that too is amazing." At the sense of this unknown dead man's long silence, my own body seemed to shrink slightly in the sunlight.

"The nurses teased me by saying they'd never come across anyone who endured in such patience. 'Enough's enough,' they told me jokingly," he went on. "The doctor also said with a smile that it might make me feel better to complain a bit when I was having a hard time of it. From my own point of view, I was aware of how much I was asking of them at the hospital, and I also felt compunction about letting myself go in front of Torizuka when we'd known each other such a short time, not to mention with my poor frail mother. But it's true, I was strangely strong-willed and stubborn about it. I met you around the time I was beginning to feel uncomfortably that I might get a bit odd if this went on, so I was grateful that you listened to me that night. I've since managed to become much more carefree and irresponsible. But a few days after the second surgery, when you'd already left the hospi-tal, I think, I had another terrifying dream."

When he said this, a difficult smile spread over his face. His eyes were on a group of young mothers sitting on a bench across the avenue from us, deep in talk while their children played nearby.

"I was with my father," he said at last. "That was fine, but all around us were couples, countless men and women, frantically making love. Well, it was a dream, remember. My father and I were in the sitting room read-ing newspapers, but all the rooms and houses around us with the couples in them were ceilingless and visible from above—not that we were exactly looking down on them, but we could see. 'What do you think?' my father asked me without raising his eyes. He wasn't talking about the newspaper item I was reading. 'It's up to them, isn't it?' I replied. 'That's not what I'm asking about,' he said. He raised a rather stern face from the paper. 'Doesn't it strike you as the embodiment of the world's prosperity?' he asked. I felt he was just being his usual inflexible and dogmatic self, and didn't reply.

259

Privately, I thought, So what's the problem with that? Then he said it slightly differently, 'Don't you think that's the motivating force for the world's prosperity?' His words surprised me by sounding suddenly young. It's uncomfortable, even in a dream, to perceive your parents as young. I looked at his face, and asked if he really thought this, and his face somehow grew sterner and sterner, and took on a look as if he was about to come out with a grave pronouncement on the world. I changed the subject by asking what he knew about men and women, anyway."

"You actually said that?" I said worriedly, almost forgetting it was a dream.

"No, not out loud," he replied. "But I babbled on: 'So what about the dead Sakae, eh? And Megumi. She apparently knew a man, but he doesn't seem to have loved her.' My father's eyes opened wide. Oh, what an awful thing I've said, I thought, shrinking, when I saw tears falling from his eyes. 'Sakae and Megumi did sad things,' he said, 'but they were born, their eyes took pleasure in the green leaves of gardens.' Then he went on, 'Take good care of your mother, she's a happy woman whatever I may have done, and it's good to take good care of a happy woman.' A strange thing to say ..."

. . . . .

"A strange thing to say ..." He was almost muttering to himself, and his eyes were now drawn to a group of men who entered the avenue from the main road. My gaze followed his, to see three elderly men, in walking shoes and the same kind of light windbreaker that Yamagoe had laid over his knees, who seemed to be out together on an expedition, though they carried nothing. Yet for all that, they didn't speak to or look at each other, and maintained an odd mutual distance, one walking ahead and the other two some way away on either side behind him, almost as if they chanced to be walking together in the same direction, though they kept pace with each other. I found myself thinking a thought quite unusual these days, that they had the step of those walking out their hunger. I now couldn't take my eyes off them. The man in the lead was of an age to be able to saunter out at his leisure like this, but the other two seemed younger, somewhere under fifty. All three seemed to have evoked for me an impression of malnutrition. All were thin, with sallow complexions and brownish skin, their cheeks sunken, and though hair and beard weren't left to grow long, there was an unclean sense about them, as though they hadn't washed for some time. As they approached us they clearly were aware of our watching eyes, for each individually showed the same look of suspicious wariness in his glance. They slowed down as they passed, and their receding figures heading toward the park entrance revealed yet more clearly how they matched pace and breath together.

"Just what was that 'economic bubble' Japan went through in the eight-

260

ies?" Yamagoe asked, apparently following his own train of thought at the sight. "The big downturn happened the year we were in the hospital, didn't it?" His eyes had returned from following the men walking toward the park entrance, and as he spoke two more men passed in front of us. They were dressed like the three before, and walked with the same slow pace, but these two were about thirty, and carried knapsacks on their backs. They had evidently seen us watching the previous three walking away, and they passed us side by side, their piercing eyes averted, obviously together yet keeping their distance from each other, and walked on toward the park, with a slowness odd in those so young, that was redolent somehow of great hunger.

"Maybe they're the companions of the old ones off on a picnic, bringing along the lunch," I said with a smile.

"No," Yamagoe replied, "I got the impression they were keeping a distant eye on the three ahead." Surprised, I recalled the two young men who had just passed us, seeming momentarily intrepid, and was about to ask him what he meant, but at that moment there came the sharp cry of a girl from across the avenue. "Mummy, it's lunchtime!" Her little brother gave a cry that reproduced the inflection of her words.

"That reminds me, I must rush home for lunch myself," said Yamagoe, rising with a spring in his legs. He tied the windbreaker firmly around his waist again, saying with a laugh, "I'm still in rehabilitation, you see," then bowed his farewell and ran off. At the far end of the avenue he raised his right hand in a breezy wave, then jogged off in impressive style. The faint aroma of his youthful sweat lingered on the bench. I thought I noticed within it a hint of sweet milk.

The earthquake receded further into the past while I hesitated over whether to call Fujisato and find out how he was doing. Around this time, I developed a late-night habit of consulting today's date in the almanac I brought back from the local shrine on our New Year's visits. It named the days according to the ancient lunar and festival calendar, with names that had no substance in my modern life—*mochi, usui, kagen*—but as I gazed at it a vague desire to count the days would rise up in me, which soon grew into a habit of fervently counting, though what I was counting I couldn't say. Busy though my life was, there was no particular need to count up its days. I did notice, though, that exactly coincidentally with my hospitalization four years earlier, each year at this time my body grew sensitive to the changes in weather.

For the most part the weather remained fair, but at the end of the month some rain mixed with snow fell, and then during the morning on the first of March snow fell thick enough to accumulate. By noon, however, most of it had melted, and the weather cleared in the afternoon, with a red sunset. It was almost the day of the Girls' Festival, on the third of the third month. I felt a renewed concern for Fujisato's household, but decided they must surely be fine. Then the following afternoon, a telephone call came from my younger cousin, and he dropped by after dinner that evening.

No relative of mine had ever come to call before. Even though this maternal cousin lived not far away, we hadn't seen each other in about twenty years. He was forty-five, and had always been a teetotaler, but four years ago he had had treatment for a tumor of the salivary gland, and now the saliva secretion had slowed to a trickle, so that he had to constantly moisten his mouth with water. We put out a jug of water for him on the table, but even this was not enough, and as he talked he kept taking out a spray he carried and spraying his mouth. Four years ago I had gone into the hospital in February, then in May my maternal cousin who was the family head had had surgery for lung cancer; in September my elder brother had passed away, and about the same time, according to my cousin who phoned when he left the hospital, this other cousin had undergone treatment for a strange lump below the ear.

He told me he had been hospitalized twice in four months, and afterwards had remained weak for a long time, so that even after he had returned to work, on his way there and back he would have to get off the train halfway along and rest. In May of the following year he visited the main family house deep in Gifu Prefecture. He and his cousin, who was still convalescing from his own surgery, compared notes on their recent illnesses, and both recognized in each other's faces the look of death. Kozo was still so weak he had to interrupt the conversation at one point and go and lie down, my cousin said, but he went on to say that the family had later said they'd been worried that he himself would die first.

He showed no signs in his healthy complexion of the illness whose aftermath he spoke of so serenely. Around eleven he left, promising to call again. When Kozo had been released from the hospital in the fall after having one lung removed, the doctor had assured him that he would feel better in six months, and he'd waited faithfully for this to happen, but once the six months were up, he began thinking of the fate of his cousins as well as his own fate, and speaking in those terms. The following year, at the end of February, he died. Apparently, at the beginning of that year he had finally begun to say that he was feeling a return of the strength to live. Looking back on it, my cousin said, he believed now that Kozo's will to live had been weak, and that he himself had experienced something similar—he had felt it was all he could do to stand his present suffering, and he hadn't feared or even thought of the possibility of a relapse.

It was hard to detain a teetotaler guest past this hour, and when he had left with a parting smile I returned to sit at my desk, though I had no intention of doing any more work that evening. Cradling my head in my hands, I recalled that my now-dead cousin had also said in a letter sent just after he left the hospital that he didn't fear death. At the time I was just getting over my own illness, and had been seized with the suffocating thought of the intense pain and grimness he would be feeling in the months after his lung had been removed—but now I began to think very tentatively that, as with the cousin who had just left, though outwardly pliant, they were men of impressive inner steel, with a fierce self-respect, and when they faced death this quality would manifest itself in a defiant resolve as death pressed in closer. But my thoughts soon came to a standstill, and returning to myself I discovered that I was idly turning the pages of the shrine almanac by my desk. Continuing to look through it, I came upon the name of the day four days previous, *keichitsu*, the designation of the day when wintering insects come out of hibernation. I would normally delight in this word each year when I saw it, but now it lingered before my eyes with a somehow sinister implication. Finally shaking this off, my eyes fell on the name of the day three days later, *jogen*, the early crescent moon. Then I recalled an article I had read somewhere in recent years about how deaths from car accidents tend to increase at this phase of the new moon, for reasons unknown—not to any remarkable degree, but the figures show a definite, though slight, increase. Puzzled, I thought that *kagen*, the time of the waning moon, would make more sense as the occasion for such things, yet it appeared that the new moon was the most dangerous time.

Days passed. On the day of the Girls' Festival, rain began to fall at night. The next day, marked in the almanac as *kyuhatsu uma*, the year's first "Day of the Horse" in the old calendar, heavy snow was forecast, but not enough fell to accumulate, and it continued to rain all day. The days of *keichitsu* and *jogen* were both fine. I calculated that about two weeks after this was when I had been lying four years ago stuck lying faceup in bed, unable to move my head. Why, I wondered in bewilderment, was I so constantly aware of the weather, like some horse trainer intent on his plans to enter his horse in an approaching race? Then I noticed in the almanac that it was the night of the ancient Omizutori festival at Todaiji Temple in Nara. It was more than twenty years ago, I thought, that I had been allowed to be part of the outer circle of worshippers in that festival, sitting in the stillness of the painful cold watching through the lattice the repentance rituals performed by the monks in the inner circle. And I recalled the vivid thuds when they had thrown themselves knees first onto the thick boards of the worship hall floor in total obeisance, and wondered just how that high temple balcony must have swayed on the morning of the earthquake, how the pillars and rafters would have groaned—and there rose before my eyes the pale faces of the monks in the midst of their long fasting practice, faces brimming with vitality, fiercely intrepid, something almost defiant and lawless about them.

The next morning was fine, but clouds gathered from about noon, and past two the house grew dark under black clouds. No rain yet fell, but thunder began to roll in the distance, and at this point the telephone rang. It turned out to be Fujisato.

"Has Sugaike told you the story?" he asked.

"No, I haven't heard anything," I replied, surprised to hear in my voice the tone of someone dismissing bad news. The odd thought crossed my mind that this was how people in fact attracted misfortune.

"Well, he really is going senile then," said Fujisato with a laugh. "It would have been the night of the Girls' Festival that we talked, ten days ago now."

Hearing this name in a dark place gave it a vivid ring.

"On the day of the Girls' Festival," Fujisato went on, repeating the name carefully, "my little sister died in an air raid, you see. I had an elder sister too, but she was always racked with guilt about having escaped unharmed when she was evacuated to the country. It was a kind of taboo in our household to set up Girls' Festival dolls after that. She got married when she was more than twenty. That was when my mother calculated how old her younger daughter would have been had she lived, realized with an ache in her heart that the girl would be almost marriageable age now, and one day she went out and bought two Girls' Festival dolls, man and wife. She started setting them up for Girls' Festival each year, like a kind of memorial ceremony for her little girl. This went on till the time when my daughter was born.'

Here he paused and said with a happy laugh, "I've immediately gotten off the subject. I'm just talking about myself. I seem to be wandering in my old age these days."

"So you had an elder sister."

"She died thirty long years ago. But before I forget ..."

Sugaike had called him on the night of the festival, with a work-related question to the "now-retired" Fujisato, but had said that more importantly, we should all three get together again when the cherry blossoms were out. Fujisato had all along wanted us to meet again there, he said. He invited us all to his house, despite the lack of a cherry tree in the garden, whereupon Sugaike said he'd love to see his daughter again, and thus his house was fixed on. As for the date, since Sugaike's plans were still a little unclear, and since Fujisato was the one who could afford to be flexible, he'd left it up to Sugaike and me. He'd been waiting to hear from one or other of us, but it had only just occurred to him, in the instant it grew dark and thunder rolled overhead, that perhaps he'd promised to be the one to make the arrangements this time after all, and he was calling to straighten the matter out.

"That's a fine idea. But I think it's wiser not to feel that we need to stick to the moment when the blossoms are out. One-third blooming, or leaves showing among scattered blossoms, that sort of moment is more suitable for us, I'd say. Or a garden that still holds the bare winter branches." I told him the three rare days I wasn't free between the end of March and into the first quarter of April, then asked, "And how has your daughter been?"

"All's gone completely quiet," Fujisato replied.

"When you say 'quiet,' she was always a quiet person, I'd have thought."

"No, I mean in the house."

"So it gets quieter than that, does it?"

"Starting with the father."

"As for you, you were as quiet as could be, surely."

"You couldn't be more wrong about that."

The conversation drifted toward absurdity while thunder rolled across the sky and the rain began to pelt down, but Fujisato didn't burst into laughter and neither did I, though I thought of that aged figure Yamagoe had described, standing under the dead hackberry with a constant happy smile on his face.

"Later I saw my own face as I had stood there at my daughter's back while she stared at the television the morning of the earthquake. It had a sinister look."

"Any face watching such a catastrophic scene would look sinister, surely."

"It was a face that was staring fixedly at someone jumping."

"Aren't you getting things all mixed up here?"

"I was the one who jumped, and I was the one who watched."

"Sure enough, you were seeing what you saw forty years ago."

"It happened while I was still asleep at home."

"If that's the case, it was over many years ago."

"No, it wasn't over."

A wave of exhaustion came over me. There could never be an end to this watching oneself poised to jump. But Fujisato's voice was full of a calm joy as he went on.

"That morning I gazed at my own sinister face as my daughter slept. So that's the face I've been living with off and on through the years, I thought. It's true, some years ago when I'd come to the decision to quit work, I felt this same kind of face, and was filled with guilt toward my dead wife. Once I'd made the final decision, things felt better. My face changed as well. Everything around grew quiet. And it's grown even quieter since I've been at home. Every day I was astonished at how tranquil a day could be, how new. But that day, while I waited for my daughter to wake up and listened to her calm breathing, I understood that in comparison to this, she hadn't really been calm at all. Oh sure, she was calm enough, but always something lurked there somewhere that was crashing down with a huge impending force. Joy swept me, and the sinister look vanished. I do hate the idea of taking that face to my coffin, I must say."

"You sure have been intense, haven't you?" I sighed. I almost added that it was no wonder those rumors about him had flown. "But how about your daughter?" I asked.

"She's brightened up," he replied. "She says those experiences of dawn paralysis have disappeared."

"It would be dreadful if they hadn't. But what does she say about you?" I said, rephrasing my question. I felt I had heard the same answer somewhere before, and exhaustion swept over me again, but I told myself that it was after all quite common for things to slowly improve through repetition, even if only in a limited way. And then I felt that I had had this thought too at some point before.

"She's grown to laugh a lot these days," said Fujisato. "One time we were facing each other silently in the living room late at night when she suddenly burst out laughing. When I asked what was funny, she pointed out that I'd laughed first. 'Recently you laugh at all kinds of trivial things,' she said, like a child being given a candy. So then I said to her in return, 'Lately when you laugh, you don't hunch your shoulders the way you used to; the laugh comes straight up from your chest through your throat and your eyebrows pop wide open, and you give a fine warm laugh, like smoke puffing out of a chimney.' 'Oh no!' she cried, and gave a laugh exactly as I'd just described."

"That bodes well," I responded with a laugh of my own, aware that it was somehow shameful to imagine the scene too clearly.

"But of course it was you rather than your daughter who was the initial cause for concern. There are cases of old people breathing their last just when everyone around is feeling glad that they're so happy and laughing these days."

"I didn't breathe my last," said Fujisato, after a brief pause. "I snapped instead. I was squatting in the garden, and when I went to stand up there was a sudden stabbing pain, and I gasped for breath. I raised myself upright ever so slowly, and thank heavens managed to stand. My daughter was laughing on the veranda. I could see her in the distance. Apparently I had the face of a startled child. But I was in bed for three days after that, and for several more days I was tottering about. When I went out for a walk in the hackberry park, my daughter came laughing out to follow me. She'd teasingly try to take my hand. She knew that if I laughed it would still reverberate in my lower back, you see."

After a moment I heard Fuisato's voice saying "Hello? Are you there?" I was facing the window, which was now white after the rain had ceased, smiling to myself as I saw the old man who had startled Yamagoe under the hackberry. I let another "Hello?" go by, as I considered that that faint, refined laugh Yamagoe had reported would actually have been a way of avoiding the jarring to his back that a louder laugh would produce. Still, I was strangely struck that the girl whom Yamagoe saw accompanying the old man had seemed to him to be a beautiful woman.

266

You sure know how to go crazy, I muttered.

. . . . .

After two days of fine weather, rain began to fall again on the third evening, and it went on raining the following day. At midday I set off with an umbrella, and when I came to the park I saw on the bare branches of the hornbeam tiny hanging clusters of yellowish brown. These are a tree's flowers, I thought, and in a few more days they will burst forth brilliantly in their own tiny way, taking on a faint reddish tinge; but right now they hung there chill and wet, and as I gazed, the word "kitten" came to mind. In German, this was the name for the hanging flower heads or "catkins" that are found on other trees, such as hazel and birch and willow. Perhaps they were compared to a tiny kitten's tail, I thought, and I looked up at them, wondering whether a drop of water would hang on the tip after rain.

It rained all day. That night, I consulted the shrine almanac and discovered that it was full moon, the second month's *mochizuki* day in the traditional calendar. Then I realized that this was the second month since the earthquake. Flipping back through the almanac, I saw that the earthquake had also happened at full moon, the last *mochizuki* of the traditional calendar year. Why should this be? I wondered vaguely, and I felt a sudden urge to call Sugaike at home.

As soon as he came on the phone, I began, "I had a call from Fujisato the other day," but then I found I couldn't count back just how many days ago it had been. It felt about two weeks earlier.

"Ah yes, the plan to get together again. I was just thinking of giving you a call about it," he responded in a heavy, drowsy voice that suggested he had been drinking. "We just seem to let plans slip," he said as he launched into a discussion of what days we had free. It was agreed that sometime when the blossoms were opening would be best, in the first or second week of April. "Sundays would get in the way of your precious horse race," Sugaike pointed out with a laugh, so it was decided to make it Saturday afternoon. He promised to contact Fujisato with the plan and get back to me, and as we were about to hang up, I asked,

"How did Fujisato seem? He was saying to me blissfully that he seemed to have entered his second childhood in retirement."

"He can see things, that man," responded Sugaike simply. "You know, I called him when I was a bit stumped by what to do in relation to some work, and I thought he might know about such things. And sure enough, he had a fine understanding of it all. He said he'd been stuck at home for six months or more now and even before he'd left work he wasn't in a position to gain much important information for quite some time, but he told me all sorts of things, considerately and honestly. That's the way he is."

"He must be pretty bright."

"But anyway, while we were talking—there'd recently been some scandal that had just begun to surface, something I couldn't really reveal to Fujisato when I called for a private discussion, and then he goes and says without any prompting that something of the sort would be likely to occur, and made a prediction about the future, though in guarded terms. And things are turning out exactly as he anticipated. It's all going quite clearly in the direction he spoke of. It's the sort of thing where after the event people would be inclined to say anyone could have foreseen it, once it's all over and done with, it seems that it was obvious all along, but of course at the time ..."

"This is difficult stuff. But could he still be getting information somehow?"

"That's what I thought too. I even wondered whether he was still playing some secret role in things. But it's just not possible that it could have been sourced through the company. Then I recalled how people had been saying four or five years earlier that this Fujisato character was a fellow who could see the future, to a scary degree, and all the scarier because he was pretending he couldn't. I remember asking whether such people still existed these days, who could see the future."

"I guess a standpoint from which you can see ahead does exist. And maybe if you've spent a long time toiling away there, even when you step down, you continue to be able to see amazingly well for a while. Or maybe it's just an innate gift he has."

"Mind you, it's all just rumor."

"For that very reason it tends to get out of control, though."

"If you don't look at it as being about any particular individual, rumor can be revealing, can't it? Even in a world without prescience, people can be prescient. But so what? You can't do anything about what you see coming, and you're left there floundering. And then, each not seeing involves a little bit of seeing too. It seems they're opposites, but in fact you can see while being almost entirely unaware of it. When you realize that time after time some judgment, some bold prediction of yours has hit the mark, no matter how coolly you appear to take it, it leaves a surprisingly strong impression. And what's more, you have the urge to embody it in some particular person. The urge can become quite excessive. So even if this is Fujisato, in a way it both is him and isn't him. It all takes place inside a narrowly confined world, after all."

"So how do you feel toward Fujisato as he is now?"

"Well, it's a funny thing. I believe him."

"And looking back?"

"When he was caught up in the maelstrom, he and I were about on a par as far as prescience goes."

"You mean he's only developed it just now?"

268

"I'd guess that now he can see things, yes."

"Why?" I asked doggedly.

"To my mind, it could be thanks to his daughter," replied Sugaike.

"Thanks to his daughter," I repeated, and then I paused. It wasn't so much that I felt I shouldn't follow this wild leap, but rather that an instant recognition of its likely truth stopped me in my tracks. Deep inside it floated an image of the daughter in front of her father, leaning backwards in laughter.

"It's not for yourself that you can foresee a crisis," Sugaike was saying softly. "If you can't see crises, you can't see either ahead or behind. You can't see a thing. Not even the next thing in front of you. It seems to me that this fellow is living in his safe and peaceful present under the knowledge of a crisis he senses from the past, for the sake of his daughter. He said another strange thing. Apparently even when he walks about the house, he feels as if an abyss is opening beneath his feet. He says he's constantly grateful that he can take each step without tumbling in."

"That's a blessing," I murmured, and the oddness of the words I'd spoken startled me. Once more the image of Fujisato's laughing daughter rose up in me.

"And what of you?" I said, intending to ask how he'd been recently.

"As for me, I'm one who's being seen, rather than seeing the future," he replied. "I've been like a wild beast these last two months."

.   .   .   .   .

"Mad with rage?"

"When I see a building I want to knock it down. Or a bridge or an expressway. What the hell are you doing building such things? I think."

"One of the aftereffects of the earthquake."

"But it's precisely when I'm thinking these frenzied thoughts that I realize my social face is quite passionately a 'constructed face.'"

"I can't imagine you having a 'constructed face,' I must say."

"It's a civil engineering kind of construction, actually. We're all civil engineers, is what it comes down to."

"Well, that's probably true enough."

"I plan to go right on kicking up a fuss throughout my life, till my strength gives out, you know. If I end up sad and lonely, well, that's my lot. But recently, I've been being looked at ..."

"Who looks at you? Girls going by?"

"The figure of the dead in the incense smoke."

"That Nakayama ghost, you mean? ... Well, even if the ghost of that woman resents you enough to haunt you, there's something sexy about that idea, so I wouldn't complain."

"Actually, it's overstating it to say I'm being looked at. It's kind of like

269

those thirty years when someone wasn't here, suddenly now they're here more substantially than I am, looking at me. Saying, what are you doing? And all I can do is hang my head in shame and agree. But I feel those eyes on me."

"Would this be something that's followed you from that inn in Nakayama back in October?"

"You know, the next morning I set off briskly down the hill to the station with my hand luggage. We took off from Narita as planned. Then, seven days later, perhaps, I suddenly found myself sitting up scared in bed, feeling I could hear someone breathing. I checked the bathroom. It was a cheap hotel—no bath, just a shower, you understand. Nothing erotic or weird in there. I pissed and went back to the bedroom."

"Maybe you hadn't turned off the faucet hard enough?"

"Till I opened the door I'd imagined an old bathtub with an antique patina to it. I was still half asleep. In the room there was a scent of incense."

"You'd be saying to yourself that the incense still clung to your clothes after all that long travel, I guess. Still ... you ought to look after yourself, you know."

"I'm looking after myself just fine."

"That's good."

"When I feel those eyes on me, wherever I am, it all grows quiet, you see."

"Isn't tomorrow the first day of Higan?"

"Right, and I've already been to Nakayama. There weren't any of those red Higan flowers blooming, though."

· · · · ·

Next morning the rain continued; it was cold all day, and the rain never really lifted. My wife and younger daughter went off to my wife's family home for Higan. In the morning I set out for a walk into town. Today, for once, the narrow lanes that ran here and there between what seemed solid wall of houses along the road caught my eye. I paused to look at a house that was being demolished, feeling the sight as not so much ugly as shameful.

The next day, Sunday, the weather was fine, but just before noon, when a guest had called in, the sky began to darken again. After we'd strolled around the park to see the plums in full bloom, we ate in a nearby restaurant, and when I was walking back home alone it seemed about to pour with rain at any moment. After a little wine over lunch my body felt slow and listless, and I took a rare afternoon nap. At one point I awoke, then sank back to sleep again, and when I woke up again the day was coming to an end and the rain finally began to fall. My younger daughter had work the next day, so she came back earlier than my wife. As I was going to bed sometime past

270

midnight, a siren that sounded a fire engine's went by outside. Then a number of sirens passed with small intervals between them, turned the corner at the three-ways nearby, blaring something over speakers to alert the traffic, then seemed to head off north down the old canal road. As the sound of the sirens grew distant, the sense of their direction became more vague; they were now like lights wandering lost here and there over the dark waters of a bay. Listening to them, my consciousness also flickered toward the phone, half expecting it to ring, but I must have dozed off, and when I woke again the fire engines seemed to be on their way back. It was at this point that I saw the dead hackberry tree and Fujisato's house standing together against a burning red sky, neither in their real location. One of the heavy shutters that blocked off the veranda was pulled back, and I could see father and daughter sitting there in profile, bathed in the red light that shone in, smiling brightly. The garden was suddenly thronged with a vast jostling crowd of singed men and women, handing around rice balls. I could see Yamagoe and Torizuka there, her stomach swollen in pregnancy. Sugaike had come running, and was pounding grimly on the hallway door.

I'm the only one absent, I thought tearfully as I was drifting back into sleep.

The next day was brilliant warm spring weather. I woke at about ten in the empty house, and when I had walked through the park aimlessly for an hour or more, I made myself lunch. Before I settled down to work at the desk after lunch, I put in a call to check up with the place I was doing the work for. "Didn't you know?" said my interlocutor in astonishment, and proceeded to tell me that that morning a large number had died when poison gas was released in the subway while people where on their way to work. When I turned on the television, it was endlessly replaying the footage of the scene. Seized with the fearful sensation that a three-day-old tragedy was being retold here, I switched it off, then sat in front of the dead screen, and began to summon the subway network in my imagination and figure times. But though the calculations should have been straightforward, they were beyond me, and I retreated into a state of dull panic. At length I stood up, noticing that my movements had slowed as well, got on the telephone, and called my daughter's at work. She answered right away. She'd gone through the city center on the subway that morning, but her company was a little to the east of where the incident occurred, so she had passed through some time earlier. I asked after her elder sister, and learned that she'd still been sleeping when the younger one left for work. This meant that my other daughter hadn't coincided with the tragedy either, so I called my wife at her family home. When my brother-in-law came on the phone, I burst out with the statement that something extraordinary had happened in Tokyo. "I'll hand you over to my sister," he said breathlessly, and retreated. He must have thought I meant that something had happened to me personally. The

271

household had not yet heard of the event. I realized that my elder daughter had left the house around the time I was waking up. When I awoke, there was not the least shadowy sense of anyone having departed.

Walking in the park before noon each day, I saw the helicopters constantly circling above. They would head off northwest, then come back in from the west. On rainy days, only their noise would pass deep in the clouds. They were still flying in a light snowfall.

. . . . .

The phone rang for some time before Fujisato answered it.

"It's one piece of bad news after another these days, isn't it?" he said. "But I've talked with Sugaike again and we decided on April eighth as the day, so please come along. Let's treat it as a way to welcome better fortune. My daughter's looking forward to it too." He went on to say that, reading the newspapers each day and putting time and place together in his mind, he realized that he himself could easily have been involved if the tragedy had occurred when he was working. He also said that it seemed a kind of miracle that he didn't know anyone among the victims.

Yamagoe telephoned on Sunday evening. When I answered, he greeted me hastily.

"What on earth was that all about?" he said almost accusingly. "Surely it would be obvious to anyone that if you go and do something like that just when the police investigations are closing in around you, it will only invite more trouble. They must have been driven by some necessity of their own. I'd guess the assessment of the situation that told them this would stop the investigation was based on the same thing. Do we really have to be content with this patently circular logic that just says Aum Shinrikyo is a weird group, so they make weird judgments?" He finally gave a thin laugh. "When this incomprehensible event happened, I started to get chills on Sunday evening, and I'm afraid I began to get really worked up late at night. It would have been right about the time the lights go out at the hospital, I guess." He reported that the pregnancy was going absolutely fine. Torizuka hadn't shown any particular interest in the tragic event.

. . . . .

"Do you get the feeling all of humanity, ourselves included, has somehow not quite grown up, and there's something grotesque in us all?" said Sugaike. "'I'm innocent, we say—or no, didn't do it—I didn't do it, I'm pure, we say glibly whenever anything happens. That's what this is all about. Just try changing the tune a bit each time you sing the chorus, and you'll hear your own voice coming through. And yet, now there's these rumors going around that long before this happened there were rumors that it would. Let's take a good look at each other when we meet, eh? I'm praying we three

272

ancients will be roaring with laughter."

At this stage in the negotiations, all three lapsed into heavy silence, and I too couldn't summon the strength to carry things on.

Only a few days remained till the end of March. Around noon on a fine day of cold wind, I witnessed a strange sight in the park. In front of the wood, there was a rectangular grassy field called the Square Paddock, where horse events were held. My usual course is to cut across the park from the east, take the gravel path past the wood and the Square Paddock, and go on around the grazing field and children's playground beyond; I then come out by the little bleachers stand to the Square Paddock, then right along the wire fence, and either turn into the wood from the north end of the fence, or go on along it, then turn left and go south past the wood. It was odd that that day, I didn't notice anything till I was turning left at the fence in front of the wood. At that point I raised my eyes, and there advancing quietly toward me was a line of elderly people, all men. They were lined up precisely in single file. Yet it was not like a march; they walked with a kind of sway, with feeble steps. All seemed quiet; no one was speaking. They weren't even looking at each other, let alone smiling. Almost all had their eyes fixed on their own feet. The man in the lead had a fine head of white hair. He walked with a style similar to that of the men Yamagoe and I had seen in the avenue the month before, stiff-legged, and though he had nothing on his back, there dangled diagonally at his waist from a string slung over his shoulder what I took at first to be one of those torches that guardsmen carry though somewhat larger, but what turned out to be a stainless steel cylindrical thermos. I stepped off into the wood to my right to let them pass, and watched as the man went by. His unflickering watchful eyes indeed held a cautious glint, and the face too resembled those of the other men we had seen. He passed with eyes averted, holding off my gaze till the very last, languidly, without a preliminary ascertaining glance in my direction. And then a faint wave seemed to move through the column of men in their fifties or forties who followed behind him. One after another the thin, spiritless faces rose up before me, and each cast a flickering glance at my own passing face beside them as if at some utterly distant outsider, some with accusing bewilderment, some with resentful jealousy, then each turned his eyes quickly back to his own feet before any real recognition of another human could register there. Five men, ten men passed by me, then I saw approaching me the men carrying knapsacks; they did not look down, and yet their eyes never even glanced sideways as they approached. They too walked on from sheer habit on legs wavering with fatigue, but these men looked young, in their twenties and thirties, and I realized the column must be organized by age; toward the rear I noticed a particularly drooping and dejected-looking foreign youth with pale hair and complexion. The line of men moved on along the fence, and headed into the distance.

When I had almost reached the southern edge of the wood I came to my senses and turned to look back. The column of men was moving at what seemed a terribly sluggish pace. They were turning east from the northern end of the Square Paddock and heading toward the front of the bleachers, when a sudden clarity of vision swept over me—I saw the sun cloud, and each man's shadow suddenly rise up black, and from the midst of this vision I counted along the line to twenty-five, twenty-six men, and then finally it struck me that all these men were seeing nothing, that there was no landscape around them, and in astonishment my gaze faltered, while the column moved around the bleachers, crossed the white gravel pathway as they would a desert and, with the same swaying gait and maintaining strict formation, not one slackening his pace, all seemed to move on out through the park's gate, into the avenue, and away toward the main road that lay beyond.

ABOUT THE AUTHOR

Born in Tokyo in 1937, FURUI YOSHIKICHI graduated from the University of Tokyo in German literature. While teaching at Kanazawa University, he translated the Austrian writers Robert Musil and Hermann Broch. He left the university in 1970 and began to establish himself as a writer. His major awards include the Akutagawa Prize in 1970 for the novella *Yōko*, the Tanizaki Prize in 1983 for *Asagao* (Morning Glory), the Kawabata Prize in 1986 for *On Nakayama Hill*, and the 1997 Mainichi Art Award in 1997 for *The White-haired Melody*. He includes very little social commentary in his novels, preferring to look into the heart of individual characters.

ABOUT THE TRANSLATOR

MEREDITH MCKINNEY'S previous translations include *The Tale of Saigyō*, the Japanese classic *The Pillow Book*, and Natsume Soseki's *Kusamakura*, as well as the award-winning short-story collection *Ravine and Other Stories* by Furui Yoshikichi. She lives in Braidwood, Australia, and teaches Japanese at the Australian National University.